Through the
French
Canals

D0823452

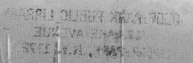

Through the
French
Canals

11th Edition

David Jefferson

DEER PARK PUBLIC LIBRARY
44 LAKE AVENUE
DEER PARK, N.Y. 11729

S

SHERIDAN
HOUSE

This edition first published 2006
by Sheridan House, Inc.
145 Palisade Street
Dobbs Ferry, NY 10522
www.sheridanhouse.com

Copyright © 1970, 1972, 1975, 1979, 1982, 1987, 1990, 1994 by Philip Bristow
© 1999, 2003, 2006 by Philip Bristow and David Jefferson

First edition published by Navigator Books 1970
Tenth edition published 2003 by Sheridan House Inc.

All rights reserved. No part of this publication may be reproduced in any
form or by any means – graphic, electronic or mechanical, including
photocopying, recording, taping or information storage and retrieval systems –
without the prior permission in writing of Sheridan House.

While all reasonable care has been taken in the production of this book, the
publisher takes no responsibility for the use of the methods or products
described in this edition.

Library of Congress cataloging-in-publication data

Jefferson, David.
    Through the French canals / David Jefferson.-- 11th ed.
      p. cm.
    Previous edition entered under Philip Bristow.
    Includes bibliographical references and index.
    ISBN 1-57409-233-2 (alk. paper)
    1. Boats and boating--France--Guidebooks. 2. Canals--France--
Recreational use--Guidebooks. 3. France--Guidebooks. I. Bristow,
Philip. Through the French canals. II. Title.

GV776.48.A2B74 2006
797.10944--dc22

                2006004774

ISBN 1 57409 233 2

Printed and bound in Singapore by Star Standard.

PAGE II–III **Mèze on the Étang de Thau.** *Photo: David Jefferson*

Contents

Introduction to the 11th edition

The first edition of *Through the French Canals* by Philip Bristow was published in 1970, and since then has become recommended reading for anyone planning a cruise on the French waterways.

Over the years, Philip Bristow carried out his meticulous research primarily in two boats – *Gay Whippet*, an 8-ton 32ft Hillyard, and the 43ft motor yacht *Carillon*. He wrote books about the waterways of France, Holland, Belgium and Germany and guides to the Spanish coast and French Mediterranean harbours.

There have been many significant changes since Philip Bristow first cruised the French waterways. Then, pleasure boats were something of a rarity in these parts, with the heavy barge traffic having the priority. Progress could be exceptionally slow, with long queues of commercial traffic waiting to enter locks, and the timing of passage through them by pleasure craft was sometimes dictated by the mood of the lock keeper.

With one or two exceptions, mostly on industrial sections of waterway, the barge traffic has dwindled. On the River Seine, for example, the lock keepers, always affable to passing boat crews, have instructions to guarantee that a pleasure boat will not have to wait more than 30 minutes in order to lock in.

Alongside the decline in barge traffic, the growth in the waterway leisure business has been dramatic. Fleet hire operators are in their hundreds and continue to prosper, with a rapid growth of yacht harbours with improved facilities to accommodate them and the *halte nautique* to provide hirers with night stopovers. There has also been a growth in hotel barges, offering conducted tours, often in converted barges that provide both a berth and *haute cuisine*.

The loss of barge traffic has meant that the upkeep of some sections of canal and river has declined. Voies Navigables de France (VNF) – the national waterway authority – has in recent years concentrated its resources on maintaining existing commercial sections of the waterways, and is in the process of handing over the running and development of those waterways primarily used by pleasure craft to local government.

On the Canal du Nivernais in central France, for example, virtually all the commercial craft have disappeared. This beautiful canal is now monopolised by pleasure boats, some of which cause excessive wash which is gradually eroding the river bank. There has also been considerable silting in recent years, with reports of problems on the Nivernais for boats drawing only 1m (officially the maximum draught is 1.2m). Those that do have a suitable draught may find, particularly in July and August, that they have to compete for space on the water with hundreds of hired cruisers.

This overcrowding is more the exception than the rule, however. There are over a hundred different canals and rivers across France, and on many of the navigable waterways a pleasure boat may well be underway for the whole day and meet only a handful of fellow travellers. Draught, too, will not normally be a problem, and a vessel drawing 1.5m can tackle most of the waterways.

France has been particularly hard hit with serious flooding and swollen rivers and some canals have had to be closed to navigation for long periods. Waterways where the water level is exceptionally high, although still navigable, will be subject to reduced air draught, strong currents and sometimes an excess of debris to cope with. Those planning an early or late cruise should contact the waterway authority Voies Navigables de France (VNF) for guidance – the addresses of 16 regional offices are listed on pages 57–58.

One change, which some might say is not for the better, is the growth of waterway regulations and documents required. A boat owner must hold an International Certificate of Competence and the vessel must have at least Small Ships Registration. A licence is obligatory for anyone using those waterways administered by VNF.

The attractions of the waterways, however, make it worthwhile gaining these qualifications. France is blessed with space and superb scenery. The waterways provide the ideal means of exploring ancient cities, small villages and mile after mile of countryside. This inland cruising cannot fail to leave a lasting impression.

David Jefferson
2006

Typically French architecture at Mareuil-sur-Ourcq. *Photo: David Jefferson*

Part 1

1 • Summary of route details

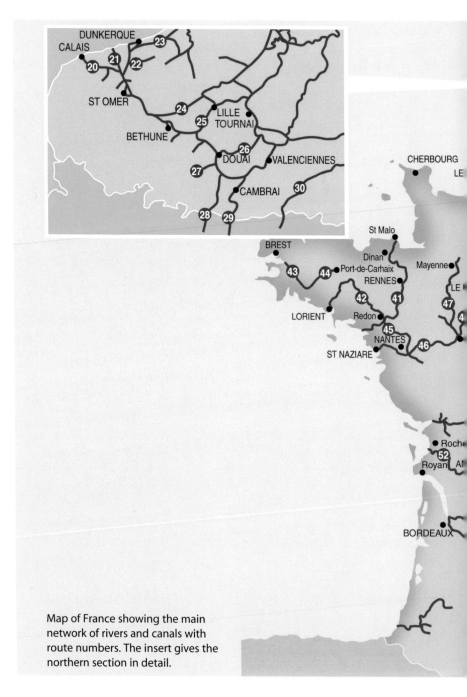

Map of France showing the main network of rivers and canals with route numbers. The insert gives the northern section in detail.

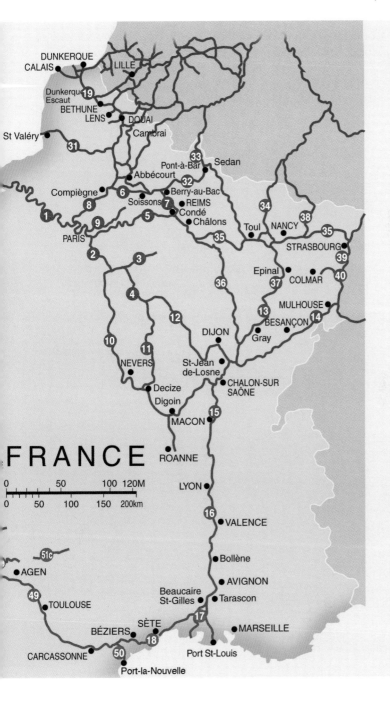

DUNKERQUE
CALAIS
LILLE
Dunkerqu **19**
Escaut
BETHUNE
LENS
DOUAI
Cambrai
St Valéry
31
Pont-à-Bar **33** Sedan
Abbécourt
32
Compiègne **6** Berry-au-Bac
8 Soissons **7** REIMS
1 **9** **5** Condé
34
Châlons
PARIS **35** Toul NANCY **38** **35**
2 **3** STRASBOURG
39
Epinal **40**
4 **36** **37** COLMAR
MULHOUSE
12 **13** BESANÇON **14**
DIJON
10 **11** Gray
NEVERS St-Jean
de-Losne
Decize CHALON-SUR
Digoin SAÔNE
15
MACON

FRANCE ROANNE

0   50   100 120M
0 50 100 150 200km

LYON
16
VALENCE

51c
AGEN
Bollène
49 AVIGNON
TOULOUSE Beaucaire
St-Gilles Tarascon
SÈTE **17**
BÉZIERS MARSEILLE
18
CARCASSONNE **50** Port St-Louis
Port-la-Nouvelle

On the Canal du Midi. *Photo: France Afloat*

2 • Through routes to the Mediterranean

Bourgogne

Of the main routes, Bourgogne involves the most locks, but for those crews with plenty of time and energy, the Canal de Bourgogne offers magnificent scenery in the heart of Burgundy. On the debit side, some locks on the Yonne have sloping sides, and there is reduced headroom through the Pouilly Tunnel (see page 7).

Commercial traffic has virtually disappeared, but this can mean canal closures for extended periods over the winter. With the decline in commercial craft, the growth in pleasure boats, particularly either side of Dijon, has been considerable in recent years, and the southern section of the Canal de Bourgogne is very crowded in July and August.

Bourbonnais

This most westerly route through to the Mediterranean is the most popular with boat owners entering the waterways at Le Havre. Not so dramatic in scenery, the route will be covered in less time, compared with the Bourgogne route, as there are 61 fewer locks to negotiate.

Marne

This route turns to the east in Paris, and within a day or two's cruising from the capital, the boat will be in France's Champagne region. In terms of numbers of locks and distance there is little to choose between the Marne and Bourbonnais routes. There is still commercial traffic on the Marne route which has been less developed for pleasure use, so there are fewer recognised stopping off places, and many miles of countryside with few signs of civilisation.

Calais to the Mediterranean

Yachts with their home ports on the east or south-east coast of England will invariably opt for the shortest Channel crossing and enter the waterways at Calais or Dunkerque or the less used entry ports of Gravelines or St-Valery-sur-Somme. At Arleux, the boat owner makes the choice between the Canal de St Quentin (105km, 40 locks and two tunnels) and the Canal du Nord (95km, 19 locks and two tunnels). Some boat owners reckon to save time by taking the busy Canal du Nord, where they will risk frustrating delays at locks; the majority will choose the less hectic and scenically more attractive Canal de St-Quentin.

From the above Channel/North Sea ports of entry, the Mediterranean can be reached either via Reims and the Canal de la Marne à la Saône or via Paris and then following the Bourgogne, Bourbonnais or Marne routes.

Atlantic to the Mediterranean

Often referred to as the Canal des Deux Mers, linking the Atlantic with the Mediterranean, the 601km route with 114 locks is made up of two rivers – the Gironde and the Garonne and then the Canal de Garonne and the Canal du Midi. Compared with the routes outlined above, there is less water (down to 1.5m in periods of drought) and less headroom beneath the bridges (see page 16).

Sète. *Photo: David Jefferson*

Le Havre to the Mediterranean via Canal de Bourgogne

Distance: 1316km **Locks**: 238 **Tunnels**: 1
Minimum depth of water: 1.8m (reduced to 1.5m or less in drought)
Minimum height above waterline at normal water level: 3.4m (except for
Pouilly tunnel with only 3.1m at sides 1.5m from centre line)

WATERWAY	Via	Route No
RIVER SEINE	Le Havre	1
	Paris	
	Paris	2
	Corbeil	
	Melun	
	Montereau	
YONNE	Montereau	4
	Pont-sur-Yonne	
	Sens	
	Joigny	
	Laroche-Migennes	
CANAL DE BOURGOGNE	Laroche-Migennes	12
	St Florentin	
	Tonnerre	
	Ravières	
	Montbard	
	Vénarey	
	Pouillenay	
Pouilly tunnel		
	Dijon	
	St-Jean-de-Losne	
SAÔNE	St-Jean-de-Losne	15
	Verdun	
	Chalon-sur-Saône	

Through the French Canals

WATERWAY	Via	Route No
SAÔNE	Mâcon	15
	Lyon	
RHÔNE	Lyon	16
	Vienne	
	Tournon	
	Valence	
	Avignon	
Craft proceeding west turn off into the Petit Rhône and the Canal du Rhône à Sète.		17 & 18
Craft proceeding south continue down the Rhône to Port St Louis.		16
This is the end of Rhône navigation.		

Le Havre to the Mediterranean via the Bourbonnais

Distance: 1330km **Locks**: 176 **Tunnels**: none
Minimum depth of water: 1.8m
Minimum height above waterline at normal water level: 3.5m

WATERWAY	Via	Route No
RIVER SEINE	Le Havre	1
	Paris	
	Paris	2
	Corbeil	
	Melun	
	St-Mammès	

WATERWAY	Via	Route No
CANAL DU LOING	St-Mammès	10
	Nemours	
CANAL DE BRIARE	Montargis	
	Briare	
CANAL LATÉRAL À LA LOIRE	Briare	
	Sancere	
	Nevers	
	Decize	
	Digoin	
CANAL DU CENTRE	Digoin	
	Montceau-les-Mines	
	Chagny	
	Chalon-sur-Saône	
RIVER SAÔNE	Chalon-sur-Saône	15
	Mâcon	
	Lyon	
RIVER RHÔNE	Lyon	16
	Vienne	
	Tournon	
	Valence	
	Avignon	
Craft proceeding west turn off into the Petit Rhône and the Canal du Rhône à Sète.		17 & 18
Craft proceeding south continue down the Rhône to Port St Louis.		16
This is the end of Rhône navigation.		

Le Havre to the Mediterranean via the Marne

Distance: 1400km **Locks**: 174 **Tunnels**: 4
Minimum depth of water: 1.8m
Minimum height above waterline at normal water level: 3.5m

WATERWAY	Via	Route No
RIVER SEINE	Le Havre	1
	Paris	
RIVER MARNE	Paris	5
Tunnel		
	Nogent-sur-Marne	
	Langy	
Tunnel		
	Meaux	
	La Ferté-sous-Jouarre	
	Château-Thierry	
CANAL LATÉRAL À LA MARNE	Châlons-en-Champagne	
	Vitry-le-François	
CANAL DE LA MARNE À LA SAÔNE	Vitry-le-François	36
	St Dizier	
Tunnel		
	Chaumont	
	Langres	
Tunnel		
	Maxilly-sur-Saône	
PETITE SAÔNE	Heuilley-sur-Saône	13
	Auxonne	
	St-Jean-de-Losne	
SAÔNE	St-Jean-de-Losne	15
	Verdun	

WATERWAY	Via	Route No
SAÔNE	Chalon-sur-Saône	15
	Mâcon	
	Lyon	
RHÔNE	Lyon	16
	Vienne	
	Tournon	
	Valence	
	Avignon	
Craft proceeding west turn off into the Petit Rhône and the Canal du Rhône à Sète.		17 & 18
Craft proceeding south continue down the Rhône to Port St Louis.		16
This is the end of Rhône navigation.		

Calais to the Mediterranean (via Reims)

Distance: 1197km **Locks**: 213 **Tunnels**: 6
Minimum depth of water: 1.8m
Minimum height above waterline at normal water level: 3.5m

WATERWAY	Via	Route No
CANAL DE CALAIS	Calais	20
RIVER AA	Watten	
LIAISON DUNKERQUE-ESCAUT	Watten	19
	Aire-sur-Lys	
	Béthune	

WATERWAY	Via	Route No
LIAISON DUNKERQUE-ESCAUT	Douai	19
	Arleux	
CANAL DU NORD	Arleux	28
Tunnel		
	Péronne	
Tunnel		
	Noyon	
	Pont-l'Evêque	
CANAL LATÉRAL À L'OISE	Pont-l'Evêque	8
	Abbécourt	
CANAL DE L'OISE À L'AISNE	Abbécourt	7
Tunnel		
CANAL LATÉRAL À L'AISNE	Bourg-et-Comin	
CANAL DE L'AISNE À LA MARNE	Berry-au-Bac	
	Reims	
Tunnel		
CANAL LATÉRAL À LA MARNE	Condé-sur-Marne	5
	Châlons-en-Champagne	
	Vitry-le-François	
CANAL DE LA MARNE À LA SAÔNE	Vitry-le-François	36
	St Dizier	
Tunnel		
	Chaumont	
	Langres	
Tunnel		
	Maxilly-sur-Saône	
PETITE SAÔNE	Heuilley-sur-Saône	13
	Auxonne	
	St-Jean-de-Losne	
SAÔNE	St-Jean-de-Losne	15
	Verdun	

WATERWAY	Via	Route No
SAÔNE	Chalon-sur-Saône	
	Mâcon	15
	Lyon	
RHÔNE	Lyon	16
	Vienne	
	Tournon	
	Valence	
	Avignon	
Craft proceeding west turn off into the Petit Rhône and the Canal du Rhône à Sète.		17 & 18
Craft proceeding south continue down the Rhône to Port St Louis.		16
This is the end of Rhône navigation.		

Calais to the Mediterranean (via Paris and the Bourbonnais canals)

Distance: 1379km   **Locks**: 208   **Tunnels**: 2
Minimum depth of water: 1.8m
Minimum height above waterline at normal water level: 3.5m

WATERWAY	Via	Route No
CANAL DE CALAIS	Calais	20
RIVER AA	Watten	
LIAISON DUNKERQUE-ESCAUT	Watten	19
	Aire-sur-Lys	
	Béthune	

WATERWAY	Via	Route No
LIAISON DUNKERQUE ESCAUT	Douai	19
	Arleux	
CANAL DU NORD	Arleux	28
Tunnel		
	Péronne	
Tunnel		
	Noyon	
	Pont-l'Evêque	
CANAL LATÉRAL À L'OISE	Pont-l'Evêque	8
	Longueil-Annel	
	Janville	
CANALISED OISE RIVER	Janville	
	Compiègne	
	Creil	
	L'Isle-Adam	
	Pontoise	
	Conflans-Ste-Honorine	
RIVER SEINE	Conflans-Ste-Honorine	1
	Paris	
	Paris	2
	Corbeil	
	Melun	
	St-Mammès	
CANAL DU LOING	St-Mammès	10
	Nemours	
CANAL DE BRIARE	Montargis	
	Briare	
CANAL LATÉRAL À LA LOIRE	Briare	
	Sancere	
	Nevers	

WATERWAY	Via	Route No
CANAL LATÉRAL À LA LOIRE	Decize	10
	Digoin	
CANAL DU CENTRE	Digoin	
	Montceau-les-Mines	
	Chagny	
	Chalons-sur-Saône	
RIVER SAÔNE	Chalons-sur-Saône	15
	Mâcon	
	Lyon	
RIVER RHÔNE	Lyon	16
	Vienne	
	Tournon	
	Valence	
	Avignon	
Craft proceeding west turn off into the Petit Rhône and the Canal du Rhône à Sète.		17 & 18
Craft proceeding south down the Rhône to Port St Louis.		16
This is the end of Rhône navigation.		

Craft entering at Calais and making for the Mediterranean via Paris can also take the Canal de Bourgogne or the Marne as alternative routes from Paris to the Saône and Rhône (see pages 7, 8, 10 and 11).

Calais ↔ Paris ↔ Bourgogne route to Port St Louis
Distance: 1365km **Locks**: 270 **Tunnels**: 3

Calais ↔ Paris ↔ Marne route to Port St Louis
Distance: 1449km **Locks**: 206 **Tunnels**: 6

Royan to the Mediterranean: Canal des Deux Mers – Royan to Sète

Distance: 601km **Locks**: 114 **Tunnels**: none
Minimum depth of water: 1.5m
Minimum height above waterline at normal water level: 3.3m (reducing to 2.4m at sides 2.75m from centre line)

WATERWAY	Via	Route No
RIVER GIRONDE	Royan	49
	Pauillac	
RIVER GARONNE	Bec d'Ambès	
	Bordeaux	
	Castets-en-Dorthe	
CANAL DE GARONNE	Castets-en-Dorthe	
	Buzet	
	Agen	
	Moissac	
	Castelarrasin	
	Toulouse	
CANAL DU MIDI	Toulouse	
	Montgiscard	
	Castelnaudary	
	Carcassonne	
	Argens-en-Minervois	
	Béziers	
	Agde	
ÉTANG DE THAU	Marseillan	
	Mèze	
	Sète	

3 • Cruising the inland waterways

On some occasions when the inland waterways of France are mentioned it is in connection with a passage to the Mediterranean, as though the waterways were only to be considered as a route to the sea. It is a pity that the Mediterranean casts such a spell, for that part of it within range of a cruise with limited time has very little to offer the small boat owner compared with the peace and interest of the French canals.

Just as mountaineers strive to get to the top of mountains so, it appears, do yachtsmen have ambitions to reach the Mediterranean which has a great deal to offer those with time to get far away from the crowded anchorages and harbours; or even for sailors who can afford to base their boats there. But for the more usual limited-time cruise, the time available would be far better spent exploring the inland waterways.

Days spent cruising at sea can be frustrating with the unpredictability of the Mediterranean weather. Sailing or motor cruising, it is easy to sympathise with the songwriter who wrote: 'we went to sea to see the world but all we saw was the sea'. One can sympathise with the lady who said that she was quite interested in leaving harbour and liked entering harbour, but found the time in between a complete bore. There is no 'time in between' when you cruise in the inland waterways, for a whole panorama is unfolding at every moment – woods, towns, fields, little villages where you can step ashore to shop and explore.

At sea your progress is determined by weather; strong winds may suddenly appear, dying away to leave complete calm. Weather never interferes with your inland waterway progress (except at times of drought and flood).

The distance down the Rhône from Lyon to the Mediterranean is around 320 km, a two to three day journey. The business of cruising the Rhône has been much simplified, but still must be treated with caution, particularly by boats with limited power.

The expedition down the Rhône to 'see the sea' can use up time and effort which might be more profitably spent in the canals. So if you have limited time and budget then consider, instead, a planned cruise through France. The Summary of route details (pages 1–4), which includes a map, shows the main navigable waterways of France arranged as 52 routes. The **towns** and *villages* on or near each of these routes are given, along with cumulative distances and the location of locks, in Part 2.

For instance, if you plan to enter France at Le Havre, Route 1 will describe the route as far as Paris. If you wish to turn off before Paris, you can do so at Conflans-St Honorine (Route 8), up, say, to Compiègne, branching right on Route 6 to Bourg-et-Comin, continuing on Route 6 to Berry-au-Bac, turning right on Route 7 as far as Condé-sur-Marne where you may take Route 5 to Paris; then back on Route 1 to return to Le Havre and you will have covered 1132km, passed through 76 locks, and sampled a little champagne on the way, perhaps.

WATERWAY	Route	Km	Locks	Route No
RIVER SEINE	Le Havre to Conflans	305	4	1
LEFT				
RIVER OISE	Conflans to Compiègne	99	7	8
RIGHT				
RIVER AISNE	Compiègne to Bourg-et-Comin	72	12	6
CONTINUE				
CANAL LATÉRAL À L'AISNE	Bourg-et-Comin to Berry-au-Bac	20	1	6
RIGHT				
CANAL DE L'AISNE À LA MARNE	Berry-au-Bac to Condé-sur-Marne	58	24	7
RIGHT	Condé-sur-Marne to Paris	202	22	5
RIVER MARNE CANAL DE CHELLES CANAL DE MEAUX À CHALIFERT				
RIVER SEINE	Paris to Le Havre	376	6	1

How long does it take?

The length of time this would take would obviously depend upon the number of hours you wished to spend in cruising every day, but the route makes a reasonable three to four weeks' cruise.

Many permutations and combinations of other routes can be planned along these lines; but the main point to be borne in mind is that anyone with even three or four weeks to spare can enjoy a cruise in the French canals. Cruises can be tailor-made to fit in with the time available.

For a leisurely passage along canals at walking pace, reckon on about 7/8 km an hour, with 15 minutes to pass through a lock (remembering that on some of the canals, the locks close for lunch). Powerful motor cruisers on passage can be opened up on the wide rivers where the speed limits are greater (eg 15 knots from the sea to the outskirts of Rouen and on the lower Saône and Rhône).

It is possible to average around 15 to 20 locks a day once you get used to the physical exertion involved. Moving a boat through locks is not a particularly strenuous occupation but after your first few days you realise what sort of physical condition you are in. It is wise to take it easy at first.

Speed limits

The speed limit varies usually between 6-10km/h. On some of the larger canalised rivers such as the Seine, between Rouen and Paris, pleasure boats not exceeding 20 tons can travel at 20km/h (10.8 knots). The limit is considerably reduced in backwaters and off moored boats, pontoons etc.

In some of the narrower canals a speed of 5 knots can set up a considerable wash, and where damage to the banks is likely to result you should slow down. Wherever the wash of your craft may inconvenience others, you should also slow down; in fact you should use your judgement and show consideration at all times. It will be seen that speed limits in the rivers are higher than in the canals but, whenever you are in doubt, you can use the barges as your guide.

Maps and guide books

In planning your cruise it will pay to consult as many maps and guide books as possible so that you go through, and near, most places of interest. The Michelin sectional maps are useful for this purpose. If you write to the local tourist office of the towns along your planned route they will be pleased to send you information regarding items of interest in their area and of events taking place at the time of your proposed visit. Minutes spent in advance planning will repay with hours of interest and pleasure on the cruise. Somehow this planning seems to be more worthwhile with a cruise than with a motor tour, maybe because you cruise along the waterways in such a leisurely fashion that stopping is no inconvenience, and you get used to stopping for locks anyway.

Cruising the French canals is the most delightful experience, catering for every taste; an active holiday for the active and a leisurely one for the leisurely – all rolled into one. For further cruising information, see also *Cruising French Waterways* by Hugh McKnight.

To get the most out of your exploring you need a bicycle for each person on board; a place on deck can usually be found for them. The Michelin maps show all the byways, and coasting along the country lanes to shop at out of the way villages is a delight. There will be no shortage of volunteers to pedal along some grassy towpath in the clear morning air to fetch the bread and milk. Shopping bags are no weight on the handlebars. When water and fuel have to be carried any distance the bike will be worth its weight in Puligny-Montrachet. And if you wish to make quicker progress through a relatively uninteresting section, a crew member can easily cycle ahead along the towpath to prepare the locks for your coming.

The details given against the place names in the Route Details Section are not by any means comprehensive, but it is hoped that the brief data given will arouse your interest sufficiently for you to want to seek further information. At each of the places named, whether described or not, it is understood that at least a shop will be nearby, and usually there will be much more.

Boat handling skills

No special skills are needed to handle a boat on the French canals but UK boat owners, taking their craft on the French waterways, must hold the International Certificate of Competence issued by the RYA. This involves a practical and oral examination (see page 36), so it follows that the skipper will already have the basic skills. Conversely, anyone who hires a boat on most of the French waterways need have no previous experience on the water to take over a hire cruiser providing, after having demonstrated the boat, the cruiser hire operator is satisfied that the skipper has mastered the basics (see pages 60–61).

Negotiating a lock.
Photo: David Jefferson

4 • Choosing the right boat

Power or sail?

What boat should you choose? Sail or power? New or second-hand? If you are a beginner you will obviously have less to learn if you buy a motor cruiser rather than a sailing yacht; but this consideration cannot be of the greatest importance because beginners are sailing away in sailing yachts every day of the week.

Quite apart from the relative merits of sailing versus motor cruising, a motor cruiser will have roomier accommodation for a given overall length than a sailing boat. The sailing boat hull needs to be a 'sailing shape' whereas the motor cruising hull does not need such fine underwater lines. The comparatively restricted accommodation of a sailing yacht is further reduced by the stowage room needed for sails and gear. The cockpit space needed for managing the business of sailing can be used for accommodation in a motor cruiser.

You would only buy a sailing boat if you were keen to enjoy sailing at times when you were not inland cruising. At these times the handling of a sailing boat involves your family, for one member usually attends to sail changing while another minds the helm. In a motor cruiser, only the one person at the wheel is involved.

These are all general considerations to be borne in mind and do not refer specifically to selecting the most suitable craft in which to explore the French canals; for this purpose alone there is no doubt that a motor cruiser would be the obvious choice.

Unstepping masts

If, however, you feel that you would like to sail sometimes and explore the inland waterways on other occasions, then there is no difficulty in unstepping the mast of a suitable sailing yacht when you want to use it for canal cruising. If this is to be a regular routine, then a yacht with a tabernacle does make life so much easier. Big sailing yachts with tall masts may not be suitable for the inland waterways because of their deep draught. The owner of such a sailing yacht, whose mast height greatly exceeds the LOA of the boat, may well have to consider arranging for the mast to be transported overland to await the arrival of the boat in a Mediterranean harbour after she has motored across France through the waterways. Carried on crutches on the boat, apart from being a nuisance when manoeuvring, the over-hang can easily cause damage, not only to the overhanging section, but to the whole mast and to everything to which it is attached.

Most entry ports into France have yacht clubs where masts can be unstepped, and stored too. In Le Havre, for instance, unstepping and stepping can be arranged at the marina by the Capitainerie. They also have details of a firm who can store the mast and, if needed, transport it overland to Port St Louis (see pages 32–33 for a list of firms that can lower/raise, store and transport masts).

Motor cruisers

With the huge interest in navigating inland waterways, boat builders have been designing craft that are equally suited to running in coastal waters or canals. With semi-displacement hulls, they are good sea boats capable of 15–20 knots for the Channel crossing, and coping with most conditions. They have engines designed for low speed running to achieve hours of economical waterway cruising, use the keel to protect all the stern gear (or bilge keels to protect twin props, shafts and rudders) and an air draught that can be reduced in minutes for particularly low bridges. And for extended stays on the boat, equipment such as hot air heating comes as standard.

Multihulls

Much in evidence on the waterways, particularly bound for the Mediterranean, the beam of these craft, unless exceptional, presents no problem. Maximum beam permitted on most of the canals is 5.0m (Brittany 4.5m).

Prop power

The ideal craft is a twin-screw motor cruiser with inside and outside steering positions and controls, but only if it is a craft with propellers protected, either by the sort of metal guards that you see on barges or by the actual position of the propellers in the shape of the hull, otherwise a prop will be the first point of contact with the sloping side of a lock or become entangled with submerged debris.

The same objections, indeed more so, apply to outdrives, inboard/outboards, transom, stern drives, or whatever other name is given to outside drive units. The less you have 'outside' of your boat the less likely you are to run into trouble. Even if remote controls could bring outside drive units completely

The removal of the mast gives much more deck space. Also, bear in mind that the cost of repair can easily be more than the cost of sending your mast by road. *Photo: Keith Harris*

inboard, instead of raising them, the point is that there is rarely any advance warning of the time when this might be necessary.

Protection is, therefore, essential for any yacht with exposed propellers. If you have a choice between single or twin, single is perfectly adequate for the French canals, and obviously more economical. A twin screw is more manoeuvrable, although a good skipper will manage a single screw better than a poorer one with a twin. In recent years bow thrusters have appeared on quite small craft and this is certainly a splendid aid to manoeuvring, particularly in confined harbours and waterways. It is also less expensive to fit a single engine and bow thruster rather than twin engines.

Professional advice

It is hardly necessary to stress that you should never buy a second-hand boat without a professional survey.

The RYA has long been active in protecting the rights of yachtsmen and if you are not a member you should join and thus help the cause. The address is Royal

Classic Boats' EuroClassic peniche (overall length 14.63m, beam 4.1m, draught .76m, air draught 2.6m) can be purchased through the boat sponsorship scheme introduced by France Afloat and earning income through chartering. *Photo: ClassicBoats Ltd www.classicboats.co.uk*

Yachting Association, RYA House, Ensign Way, Hamble, Hampshire SO31 4YA (tel 0845 3450400) and they are always most helpful and willing to advise you on the current situation regarding documentation needed for craft entering France (and, of course, on many other matters).

Boat sponsorship

Of the various choices for financing the purchase of a boat for the French waterways, 'boat sponsorship' is an interesting option.

In a scheme introduced by France Afloat (see page 61), the EuroClassic range of river/canal boats can be purchased through Classic Boats in the UK and transported to France Afloat's bases where the vessel will form part of the Burgundy Cruisers hire fleet. France Afloat handle all the chartering and pay most of the running costs such as insurance, licensing and general maintenance, and provide the mooring when the boat is not in use. The owner receives 30 per cent of the income from chartering which can give a reasonable return on the investment plus the attraction of an annual four-week holiday cruising the French waterways in your own boat.

Comfort and safety

In considering a suitable boat for the waterways you will be thinking in terms of living onboard for several weeks at a time and you will want as much room as you can afford, certainly headroom. An aft cabin is a good idea for families with children or for two families. It also makes for easier living to have the separate bedroom that an aft cabin makes possible. Two toilets make for harmony, two toilets and showers make for luxury indeed, but naturally you have to monitor the water supply, pumps, heaters and drain away.

The ideal accommodation layout that has developed in suitable motor cruisers provides a bedroom or cabin at either end of the boat, each with its own toilet and shower; a central galley with dining area opposite which makes up into a double berth and a secondary steering position on the aft deck.

You should bear in mind the question of freeboard when you are going about the delightful business of choosing your dream yacht for the French waterways. The seller of any 'high-out-of-the-water' luxury yacht will have thoughtfully provided a stepped platform alongside for your ease of access and descent when you come to view; but when emergencies arise later, and you need to quickly leap off or on, there will be no one alongside with a stepped platform. You will need to be stepping off and on at high speed on occasions and you should choose a boat that allows all of your crew to do this easily.

Draught above and below the water

Shallow draught, bilge keel or lifting keel craft are an advantage in the waterways because they enable you to go alongside attractive river banks and villages denied to a deeper draught. For the ideal French waterway yacht a 1.2m (4ft) draught is about right despite the average waterway depth of 1.8m (5ft 10in) in normal conditions on the main routes to the Mediterranean.

The most critical dimension is air draught, or height above the water. The modern design of sea-going motor cruisers provides for a flying bridge which may well debar the craft from the French inland waterways. When salesmen tell you that their boat will go through the French canals, they are referring to the main routes from Le Havre or Calais to the Mediterranean but, even here, the Burgundy Canal maximum air height is 3.4m, with less clearance for a fly bridge through the Pouilly tunnel (see page 7). The Bourbonnais and the Marne minimum bridge clearance is 3.5m. Every height above the waterline limit is shown in the Route Details section, and you should study them before falling in love with a boat that is too high out of the water.

Cruising in retirement

Many more people approaching retirement are now seeking to spend their early retired years in cruising the European waterways and wintering in the Mediterranean. 'For a year or so, maybe', they protest tentatively, but years later are happy, bronzed nautical tramps who could never consider giving up the marine gipsy life and whose only regret is that they did not embark upon it years earlier.

An odd observation is that personal relationships sometimes improve when confined to the waterway life. You would imagine the reverse to be the case, indeed we have all heard women protesting that 'they do not know what they will do when they are shut up with him all day long on his retirement' – and they are usually referring to life in a house! The intimacy of the boating life must act like an emotional pressure cooker bringing out only the best; the most unlikely couples can be seen wandering ashore hand in hand...

When you plan on boating in retirement you must plan for comfort first of all. You can forget all about sailing on your ear. Make sure you have a superb kitchen and dining area, a comfortable bedroom, toilet and shower and then – and only then – can you start deciding how much sailing performance and paraphernalia you can wrap around that.

Even for those who openly object to sailing, who have simply never gone along with boating ideas at all, there is still the avenue of persuasion represented by the inland waterways of Europe. Obviously you would not go across Seine Bay by way of introduction; but to have the boat alongside some charming French village where you have arranged for dinner ashore perhaps, and then next day to commence gliding through the beauty of France, bounce-free and passing by a never ending panorama of interest... you can more easily than you think have anyone hooked on the boating life. After a week or two, the boat will have become a way of life and the odd bounce will be accepted.

By the time you get to the Mediterranean you will also be very much fitter and perhaps this is the time to mention that if you have been accustomed to a sedentary life you should adjust to the boating life by easy stages. If you make yourself competent at handling your craft, the passage through the many locks should present no physical stresses but after the first few days of rope throwing and hauling and maybe some lock ladder climbing you can expect to be exhausted. However after a day of rest and recovery and a bottle or so of Côtes du Rhône you will recover. So to fully enjoy the French canals, don't try to do too much too soon.

The Dutch builders Linssen Yachts produce a prestigious range of steel displacement motor yachts designed for coastal work and inland waterways. Shown here (ABOVE) is the Grand Sturdy 299 Sedan (overall length 9.35m, beam 3.35m, draught 1.00m, air draught with folded mast 2.48m) and (BELOW) the Dutch Sturdy Evergreen (overall length 10.10m, beam 3.60m, draught 1.05m, air draught with folded mast 2.45m). *Photos: © Linssen Yachts B.V. www.linssenyachts.com*

5 · Equipment

When cruising the beautiful waterways of France, you can forget all about plotting courses, and fixes, and sail changing, bouncing around and hanging on. You can forget all about the need to work out your direction – it is there, ahead, the water-road.

The equipment needed will be for: protecting your yacht against the odd encounter with other craft and with lock walls, providing adequate securing and getting ashore facilities, spare fuel cans and transport, and safety onboard.

Fenders and planks

Adequate fenders are necessary, a minimum of four, large, sausage shape, but preferably more because they can come under considerable strain when being squeezed along the sides of steel barges. And they can be easily broken off on

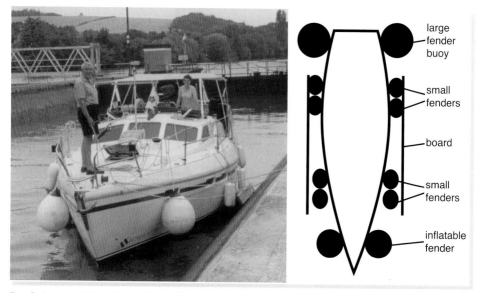

Fendering in a V lock. You will need a combination of small, medium and large fenders (see diagram). *Photo: Keith Harris*

entering those locks where it is necessary to put a crew member ashore with a warp; for the lock ladder is usually just inside beyond the lock gate and in manoeuvring to put your crew on the ladder you must obviously be close in – so close that fenders get pressed into the gate recess and held there while the yacht moves on. It does not often happen, but there are times when concentration wavers, for instance when you are nearing the end of the 37 locks (which are almost joined together) approaching the summit of the Bourgogne.

The use of tyres as fenders is not permitted as, without an inflated inner tube, they can come adrift in a lock and sink, sometimes jamming the sluices.

Fender sox are a useful addition to protect your boat in grimy locks. A plank or two comes in very useful for hanging outside the fenders when alongside pontoons or piles that otherwise work their way inside the protective fenders and make contact with the hull. The plank is sure to come in handy doubling up as a gangplank when, for some reason, there is too big a gap between the boat and the shore. A hole in each end of the plank will make for easy attachment.

Sometimes, when it is desirable to come alongside an unscalable quay wall, a ladder onboard then makes all the difference between getting ashore and not.

Boathooks, stakes and warps

Take the largest boathook you can conveniently stow on deck. If you are a congenital boathook loser, take two. If you have only one, obtain a long pole on the canal bank as soon as you can. Lock keepers in the country sections invariably have a fine selection. You will need the pole for fending off, not only from the walls of locks with sloping sides, but from canal banks when you secure in just sufficient depth of water. You see barges moored in this way with poles almost big enough to do duty carrying telephone wires.

You will need two stakes, preferably of metal; these you will find useful, necessary even, to hammer into the bank alongside, when there is no other attachment for your warps. Also, of course, you will need a mallet or large hammer for banging the stakes into the ground.

Warps have a hard working life on the waterways and four 27m (88ft) 38mm (1½in) to 50mm (2in) warps are the minimum that should be carried on an average cruiser of around 8 tonnes. Every lock puts a strain on them that they do not experience in harbour. The water surges to or from the lock with the warps straining, sometimes chafing over the edge of a lock wall, finding sharp cracks and crevices. Warps are your waterway friends and you should look after them most attentively.

Dinghies

On most waterways, towing a dinghy is prohibited, and to do so may earn a sharp rebuke from the lock keeper. Yet one must have a dinghy so it must be capable of being stowed inboard out of the way. The advantage of an inflatable is that when entering the inland waterways this can be bagged up and stored. Occasionally it can be useful secured alongside to keep the boat off a quayside or river bank.

Flags and sirens

As far as flags are concerned, a French courtesy flag will be needed.

You will need a hooter or fog horn to warn of your approach. In the peace of the country locks you could almost shout to announce your arrival, but in the commercial sections and harbours, with noise all around, you need something fairly drastic.

Torches and searchlights

Two or three good torches are necessary, for you will often be returning to your boat at night, perhaps on unlighted canal banks. Replacement batteries and torches are easy enough to buy anywhere in France.

A good searchlight with a wide beam will be essential for the tunnels. In some tunnels you can be towed if you have no searchlight, or if the light you have is considered unsatisfactory. Towing times and charges are available at the lock nearest the entrance.

Containers and hoses

The only other necessary items that might be classed as deck equipment are portable containers for fuel, water, and paraffin, as many as you can stow. There are so many different shapes and sizes of container that it is well worth going to the trouble of finding ones that fit your available stowage space; you will also need filling funnels for each. A boat hose is also worth investing in for use with lock-side water taps. The type that packs flat on a reel is best. Obtain a variety of threads. Also, your filler caps should be attached inboard by a wire or line.

Holding tanks

Pump-out facilities along the waterways for disposing of 'black water' (toilet) and 'grey water' (washing-up etc) are few and far between on the French waterways. Waste water from most of the charter boats is pumped straight into the canals and rivers. Offshore in parts of the Mediterranean, and in certain French ports in the south, legislation is starting to dictate the use of holding tanks, but on the waterways, implementation of environmental policy with regard to the disposal of waste from the heads, shower or galley is primarily in the hands of the local authorities and varies from region to region. Some ignore the problem completely; others encourage the provision of holding tanks but are still reluctant to provide adequate pump out stations.

Legislation is strict on the UK waterways where holding tanks are standard equipment, and ashore there is an abundance of pump-out stations. If a canal boat with a holding tank operated in the UK is taking up a new location on the French waterways, the dearth of pump-out stations may cause major problems. Conversely, the owner of a sea boat with no holding tank based in the UK considering moving to the Mediterranean may well require a holding tank when based in the south of France.

The experts in the UK who will advise on pipe work, pumps, deck fittings, hull outlets and holding tanks are Lee Sanitation Ltd, Wharf Road, Fenny Compton, Warwickshire CV47 2FE. Tel 01295 770000 Website: www.leesan.com. They normally have a stand at the London and Southampton boat shows.

Masts

Sailing yachts will need stowage planned in advance on deck for the mast when it is unstepped. Trestles at each end of the boat are simplest, with the centre of the mast resting on the top of the coachroof, in the tabernacle if there is a convenient one. Pieces of foam rubber are useful for protecting the masts at points of contact and at each end if there is an overhang. An overhang of 2.5m at each end is about the limit one should contemplate. The difficulty arises in the smaller locks when you are below the level of the lock wall, and the rush of water causes the boat to swing strongly. Stationing oneself right forward with a boathook at the ready is the answer but it can be a bit of a strain at times.

Some boat owners lash timber athwart the bows when the overhang of the mast is considerable. This prevents damage to the mast by swinging in locks but such an arrangement is viewed with apprehension by other craft alongside.

Sailing yachts should take a supply of strong, stringed labels to mark each item of standing and running rigging, blocks and shackles before the mast is unstepped; as soon as it is laid on the deck the shambles of rigging will resemble a fallen tree.

Masts can be left at Le Havre and stepped on return, or transported overland to await the boat's arrival at Port St Louis. Leaving the mast ashore can be the best arrangement, for the mast and rigging are always in the way on deck and the overhang of the mast can be a nuisance as already mentioned. Regular visitors to the inland waterways would be best suited with a motor cruiser.

Capitaineries at the following ports will arrange the lowering or raising of masts (they rarely have permanent storage facilities):

North Sea/Channel: Dunkerque, Gravelines, Calais (plus storage), St-Valery-sur-Somme, Le Havre, Honfleur, Rouen, St-Malo (Bassin Vauban – self-operated 1-ton), Saint-Servan (Port des Sablons), Dinard, Dinan (500kg)

Biscay/Atlantic: Redon, La Roche Bernard, Port d'Arzal-Camoël, Royan, Port Medoc (mouth of the Gironde), Pauillac, Bordeaux (Lormont)

Mediterranean: Port St-Louis (Port Napoleon – plus storage), Cap d'Agde, Sète

If more than raising or lowering the mast is required, the following firms also undertake storage and transport of masts in addition to removing/stepping:

North Sea/Channel

Devriendt-Hansmar NV
Industrieterrein 'De Arend' 13
B-8210 Zedelgem
Belgium
tel 050 250 310
fax +32 (050) 208 281
e-mail: info@decamar.be
www.decamar.com

Marine Plus
Hangar 27
Quai Frissard
76600 Le Havre
tel 02 35 24 21 14
e-mail: marine-plus@wanadoo.fr

Honfleur Nautique
Tec Ocean
Route de Bassin Carnot
14600 Honfleur
tel 02 31 89 55 89
email: tec.ocean@wanadoo.fr

Chantier Naval de la Baie de Seine,
Bassin Vauban
136, Quai Frissard,
76600 Le Havre
tel 02 35 25 30 51
e-mail: stephan.reiset@cnhm.fr

Mediterranean

Navy Service
Ave de la Première DFL
13230 Port St Louis
tel 04 42 11 00 55
e-mail: navyservice@voila.fr

Littoral Marine
Zone Technique
34300 Cap D'Agde
tel 04 67 26 44 37
e-mail: littoral.marine@wanadoo.fr

Gas, paraffin and fire extinguishers

Below deck, an inland waterway cruise calls for no special equipment. The UK Calor bottles are not available in France. Empty bottles of butane/propane can only be exchanged for full ones of the same brand. Those spending several months on the French waterways should consider adopting the French type bottles and fittings. Although the small 4.5kg Calor cylinders cannot be exchanged, the French Primagaz of the same capacity does have the same thread and hose connections. The larger capacity Calor cylinders do not have compatible threads with French cylinders. Camping Gaz in various sized cylinders is widely available in France, and a simple adaptor to run Camping Gaz with Calor fittings is available in the UK at many camping shops.

If you happen to have paraffin appliances on board you will find that paraffin is widely available under the name of *Pétrole Supérieur*, from *Peintures* and *Drogueries*. Methylated spirits are obtainable from the same source, also from some food stores, and known as *Alcool à Brûler*.

It is essential to have fire extinguishers strategically sited. There may be occasions when the boat is inspected by the French authorities to make certain basic safety equipment is on board.

6 • Planning the cruise

Having decided upon your boat, the next step is to plan your cruise through the French canals.

The limits of your cruise will obviously depend upon the time that you have available and whether, in this time, you propose a return trip or a one-way trip, leaving your boat in France ready for your next cruising adventure (in which case you would either return by train or, more conveniently, in a hire car (see page 62)).

You should apply to Chambre Syndicale Nationale des Courtiers du Frêt Fluviale, 32 Rue de Londres, 75009 Paris, tel (0)1 42 85 54 26, fax (0)1 42 85 00 22, for the current list of *chomages*, which shows which locks are closed for maintenance work and when; this maintenance work is usually carried out during the winter. The list is published in March/April showing the autumn/winter closures for the current year and for the first three months of the following year.

In addition to these lock closures for fixed repair periods some lock sections are closed on Sundays.

Use the route map in conjunction with the route details and the appropriate Michelin map, noting the names of the towns that lie on or near the route of your proposed cruise. As already mentioned, the tourist office at these towns will be pleased to send you details of items of interest or of any special event planned for the time that you will be there. See pages 305–6 for a comprehensive list of waterway guides and other recommended reading.

Since 1 January 1992, boats cruising the French waterways have been required to pay a fee. It is fair that all waterway users should help to pay for their considerable upkeep, and no yachtsman is likely to object to the modest charges. The Voies Navigables de France (VNF) is the independent authority set up by the French Government to manage the state waterway system.

The fee is due for any boat over 5m LOA fitted with an engine exceeding 9.9 bhp. On payment, a licence is issued for display on the front of the boat, starboard side, visible from the exterior at all times.

The amount of the fee is based on the boat's surface area of length by beam, excluding pulpit or other 'outside' fittings. You can pay for 16 consecutive days, 30 consecutive days, 4 months or the whole year.

VNF licence fees 2006 (euros)

Categories 2006		I	II	III	IV	V
	manual propulsion*	up to 12m²	from 12 to 25m²	from 25 to 40m²	from 40 to 60m²	over 60m²
Option						
Year	34.40	79.60	113.90	228.90	369.80	457.90
Season	—	71.70	102.50	206.00	295.80	366.30
Leisure	—	29.00	60.00	89.00	118.00	148.70
Holiday	—	17.20	35.50	52.70	69.90	88.20
Day	8.70	8.70	17.20	25.90	34.40	43.00

The Yearly Card: A 10% discount may be available at certain times.
The Season Card: 4 months taken consecutively.
The Leisure Card: The leisure card is valid for 30 days taken consecutively.
The Holiday Card: Valid for 16 consecutive days, this is issued with an expiry date. If taken out on a Saturday, it gives you access to three consecutive weekends.
The Single Day Card: It is valid for one day, and cannot be delivered in more than two separate issues.

*Regardless of the surface area of the boat.

Thirty-seven VNF payment centres are situated throughout France, at Calais, Dunkerque, Le Havre and Rouen, for instance, although not at all points of entry into the country; see pages 57–8 for full list of VNF payment centres. You can apply by post for a licence, giving name and address, name of boat, overall length and beam, draught, proof of engine output, registration number, desired duration of licence and corresponding dates of validity to: VNF, 175 rue Ludovic Boutleux, 62400 Béthune, France. Postal applications should be accompanied by a photocopy of the Registration Certificate, the International Certificate of Competence and a cheque in euros payable to VNF. Apply in advance for the current rates to the Béthune address or internet site: http://www.vnf.fr.

7 • In the waterways of France

Documentation

On UK-flagged vessels, the owner (or strictly speaking the helmsman) should possess the International Certificate of Competence (which includes the CEVNI test). This covers handling boats up to 24m. Above 24m, the French Certificate PP is required. Obtain details from the RYA. Since 1 January 2005 the powered craft category of the certificate is divided into two groups, dependant upon the type of course or assessment you take: Powered craft up to 10m in length *or* powered craft up to 24m in length.

Sail is still in one category allowing use of a yacht with auxiliary on the waterways up to 24m in length. The British cruiser hire company France Afloat, 1 Quai du Port, 89270 Vermenton, France, is a recognised RYA examiner and can offer a combined cruising holiday and the opportunity of gaining the ICC qualification from their base at Vermenton, nr Auxerre on the Canal du Nivernais (see page 61). It is also compulsory to carry a copy of the CEVNI Rules (obtainable from the RYA or from Adlard Coles Nautical: *The Adlard Coles Book of EuroRegs for Inland Waterways: A pleasure boater's guide to CEVNI*). Evidence of third party insurance cover should be available. Some insurance companies provide an extract of the terms of a boat's insurance in several languages to meet this requirement.

The boat owner should always be prepared for a spot check by French Customs of ship's papers which must include registration certificate, VHF licence, along with passports for all the crew.

When hiring a boat, no special documentation is required apart from the *Carte de Plaisance* which is issued by the cruiser hire operator.

Rules of the water-roads

The rule of the road is generally to keep to the right. However, this does not apply on some sections of waterway. On the Seine, for example, traffic is continuously switching from one side to the other. These cross-over points are shown on the river bank (sometimes obscured) and in the more detailed river guides. A helpful general guide to the 'rules of the road' is given in *The European Waterways* by Marian Martin, published by Adlard Coles Nautical. When you

Waterway vocabulary

accostage – alongside mooring
amarrage – mooring
amasse – grouping of boats to enter lock
amont – upstream; upper reaches
appontement – pontoon
aval – downstream; lower reaches
avalant – descending
avis à la batellerie – notice to boat owners
bâbord – port side
bac – cross-river ferry
bajoyer – lock wall
barrage – weir/dam
batillage – boat's wash
bief – stretch of water between two locks

chemin de halage – tow-path
chômage – period of closure of locks for maintenance
clapot – small waves
confluent – the meeting of two or more rivers
darse – basin
délaissé – closed canal
dérivation – section of canal bypassing a nearby river
digue – dyke
duc d'albe – mooring post
échelle d'écluses – staircase of locks
écluse – lock
éclusier, -ière – lock keeper
espar – post used as navigation mark
halage – towing
halte fluviale – bankside mooring

haut fond – shallows
mouillage – deep water for mooring
NNN – guaranteed normal water level
perche – suspended rod turned to operate lock
portes de garde – lock gates used only in flood conditions
radier – bottom of a lock
régulation – lock operation outside normal hours
sas – lock chamber
tirant d'air – air draught
tirant d'eau – draught
trémater – overtake
tribord – starboard side
vantelle – lock sluices

get on to the shallower sections a heavily laden barge will have to follow the deep water channel whichever side of the waterway this takes him. If he comes over to 'your side' he will put out from starboard side of his wheel-house a large blue board with a flashing white light at its centre, you then alter course to pass him on this side.

Whilst on the subject of passing it may be the moment to explain that when, later on, you come to the narrower canals you must slow down on meeting an oncoming barge and inch your way in towards the bank on your side as far as you dare. As his bow wave approaches you increase your speed and again when you are amidships of him, aiming back into the centre of the channel through the wash of his screw.

Right from the start you should keep a good look out for dredgers. They are usually held in their dredging position by a line to the bank and will be exhibiting a signal showing which side to pass. Sometimes dredgers are secured by lines to both banks and they will lower one of them into the water on your approach; but it is as well to look through the binoculars to be sure that they have seen you, not that your siren will be of much avail to announce your approach, for it would take an atomic explosion to compete with the racket of the dredging buckets.

If you see a barge displaying a red flag amidships it is an indication that he is turning in that direction and should not be overtaken on that side.

Overtaking

It is likely that you will be the overtaken vessel most of the time, particularly on the wide waterways, and you will be overtaken without comment, just as you will overtake the odd slower craft that you come up on. Some yachts fit a rear mirror so that they can see what is coming up astern without turning round, but you do not really need this eye in the back of your head to the extent that you do in a car; boats and ships move relatively slowly, and since it is likely that you will be interested in looking all around you all the time, it will be a rare occasion that a craft will creep up on you unobserved. If you are in the way you will hear about it. If you keep well over to your side of the channel you will not attract attention.

In the narrower waterways where there is just room to pass, one is supposed to signal. Request to overtake by hooting two long and one short blast if it is desired to pass to starboard and two long and two short if it is desired to pass to port. The answering signal indicating that it is OK to overtake to starboard is two short blasts; OK to pass to port is one short blast. Five short blasts means a refusal to let the overtaking vessel pass. This should not be construed as an outburst of bloody-mindedness, but simply that the skipper ahead can see a hazard that has not come into the view of the overtaking craft.

On some of the narrower canals, if you come up behind a barge going your way it is not likely that you will be able to pass him however much you toot. At each lock he will get ahead temporarily while the lock chamber is being refilled or re-emptied for you. It is foolish to allow yourself to become frustrated at being continually held up in this way. Far better to stop at some pleasant spot for sightseeing or shopping and thus allow the barge to get clear ahead. It may be that, by waiting, you will allow for the possibility of a barge coming from the opposite direction; then you will have all the locks 'set up' ready for you to enter (except in a few sections where the lock gates are always put one way after traffic has passed).

In case it may be wondered how barges going opposite ways can pass if it is impossible to pass when going the same way, the answer is that they squeeze past somehow. It takes so much longer to pass a barge when going the same way. You cannot blame him for keeping going, and it is a hair raising experience to try to squeeze slowly by over his stern and bow wave with only inches to spare. Hotel barges will invariably increase speed to prevent being overtaken so that they can claim a night stopover ahead or be first into an upcoming lock.

Bridges

When approaching bridges with a number of arches you will see signals on the bridges showing you which arch to take, as follows:

or	**2 red horizontal bars with a white stripe between**	*No entry* from the direction you are coming from
	1 yellow diamond	*Two-way traffic through arch*
or	**2 yellow diamonds**	*Entry* from your direction only (*one-way traffic through arch*)

In the canals there are many narrow sections underneath bridges, and you will need to be ready to 'put your brakes on' urgently if a barge suddenly appears from round the corner ahead as you approach. Never attempt a race to the opening, for it is likely that you will be able to stop much quicker than the opposition. In going astern, as you will have to, be sure to go astern far enough, for the barge will sometimes clear the opening with maddening slowness; if you have gone ahead too soon it is an alarming experience to have the barge alongside you and no room ahead.

In fact, these encounters with barges are very rarely met, for it is usual to cruise all day long on the smaller canals without seeing more than two or three. But when you do meet them it is as well to be prepared.

Where 'traffic lights' are positioned at bridges, tunnels, locks, etc, the signal is:

●	**Red**	*Stop*
●	**Green**	*Go*
●● }	**Red and Green**	*Stand by*

Turning off

The channel that you are to follow is usually obvious, but not always so. The entrance to a lock might turn off quietly left or right, leaving what appears to be a splendid waterway ahead ... until you observe the spray haze rising up from the falling water of a weir. Near towns there are sometimes bridges busy with traffic

River signs: prohibition

No passing

Navigation not allowed except for non-motorised minor craft

Overtaking and passing forbidden

No overtaking between convoys

No crossing
No overtaking

No parking   No anchoring   No mooring   No veering No turning   No waves   or

No passing outside the indicated area   or   No passing but get ready to start up   No entering harbour or tributary waterway   Navigation not allowed to all engine-powered craft

No pleasure-boat allowed   No waterskiing   No sailing   No rowing boat   No wind-surfing   No swimming or bathing   No jetskiing

River signs: restriction

| Beware! Limited depth of water | Beware! Limited available height above the water-way | Beware! Restrictions imposed on navigation | Beware! Restrictions imposed on navigation | The channel is 40m away from the right bank |

River signs: recommendations

Channel recommended in both directions   Channel recommended only in the indicated direction. Passing in the opposite direction is forbidden   Recommendation to keep the boat within the indicated area   Recommendation to follow the direction of the arrow   Recommendation to follow the direction from the steady light to the flashing light

Reproduced courtesy Voies Navigables de France VNF.

River signs: obligation

Follow the direction indicated by the arrow	Make for the port side of the channel	Make for the starboard side of the channel	Keep on the port side of the channel	Keep on the starboard side of the channel	Crossing the port side channel compulsory	Crossing the starboard side channel compulsory

Stop under certain conditions	Do not exceed the indicated speed	Sound your horn	Be careful!

River signs: indications

Passing allowed

Crossing of an electric wire	Ferry not navigating freely	Parking allowed	Anchoring allowed	Mooring allowed	Turning area

The waterways are considered as tributaries to the waterway encountered	The waterway is considered as tributary to the waterway encountered	End of an obligation	Indications of vessels leaving (port)

Drinking water tap	Telephone	Waterskiing area	Navigation allowed to all engine-powered	All pleasure-boats allowed	Sailing boats allowed	Rowing boats allowed

Windsurfing allowed	Bathing allowed	Jetskiing allowed

A light beam operates the ancient lifting Pont de Crimée which spans the Canal St Martin, Paris. *Photo: David Jefferson*

that holds your attention, until it is diverted by a local citizen on the nearby bank afflicted, apparently, with St Vitus's Dance; you realise that he is only trying to attract your attention to dangers ahead. Going back you find that you have missed the proper turning. Sometimes it is not obvious which side of an island you should pass, although this should be marked by an arrow.

A quiet mooring. *Photo: David Jefferson*

Mooring

No traffic moves on the majority of French waterways at night and it is a delight to tie up to trees, by some grassy bank, in the knowledge that your sleep is going to be undisturbed. But never moor up with lines across the towpath which may be used by walkers, joggers or cyclists.

Barges have priority over pleasure craft. *Photo: David Jefferson*

Times of opening

These vary from one waterway to another. In 2003, the 35-hour week was introduced in France which had the overall effect of reducing the number of hours traditionally worked by the lock keepers. Consult the routes section for opening/closure times. Some canals, eg the Canal de Bourgogne, Canal du Midi and Brittany canals, with no commercial traffic, are closed during the winter months.

On many of the canals, locks are not operated for an hour between 1200–1330 for lock keepers to take a lunch break.

Locks generally close on public holidays (see page 59). However on some holidays (eg Bastille Day, 14 July, Assumption Day, 15 August) it might be possible to make prior arrangements with the lock keeper to pass through the lock for a modest fee (billed to the boat owner's home address). Enquire the previous day at an earlier lock, and the lock keeper will invariably telephone to find out whether a particular lock or locks will be manned over the holiday, and fix up a time to be at the lock/s. Alternatively you can ask for the telephone number of future locks and make your own arrangements for the following day.

8 • Locks

What to expect

A certain competence in handling a boat is necessary in order to make the trip through the canals, and no special skill is needed to go in and out of locks. As for being worried about locks simply because of their size, the biggest of all, the Bollène, raises or lowers you in its 25m (82ft) cathedral-like chamber without a ripple. By comparison, a lock keeper can cause discomfort by changing a 1.50m (5ft) level too quickly if you are not secured properly.

Locks can vary in size and operation according to the traffic carried. Some locks have a gate in the centre, so that it can be a half-size or a full-size lock according to the traffic. Busy waterway sections have big locks, often automatically operated. More and more automatically controlled locks are now triggered by radar or photo-electric cells, which recognise the approach of your craft. If it fails to do so, go ashore and use the lock telephone which is a direct line to help. Many automatic locks need to be operated yourself.

The quieter country sections have small single locks, manually operated by the lock keeper or, more usually, by his wife assisted by a crew member of the boat passing through.

Entering the French waterways from England, the commercial size locks will be the first to be encountered, and it may be as well to consider the big locks first; also ascending locks, since these will need to be dealt with before the descending.

Ascending your first lock

The invariable rule for pleasure craft is to keep out of the way of all commercial craft, displaying to them 'after you' politeness which they will appreciate. Seek no preference over a barge because you arrived at the lock before him.

Before entering, your foredeck hand should have a coiled rope in hand ready to throw in case the lock keeper shows any interest in receiving it and assuming that he is near. It is probable that he will be if the lock gates are manually operated. Some of the bigger locks and all of the huge ones are operated by the remote control of a lock keeper in a control tower. The really big locks have vast steel shutters that rise up and down instead of gates.

Floating bollards on the Rhône (detail, right). *Photo: Keith Harris*

Whilst securing, keep your eye on the lock gates closing behind you to make sure that your stern has not drifted back into them.

Soon after the gates close, the water level will begin to rise. If you are secured to one of the lock bollards you must take up on your rope as you rise, to keep your station; secured alongside some other boat, you have no worry in this respect.

Barges in the lock will be getting ready to move out as soon as the gates ahead open; when their screws start turning you will need to be secured. The swirling water will create no problem if you are tied to bollards.

Allow any barges to go on ahead before you let go.

Securing lines

In very deep, large, locks there are set in the lock walls, recessed fixed bollards or movable bollards that slide up and down with you so that there is no need to adjust your ropes as the water level changes. Or sometimes, in smaller locks, the lock keeper of a deep lock will reach down a long pole with a hook on the end to take your warp. Some yachts carry such poles, with hooks on the end, for passing warps to lock keepers and for reaching around bollards.

Not all locks have straight sides; where they are sloping, V shaped, it can be more difficult to get a line ashore, although V shaped locks usually have a small pontoon to facilitate landing. (Some locks have one side sloping and one straight.)

When you enter a sloping-sided V shaped lock, a crew member steps onto the pontoon as the steps are too slippery with mud and slime. The crew takes the lines along the bank. When the lock has filled he can step back onto the boat as by then it is near the bank. *Photo: Keith Harris*

Smaller locks

Small locks will be the ones most frequently encountered. Since they fit the type of barge using them like a glove, there is no question of sharing these locks with a barge.

The smaller locks are on the waterways with little traffic, and it is usual to go for a whole day without meeting more than two or three barges.

Two or three yachts can be accommodated in the smaller locks, and the lock routine can then be shared between crews.

On approaching a small lock, if the gates are closed against you and no one is in view, a toot on your siren/hooter will usually bring someone from the lock house to start opening one gate for you. Whether anyone appears or not, nose your craft into the bank and put a crew member ashore, to find the lock keeper, if necessary, and to open the other gate. If the beam of your boat allows you to enter through one opened gate, your crew member will go up the lock ladder once inside.

Should it be lunch time, this will be the moment to have your own lunch, too. Many lock keepers like to have their lunch undisturbed, and who can blame them?

Obviously the gates will not be opened for you until the water in the lock chamber is equalised on your level.

RIGHT Seine locks are deep and long lines are not practicable. There are a series of recessed cleats or 'antlers' in this lock; you need to move the mooring lines up or down on the antlers as the boat moves. Use the top bollard at the top level only. Never make lines fast – run them around the bollards and hold them.

LEFT An example of how a single line system is used on a square hire boat. The line positions will be different on a sailing yacht. The engine is left running in 'slow ahead'.
Photos: Keith Harris

If, on approaching, the lock gates are open, look to see whether the iron rung ladder is set in the right or left wall. They are situated fairly constantly, all right or all left, for long sections of locks at a time, and only appear to change when you get too confident in your anticipation.

Nose your craft up to the ladder so that your crew can step off on to it carrying a suitable length of attached (to the boat) bow warp coiled over his or her shoulder like a mountain climber. The crew should get into the habit of gaining the quay quickly and allowing for the pull on the warp once the boat starts moving into the lock. Move on into the lock, and instruct the crew to take a turn round a bollard and throw the end of the warp back down to you. If your crew is already ashore to open the gate, you will need to have your warp ready coiled to throw and to stand by for its return. Secure aft and be ready to take up as the water rises.

Do not expect the lock keeper to assist with the warps. With inexperienced crews from charter boats, the lock keeper must concentrate on making sure all the craft in the lock remain suitably secured and that warps are not slipping or becoming dangerously taut.

The lock keeper will close one gate behind you, and if the second gate has been opened your crew will close that. They will then walk up to the gates ahead and wind up the sluice handles to let the water in.

When the lock water level is equalised, the lock keeper and your crew will wind open the forward gates; you toss your warp from the bollard (having taken up on it the whole time that the water was coming into the lock), your crew steps on board, and you wave goodbye to the lock keeper.

Automatic locks

More and more locks are being converted to automatic operation. On many sections of canal used almost exclusively by hire cruisers, the only manual operation is the insertion of a key and then button-pressing, following instructions displayed in French, English and German. Automation on commercial canals is achieved by light beams, radar or swinging arms. There are also rigid poles requiring a quarter turn to start the locking-in sequence. Pleasure craft should motor slowly by whatever device triggers off the lock opening, remembering that it may have been designed for slow-moving barge traffic.

Press-button operation of a lock on the Canal de l'Ourcq. *Photo: David Jefferson*

Automatic lock controls in the Canal du Loing. Detectors outside the gate open the closed gates to let you in. In an unmanned lock, the blue rod is lifted up, then the lock operates automatically. The red rod is pulled down to stop the process in an emergency.
Photo: Keith Harris

Lock types

There are many different types of lock: large, small, straight-sided, sloping, rectangular, circular, but they all follow the same pattern in the same waterway section.

Staircase locks are a series of locks joined together, the inside gates of the first lock chamber being the outside lock gates of the next and so on. When you are going through staircase locks, having put your crew ashore at the first one as already described, you move out of one lock into the next one, your crew remaining ashore to carry your warp up (or down) the staircase.

In cases where there are no facilities to put your crew ashore and there appears to be special difficulty in getting a warp ashore without help, it will invariably be found that the necessary help is readily available to greet you. It is sometimes easy to forget that one is not the first to pass that way.

Descending locks

So far, the procedure for ascending has been outlined. Descending is easier in that you enter the lock at quay level and can reach out to loop your warp over a bollard.

When descending, the lines should be doubled up (so twice the length required compared with ascending). It is essential that these can run freely round the bollards, so that they can be slipped with no assistance from ashore. Some boat owners have at least two 20m mooring lines for this purpose to cope with a considerable drop and bollards that are a long way apart (sometimes positioned for the length of a barge).

If, on approach, the gates are closed against you it will be appreciated (by the lock keeper) if you put your crew ashore to open the second gate should your boat be unable to fit through the space left by the gate opened by the lock keeper. (Incidentally, whether ascending or descending, if you do not put crew ashore to help the lock keeper he will, of course, do it all himself – in time.)

Your crew and the lock keeper walk ahead to the forward gates to open the sluices. It is now of the utmost importance to ensure that your warp is not secured both ends on board. If they are, the rope will tighten up as you are lowered in the lock, the deck fitting will be pulled out; or the rope will break; or your boat will be left hanging on the lock wall.

This can happen to the best of us; in fact it is easy enough to be diverted at that vital moment when the level of water is going down in the lock chamber and your warp is coming up taut. Kettles always whistle at such moments, and you just pop into the cabin to turn the heat off; or you may be searching in the cabin for something that a comment by the lock keeper has brought to your mind.

Your turn round your cleat may be impossible to undo when it comes under considerable strain. If you are faced with this situation, shout immediately to have the sluices closed; it may then be necessary to let in some water again (from the other end of the lock, of course) to take off the strain and get your warp free.

Locks with sloping sides obviously need a special routine, for when descending in them your hull will quickly make contact with the sloping lock wall. If you have bilge keels they will be caught in the uneven stonework of the wall and your boat will heel over as the water level falls away. Should this happen you must again shout for the sluices to be closed; if you then cannot push yourself free, the lock must be refilled until you can.

A simple routine to avoid these problems in descending sloping locks is to position yourself amidships holding the boathook and/or a long pole to push your boat away from the lock wall as you descend. You will need to have the free end of your warp in your hands as well, gently pulling on the warp (which will be around a bollard ashore) and pushing on the boathook to maintain position. If you have sufficient crew to 'pole off' at either end of the boat, so much the better. Another point to watch in descending is that you are far enough forward in the lock (away from the gates you have entered) to avoid the possibility of your rudder lodging on the shelf or step just inside the lock. When you are down to the required water level, your warp is pulled back on board; for this reason the warp is passed round the bollard and not tied to it.

In an oval lock it is impossible to keep all of the boat alongside. Watch for occasional sluices causing cross-currents. *Photo: David Jefferson*

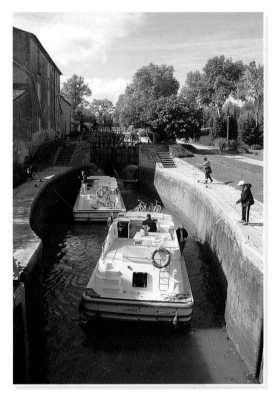

Whether in sloping or straight-sided locks you are now 'low down' and your crew is 'high up' ashore. If there are iron rungs set in the lock wall your crew will come down them to you. Sometimes, in place of rungs in the lock wall, there are steps at the end of the lock, and your crew can rejoin the boat from there The steps down the sloping side of a lock will invariably be too slippery to use, and a pontoon is provided in the lock from which the crew can be picked up.

In ascending locks the chamber will obviously be filled by water flowing in from ahead of you and often a bow warp only would suffice to secure you; in descending locks, with the flow going past from astern of you, a stern warp would often suffice. But it is wise to make a habit of securing fore and aft at all times. You will then be safeguarded against swirls and eddies. If you swing out of line, look to your helm. Your boat will steer in the moving water filling or emptying the lock and the position of your rudder is clearly of great importance.

VHF

On some waterways, you can alert the lock keeper to your arrival. Many locks including those on the Seine, Saône, Rhône and Yonne use VHF radio. You can call up the lock keeper, telling him that you will be arriving in 10 minutes and that you are on passage upstream (*montant*) or downstream (*avalant*). This call, indicating that you are a yacht and giving the name, will invariably produce a friendly response. The lock keeper may then prepare the lock for your arrival or perhaps delay closing the lock gate if you are in the vicinity.

Entry into the lock at Montbard, Canal de Bourgogne. Note that the loop is being put over the bollard with a boat hook. This is a good technique but sometimes difficult. *Photo: Keith Harris*

The lock at St-Jean-de-Losne which links the Canal de Bourgogne and the River Saône. *Photo: Keith Harris*

9 • Cost of living, shopping and stores

One of the greatest joys, of course, is the cheapness of the best wine in the world and many other drinks. There are so many different brands, so do not be put off if you do not fancy the first one you try. At around 4.00 euros for a respectable *Appellation Contrôlée* wine, you can afford to experiment.

Living is no dearer in France than it is in England at the present time and the choice and arrangement of French food for sale generally has always been preferred by a lot of people. Shopping in France can be a joyful and fascinating part of the whole holiday experience. The yachtsman in France has with him his cruising home so that he can appreciate the delight of browsing in French shops, supermarkets and open markets.

Eating out, to many, is one of the key attractions to cruising in France. Coffee and snacks will work out to be relatively expensive but you will find marvellous value in the *prix fixe* meals in France, also they will be beautifully presented and served long after the 'chef's gone home' time in Britain.

It should be obvious that bacon and eggs for breakfast are as relatively expensive in France as croissants are in England. Holidaymakers who insist upon continuing English eating habits when abroad are usually the loudest to complain about the cost of living.

Provisions

Every town and village seems to have its charming little market where vegetables, eggs, and chickens are brought in fresh from the country and cost no more than they do in the UK, if as much. The chickens are not always dressed, it is true, and sometimes your purchase is handed to you alive, trussed by the feet, in which case you will have a most interesting cycle ride in getting it back to the boat. And once on board it is likely that your meal will be long deferred.

Lock keepers in the country sections sometimes have eggs and vegetables to sell and occasionally a cooked dish such as a delicious quiche. Often there are a variety of shops near locks. The most constant shopping need is for bread and

Shopping vocabulary

apple – *pomme*
apricot – *abricot*
artichoke – *artichaut*
asparagus – *asperges*
avocado – *avocate*
bacon – *lard*
baker – *boulangerie*
banana – *banane*
beans, green – *haricots verts*
beef – *boeuf*
beefsteak – *bifteck* (well done
  – *bien cuit*; medium – *à
  point*; rare – *saignant*)
beer – *bière*
beetroot – *betterave*
blackcurrant – *cassis*
bread – *pain*
broccoli – *brocoli*
Brussels sprouts – *choux de
  Bruxelles*
butter – *boucherie*
butter – *beurre*
cabbage – *chou*
can opener – *ouvre-boîte*
carrot – *carrotte*
cauliflower – *choufleur*
celery – *céleri*
cheese – *fromage*
chemist – *pharmacie*
cherries – *cerises*
chicken – *poulet*
chop – *côte*
cocoa – *cacao*
cod – *morue*
coffee – *café*
confectioners – *confiserie*
crab – *crabe*
cream – *crème*
cucumber – *concombre*
custard – *crème anglaise*
cutlets – *côtelettes*
duck – *canard*
eel – *anguille*
egg – *oeuf*
figs – *figues*
fish – *poisson*

fishmonger – *poissonnerie*
flour – *farine*
French beans – *haricots verts*
frogs – *grenouilles*
fruit – *fruit*
fruit shop – *fruiterie*
garlic – *ail*
grape – *raisin*
grapefruit – *pamplemousse*
grocer – *épicerie*
haddock – *eglefin*
hake – *colin*
halibut – *flétan*
ham – *jambon*
herring – *hareng*
honey – *miel*
ice – *glace*
jam – *confiture*
kidney beans – *flageolets*
kidneys – *rognons*
lamb – *agneau*
lamb chop – *côte d'agneau*
leek – *poireau*
lemon – *citron*
lettuce – *laitue*
liver – *foie* (beef liver – *foie de
  boeuf*; calves' liver – *foie
  de veau*; lambs' liver – *foie
  d'agneau*)
lobster – *homard*
mackerel – *macquereau*
margarine – *margarine*
marrow – *moelle*
meat – *viande*
milk – *lait*
mushrooms – *champignons*
mussels – *moules*
mustard – *moutarde*
mutton – *mouton*
oil – *huile*
olive – *olive*
onion – *oignon*
orange – *orange*
oysters – *huîtres*
parsnip – *panais*
pastry shop – *pâtisserie*

peach – *pêche*
pear – *poire*
peas – *pois*
pepper – *poivre*
pineapple – *ananas*
plaice – *carrelet* or *plie*
plum – *prune*
pork – *porc*
potato – *pomme de terre*
prawns – *bouquets* or *crevettes*
prune – *pruneau*
rabbit – *lapin*
raspberry – *framboise*
rhubarb – *rhubarbe*
salmon – *saumon*
salt – *sel*
sausages – *saucissons*
shellfish – *coquillage*
shrimp – *crevette*
slice – *tranche*
snails – *escargots*
sole – *sole*
soup – *potage*
spaghetti – *spaghetti*
spinach – *épinards*
steak – *bifteck*
strawberry – *fraise*
sugar – *sucre*
sweetbreads – *ris de veau*
tart – *tarte*
tea – *thé*
thrush – *grive*
tin – *boîte*
tomato – *tomate*
tongue – *langue*
tripe – *tripes*
tripe sausage –
  andouille/andouillette
trout – *truite*
tuna – *thon*
turbot – *turbot*
turnip – *navets*
veal – *veau*
vegetables – *legumes*
vinegar – *vinaigre*
water – *eau*

milk, of course, which costs much the same as it does in the UK. You can buy bread every day including Sundays and holidays; if one boulangerie is closed it is likely that there will be another one open nearby.

Long-life milk (*longue conservation*) should always be carried for emergencies (it is sometimes difficult in France, even in quite large stores, to find any milk other than long-life).

A longish lunch period is usual for all shops, but they stay open until quite late in the evening. Many shops close on Mondays, but the village store type of shop seems to be open for long hours every day and often on Sundays and holidays.

Engine breakdowns

If you are unfortunate enough to have an engine breakdown you will find that the average French mechanic is quite resourceful in dealing with purely motor departments of your engine. To take a kit of spares is a reasonable precaution, for it usually ensures that the parts you have duplicated will keep running satisfactorily. A spare impeller is a must, for a jammed water pump can cause days of delay awaiting a replacement impeller.

Mechanical vocabulary

acid – *acide*
armature – *armature*
battery, to top – *reniveler la batterie*
bolt – *boulon*
carburettor – *carburateur*
choke – *starter*
diesel – *gas-oil*
dipstick – *réglette-jauge*
distributor – *distributeur*

distributor head – *distributeur de courant*
dynamo – *dynamo*
engine – *moteur*
fill up – *faire le plein*
fuel tank – *réservoir de gas-oil* (or *d'essence*)
insulating tape – *chatterton*
jet – *gicleur*
nut – *écrou*

oil – *huile*
petrol – *essence*
screw – *vis*
screwdriver – *tournevis*
self-starter – *démarreur*
spanner, adjustable – *clé à molette*
washer – *rondelle*
water – *eau*

10 • Useful information

Weather • VNF regional offices and payment centres • Public holidays • Cruiser hire • Hire cars • Mail • The Pet Travel Scheme (PETS) • Health • Weights and measures

Weather

In recent years, navigation of some of the French waterway system in the spring and autumn has been affected by serious flooding which has actually closed some sections or made navigation impossible for boats with limited power. If contemplating a cruise early or late in the season, it is essential to contact the regional VNF office (see pages 57–8) to find out if there are any local navigation problems. Where the draught is critical (if, for example, you have a boat that draws 1.2m and you are contemplating the Brittany canals or the Nivernais after extended periods with no rainfall) you must contact the regional VNF office. The seasonal climate of France is not all that much different from our own except, perhaps, for the winter-protected Côte d'Azur. Marseille in December can be as cold as London; and from December, incidentally, the French canals can be ice-bound.

Weather forecast terms

abondant – heavy	*éclairs* – lightning	*neige fondue* – sleet
affaiblissement – decrease	*épars* – at times	*nuages* – clouds
augmentant – increasing	*faible* – slight	*occasionnels* – occasional
averses – showers	*forte* – rough	*orage* – thunderstorm
avis – warning	*frais* – strong	*pluie* – rain
beau/belle – fair	*froid* – cold	*prevision* – forecast
bon (nne) – good	*front – chaud* warm front	*rafale* – gust
BMS – warning	*front – froid* cold front	*sporadiques* – scattered
brouillard – fog	*grains* – squalls	*tempête* – storm
bruine – drizzle	*grêle* – hail	*temporaires* – temporarily
brume – mist	*isolé* – isolated	*thalweg* – trough
chaud – warm	*lentement* – slowly	*tonnerre* – thunder
couvert – overcast	*mauvais* – poor	
dorsale – ridge	*neige* – snow	

VNF addresses

Regional offices

Direction régional de VNF
37 rue du Plat 59034 LILLE
Cedex
Tel: 03 20 15 49 70

Délégation locale de
Dordogne
Service de la navigation
Cité administrative Bugeaud
24016 PERIGUEUX Cedex
Tel: 05 53 03 65 00

Direction interrégionale
de VNF
2 port St Etienne BP 7204
31073 TOULOUSE Cedex 7
Tel: 05 61 36 24 24

Direction interrégionale
de VNF
2 rue Louise Michel
58640 VARENNES-
VAUZELLES
Tel: 03 86 59 77 77

Délégation locale du Lot
et Garonne
Service de la navigation
1722 avenue de Colmar
47916 AGEN Cedex 9
Tel: 05 53 69 33 33

Direction interrégionale
de VNF
2 quai de Grenelle
75732 PARIS Cedex 15
Tel: 01 40 58 29 99

Direction interrégionale
de VNF
2 rue de la Quarantaine
69321 LYON Cedex 1
Tel: 04 72 56 59 00

Délégation locale de Haute-
Marne
Service de la navigation
82 rue du Cdt Hugueny
– BP 2087
52903 CHAUMONT Cedex 9
Tel: 03 25 30 79 79

Direction régionale de VNF
34 boulevard de Boisguilbert
– BP 4075
76022 ROUEN Cedex
Tel: 02 35 52 54 56

Direction interrégionale
de VNF
28 boulevard Albert 1er
– Case officielle No 62
54036 NANCY Cedex
Tel: 03 83 95 30 01

Délégation locale du Canal
de Bourgogne
Service de la navigation
57 rue de Mulhouse
21033 DIJON Cedex
Tel: 03 80 29 44 44

Délégation locale de la
Gironde
BP 61
33028 BORDEAUX Cedex
Tel: 05 56 90 58 00

Direction régionale de VNF
Centre des Salorges
18 quai Ernest Renaud
– BP 3139
44031 NANTES Cedex 04
Tel: 02 40 44 20 20

Direction interrégionale
de VNF
25 rue de la Nuée bleue
– BP 367 R/10
67010 STRASBOURG Cedex
Tel: 03 88 21 74 74

Délégation locale de la
Saône-et-Loire
37 Bd Henri Dunant
71040 MACON
Tel: 03 85 21 28 00

Délégation locale du Canal
de Rhône à Sète
7 rue Richer de Belleval
34000 MONTPELLIER
Tel: 04 67 14 12 00

Payment centres

Offices (1) open at weekends
during the lock opening
hours.

AGDE (1)
Service de la navigation du
Sud Ouest
Tel: 04 67 94 10 99
Ecluse ronde d'Agde – 34034
Tel: 04 67 94 23 09

ARLES
1 quai gare maritime - 13200
Tel: 04 90 96 00 85

ARMENTIÈRES
Ecluse d'Armentières – 59280
Tel: 03 20 77 15 67

BERLAIMONT
Écluse de Berlaimont – 59145
Tel: 03 27 58 81 70

BÉTHUNE
175 rue Ludovic Boutleux –
62400
Tel: 03 21 63 24 30

CALAIS
45 quai de la Meuse – 62100
Tel: 03 21 34 25 58

VNF addresses

CONFLANS Ste HONORINE
Cours de Chimay – 78700
Tel: 01 39 72 73 09

DOUAI
263 Quai d'Alsace – 59500
Tel: 03 27 94 55 70

DUNKERQUE
Terre plein du jeu de Mail –
59140
Tel: 03 28 58 71 25

FONTET (1)
Ecluse 49 – 33190
Tel: 05 56 61 28 74

GIVET
Ecluse 59 des 4 cheminées –
08600
Tel: 03 24 41 26 73

LE HAVRE
La citadelle – avenue L
Corbeaux – 76600
Tel: 02 35 22 99 34

LILLE
37 rue du Plat 59034
Tel: 03 20 15 49 70

LYON
11 quai du Maréchal Joffre –
69002
Tel: 04 78 42 74 99

MARGNY-lès-COMPIÈGNE
92 rue du 14 juillet – 60281
Tel: 03 44 83 65 42

MARPENT (1)
Ecluse de Marpent – 59164
Tel: 03 27 39 54 52

MULHOUSE
14 rue de l'Est – 68052
Tel: 03 89 45 22 46

NANCY
2 rue Victor – Pont des
Tiercelins – 54000
Tel: 03 83 17 01 01

NANTES
2 rue Marcel Sembat 44049
Tel: 02 40 71 02 17

NARBONNE
9 bis quai d'Alsace –
Écluse de Gua – 11100
Tel: 04 68 42 23 27

NIFFER (1)
Écluse de Niffer – 68680
KEMBS
Tel: 03 89 74 57 44

PARIS
18 quai d'Austerlitz – 75013
Tel: 01 44 06 63 60

QUESNOY sur DEÛLE
Nouvelle écluse de Quesnoy
– 59890
Tel: 03 20 39 87 67

REIMS
11 boulevard P Doumer –
51084
Tel: 03 26 85 75 95

RHINAU (1)
Écluse de Rhinau – 67860
Tel: 03 88 74 63 33

ROUEN
71 avenue J Chastellain –
76000
Tel: 02 32 08 31 70

St JEAN-DE-LOSNE
17 quai National –
BP16 – 21170
Tel: 03 80 29 01 37

SAINT-MAMMÈS
10 quai du Loing – 77670
Tel: 01 64 70 57 70

SAINT-QUENTIN
2 rue Léo Lagrange – 02100
Tel: 03 23 62 60 21

SARREGUEMINES
30 rue Raymond Poincaré –
57200
Tel: 03 87 98 11 15

SARREGUEMINES (1)
Ecluse 27 – 57200
Tel: 03 87 98 13 47

SÈTE
1 quai Philippe Régy – 34200
Tel: 04 67 46 34 67

STRASBOURG
5 rue du Port-du-Rhin –
67016
Tel: 03 90 41 06 06

THIONVILLE
Terre plein de l'écluse
R Schuman – 57105
Tel: 03 82 88 22 80

TOULOUSE
2 port Saint-Etienne – 31073
Tel: 05 61 36 24 24

VOLGELSHEIM (1)
Ecluse de Neuf-Brisach –
68600
Tel: 03 89 72 54 33

VARENNES-VAUZELLES
2 rue Louise Michel – 58640
Tel: 03 86 59 77 86

Submerged quayside on the swollen Marne with only a bollard above water.
Photo: David Jefferson

Public holidays in France

New Year's Day (Jan 1), Easter Sunday and Monday, Labour Day (May 1), VE Day (May 8), Ascension Day (May 21), Whit Sunday and Monday, Bastille Day (July 14), Assumption Day (Aug 15), All Saints' Day (Nov 1), Remembrance Day (Nov 11), Christmas Day (Dec 25).

Banks close on these public holidays, also all day on Saturdays (and Sundays, needless to say); on weekdays they are open from 9 am to 4 pm, many closing for an hour or so at lunchtime.

Cruiser hire

With just one or two exceptions, those who decide to charter a cruiser on the French waterways need no special qualifications. All charter craft must have been inspected by VNF, and then it is the responsibility of the hire operator to demonstrate the boat, taking the skipper through boat handling, safety equipment and waterway regulations. The operator will then issue a *Carte de Plaisance* for the duration of the holiday. If the hirer wishes to venture onto the River Seine below Paris or the Rhône, then the skipper must already possess the International Certificate of Competence (see page 36).

British hire companies

Crown Blue Line and **Connoisseur Holidays Afloat** are both within the First Leisure group of companies.

Crown Blue Line
The Port House,
Port Solent, Portsmouth,
Hampshire PO6 4TH
Tel +44 (0) 870 240 8393
www.crownblueline.com

Crown Blue Line are a long-established British company building their own boats, mostly in Norfolk, for transporting to their many bases in Europe. In France, they have cruiser hire bases in Alsace-Lorraine, Aquitaine, Brittany, Burgundy, Camargue, Charente, Lot and Midi.

Connoisseur Holidays Afloat
The Port House,
Port Solent, Portsmouth,
Hampshire PO6 4TH
Tel: +44 (0) 870 774 9933
www.ConnoisseurAfloat.com

A British firm, originally based at Wroxham, where they still build their own cruisers which they operate in Alsace-Lorraine, Anjou, Burgundy, Camargue, Midi and the Rivers Lot and Baïse.

French hire companies

There are numerous French cruiser hire operators, ranging from family businesses, operating just two and three boats from a single base, to large operators with fleets of charter boats in excess of 100, operating all over France. In the latter category are:

Nicols
Route du Puy St Bonnet
49300 Cholet
France
Tel: (0)2 41 56 46 56

Nicols have built all their charter boats in their boatyard at Cholet. They have a large choice of craft located at 24 bases across France. As an optional extra, they can also provide heated and filtered bathing pools, which can be attached to the stern of many of their craft.

Locaboat Holidays
Port au Bois – BP 150
89303 Joigny
France
Tel: (0)3 86 91 72 72

This operator, with its affiliates, has 25 bases spread across France, offering self-drive *penichettes* (mini-barges) which are popular on the waterways.

France Afloat
1, Quai du Port
89270 Vermenton
France
Tel and Fax: 08700 110 538
e-mail: boats@franceafloat.com
www.franceafloat.com

This company has its own fleet of hire cruisers (Burgundy Cruisers), based at Vermenton located at the end of a small embranchment off the Canal du Nivernais. With another base at Marigny-sur-Yonne on the Nivernais, France Afloat can offer a week's leisurely one-way cruising between the two bases.

In 2006, France Afloat took over two more bases: Moissac on the Canal de Garonne and Gannay-sur-Loire on the Canal Latéral à la Loire near Decize.

France Afloat also act as agents for many other smaller, family-run French operators on most of the French waterways. Regions offered are Alsace-Lorraine, Anjou, Aquitaine, Brittany, Burgundy, Camargue, Charente, Midi and Saône.

The main office of France Afloat is at their Vermenton base, near Auxerre, on the Canal du Nivernais. Telephone enquiries on the UK telephone number cost the UK tariff, but are automatically switched to the Vermenton office, where callers can receive on-the-spot advice about the various options. France Afloat also offers a combined cruising holiday and the opportunity of gaining the ICC qualification from their base at Vermenton on the Canal du Nivernais.

Crewed boats

For anyone who wants to sail sedately along the waterways, with someone else running the boat and providing the meals, there are many crewed boats available for charter. There are a surprisingly large number of British couples who have converted barges, providing guided tours, comfortable accommodation and haute cuisine. Many of these operators can be contacted on UK telephone numbers available from the Maison de la France, 178 Piccadilly, London W1V 0AL. France information line: 0906 8244123.

Hire cars

It is quite possible to leave your boat in France so that you can continue your cruise when next you have time available. If you can make it convenient to leave your boat at a place where 'drive-yourself' hire cars are available, you will be able to bring off your personal gear with the minimum of inconvenience. Hertz and Avis cars are available at many towns throughout France; wherever you hire them from, you can drive them to Le Havre or any other Channel port and leave them there.

Mail

Mail can be sent to you c/o poste restante at any town and is reliable. A small charge is made on the collection of any letters. Many post offices now provide e-mail.

The Pet Travel Scheme (PETS)

The Pet Travel Scheme allows pet dogs, cats and ferrets to enter or re-enter the UK from France without quarantine as long as they meet certain rules. Animals which do not meet the rules will be subject to up to six months quarantine on entering or re-entering the UK. Boat owners' dogs, cats and ferrets can travel out to France on board, but must return on an authorised route with an approved transport company (many of the cross-channel ferries and Eurotunnel operate the scheme).

For full details of all the rules contact the PETS Helpline on 0870 241 1710 (Mon–Fri 8.30am–5.00pm) and request fact sheets or visit Defra's website at www.defra.gov.uk/animalh/quarantine/index.htm

Health

From 1 January 2006 the European Health Insurance Card (EHIC) – a plastic credit-sized card – replaced the E111 form. The EHIC entitles holders to free or reduced-cost state-provided medical treatment if anyone included on the card falls ill or has an accident in any country in the European Economic Area. The card can cover the spouse/partner and dependent children in addition to the applicant.

Application forms are available from post offices or on-line by visiting the Department of Health website: www.dh.gov.uk/travellers or direct to www.ehic.org.uk. Alternatively, you can apply by 'phone by calling the EHIC application line 0845 606 2030. There is no charge for the EHIC although the Post Office offer a £2 'Check & Send' service. They will process your application but this still takes longer than applying on line or by 'phone.

UK travellers in France are entitled to reduced-cost emergency medical and dental treatment on production of their EHIC. After treatment, a signed statement of treatment given (*feuille de soins*) must be obtained. With this document, around 70 per cent of the doctors' and dentists' standard fees will be refunded, and between 35 per cent and 65 per cent of the cost of most prescribed medicines. The doctor or dentist must be *conventionné* (working within the French insurance system). Fees and costs of medicines must be paid for in full and then reclaimed. See the booklet issued with the EHIC for details of how to claim for refunds, including part of the cost of hospital in- and out-patient treatment.

Weights and measures

Litres		Gals	Km		Miles	Kg		Lb
1	=	0.22	1	=	0.62	0.453	=	1
2	=	0.44	2	=	1.24	0.907	=	2
3	=	0.66	3	=	1.86	1.360	=	3
4	=	0.88	4	=	2.48	1.814	=	4
5	=	1.10	5	=	3.11	2.268	=	5
6	=	1.32	6	=	3.73	2.721	=	6
7	=	1.54	7	=	4.35	3.175	=	7
8	=	1.76	8	=	4.97	3.628	=	8
9	=	1.98	9	=	5.59	4.082	=	9
10	=	2.20	10	=	6.21	4.535	=	10
15	=	3.30	15	=	9.32			
20	=	4.40	20	=	12.43			
30	=	6.60	30	=	18.64			
40	=	8.80	40	=	24.85			
50	=	11.00	50	=	31.07			
100	=	22.00	100	=	62.14			

Looking down a flight of seven staircase locks. *Photo: David Jefferson*

Part 2 • The Routes

Facilities for boats are indicated as follows:

⚑ *Port de plaisance* – all facilities for crews and yachts, including electricity, showers and usually fuel.

⚓ *Halte nautique* – pontoons or quays with limited facilities.

A *port de plaisance* or *halte nautique* may be operated by cruiser hire operators, who may not always be able to accommodate visiting private yachts, particularly over the change-over periods, usually Friday/Saturday.

Maximum boat's height above waterline and draught are shown in metres at the start of each route.

The symbol ≪ indicates a lock. The outline maps show routes in red.

Limits of boat length and beam

River/Canal	Length m	Beam m
River Seine – from Rouen to Montereau	121.00	10.50
Canals linking Paris with Lyon via Burgundy	38.50	5.00
Canals linking Paris with Lyon via Nevers and the Bourbonnais	38.50	5.00
Canals linking Paris with Lyon via the River Marne	38.50	5.00
Canals linking Paris with Northern France	38.50	5.00
Canals linking Paris with Strasbourg	38.50	5.00
Canal de la Marne à la Saône	38.50	5.00
Canal du Rhône au Rhin	38.50	5.00
Canal du Midi	30.00	5.45
Canal de Garonne	40.50	5.80
Nantes – Redon – Rennes – St Malo	27.10	4.50
Baïse	30.00	4.00
Lot	27.00	4.80
Charente	31.00	6.30

The Lower Seine (*la Seine aval*)

Le Havre ←→ Paris

There is something special about entering Paris, and viewing the capital's sights from your own boat. Motoring under the famous bridges, some of which have spanned the Seine since the 14th century, is an unforgettable experience. Prominent amongst the many famous landmarks is the vast building housing the Louvre Museum, with the Eiffel tower on the left bank. The boat glides beneath the Pont Neuf, in the shadows of Notre Dame Cathedral on the Île de la Cité. A mere 3km upriver of Notre Dame is Paris's yacht harbour – Port de Plaisance de Paris-Arsenal, just off Place de la Bastille.

It would be wrong to give the impression that the only hightlight of a cruise up the Seine is the arrival in Paris. Upriver of the first of the Seine's locks are miles of backwaters to explore, behind the river's numerous islands. There are delightful well-established stopping-off places, or the boatowner can simply drop the anchor in some secluded spot for the night, or for a couple of hours around lunchtime.

Stunning scenery

For those making their first cruise to Paris, the spectacular scenery comes as something of a surprise. Once clear of the Seine estuary, the river winds through valleys below forests and chalk cliffs. In other sections, often lined with poplars, the fields stretch into the distance. There are many of the distinctive Normandy farmhouses, and the occasional magnificent château. Parts of the river resemble the more fashionable frontages of the upper Thames, with weeping willows and boathouses.

Cruising to Paris

A cruise to and from Paris is possible in most pleasure craft capable of crossing the Channel, providing they do not exceed the maximum dimensions (see page 68).

Masts of sailing yachts have to be removed before entering Rouen, but this presents no problem (see pages 31–3). Boats with modest engine power (10bhp/5kn) are not precluded from a cruise between Le Havre and Paris and beyond on the network of waterways. Owners of these craft can still complete the 365km to the capital from the sea in five to six days, without the passage becoming too much of an endurance test.

The Paris cruise is certainly not restricted to those fortunate enough to have many weeks available for cruising during the summer. With careful planning, boat owner and crew can cruise the Seine over a three-week period, and still have plenty of time for sightseeing in Paris, perhaps venturing along more waterways, including sections of the Canals of Paris (pages 114–121). The best-laid plans can always be frustrated by the weather, delaying the Channel crossing. For small craft, there is much to be said for getting the boat over to the other side early, perhaps the weekend before the start of the cruise proper.

For boat owners planning to reach the Mediterranean via the inland waterways, entry via the River Seine will invariably be the first choice, unless it is felt that there are too many sea miles to cover to reach Le Havre if the boat is based on the UK's east coast, for example.

The distance from Calais to Paris is 438km with 38 locks by way of the Canal de Calais, Liaison Dunkerque-Escaut, Canal du Nord, Canal latéral à l'Oise, canalised l'Oise river and the Seine from Conflans-Ste-Honorine. Compare this with the Seine route from Le Havre to Paris. This is tidal to the first lock (Amfreville) 176km inland, and well upstream of Rouen. There are then only another 5 locks and 202km to negotiate to reach the Port de Plaisance de Paris-Arsenal which is right in the heart of the capital.

It is not just the number of locks that will determine progress but also the speed limits on the various waterways. On the Le Havre route a boat can maintain 15 knots to the outskirts of Rouen and then 10 knots to Paris; for much of the waterways route from Calais, however, the top speed limit is around 6 knots.

Tidal Seine: Le Havre ↔ first lock (Amfreville)

Passage-making restrictions

On the tidal Seine, pleasure craft must not be underway between the giant Pont de Normandie, spanning the Seine estuary above Honfleur, and Rouen over the period between 30 minutes after sunset and 30 minutes before sunrise. Pleasure craft are also prohibited from using the tidal Seine in bad visibility.

Maximum boat dimensions: *Length and beam* **N/A** (large merchant ships and cruise liners use tidal Seine below Rouen). *Height above waterline* **6m** (to clear Rouen's bridges on highest tide with safety margin). More precise calculation is 15.3m less height of tide (see pages 31–3 for details of mast lowering).

Speed limits: From the sea to the downriver outskirts of Rouen (PK 260): **28km/h (15kn)** Downriver outskirts of Rouen (PK 260) to first of Rouen's bridges (PK 242): **14km/h (7.5kn)** First of Rouen's bridges (PK 242) to upriver outskirts of Rouen (PK 233): **18km/h (9.7kn)** Upriver outskirts of Rouen (PK 233) to the first lock Amfreville (PK 202): **20km/h (10.8kn)**

Distances: Le Havre to Rouen Port de Plaisance (PK 241.5): **137km** Honfleur to Rouen Port de Plaisance (PK 241.5): **115km** Rouen Port de Plaisance (PK 241.5) to first lock Amfreville (PK 202): **39.5km**

Tides

As will be seen from the graphs on pages 72 & 73, the flood in the lower reaches is almost 5 knots at springs. The flood starts in the estuary at LW Le Havre +1 and slack water in Rouen is about LW Le Havre +11, giving passage-making boats 10 hours of favourable flood. In the reverse direction, passage-making to the sea from Rouen and leaving on the first of the ebb, after about 3 – 4 hours the benefit of the ebb will be slipping away as the tide turns.

Boats making for Rouen at the maximum permitted speed of 15kn as far as La Bouille (PK 260) and then 7.5kn for the next 10nm should complete the passage from the estuary to the centre of Rouen in about 4 hours with the flood. Boats with an engine capable of 10kn, again taking the flood all the way, will be underway for about 6 hours.

Owners of craft with 10bhp engines, capable of a maximum 5kn, have to plan the passage carefully, making the optimum use of the tide, and at the same time conforming with the regulations prohibiting pleasure craft from being underway between sunset and sunrise.

It must be appreciated that, apart from the somewhat exposed landing stages at Caudebec (where there are also some visitors' moorings) and Duclair, there are no other recognised stopovers between the sea and Rouen. The piles to which barges may secure, the huge mooring buoys used by large ships, and the occasional inviting-looking quay, are not for pleasure craft, as they will invariably be in the tide and unprotected from the considerable wash of passing traffic. Anchoring in the tidal Seine should only be attempted in an emergency – because of the wash, strong current and poor holding ground.

Port de Plaisance, Le Havre. *Photo: David Jefferson*

Boats making 4½ to 5kn through the water, can complete the upstream passage in about 12 hours from Ratier NW buoy in the estuary (10½ hours starting from Honfleur) if, by careful planning, the tide is carried almost all the way up to Rouen. The ebb in Rouen is rarely more than 1kn, so reasonable progress will still be made if arriving in the outskirts as the tide turns.

Starting times for boats with limited power (10bhp)

Le Havre	LW Le Havre -30 min
Ratier NW	LW Le Havre +30 min
Honfleur	LW Le Havre +2 hrs

A passage between the sea and Rouen on one tide during daylight hours is naturally more likely to occur between May and early August, with the shorter nights.

Return passage planning from Rouen to the sea ———————

For boats with limited power (maximum 5kn), the opportunities of completing a daylight passage between Rouen and Honfleur/the sea are restricted to only a few days in the month. Interpreting the tidal charts on pages 72 & 73 correctly is essential. The charts illustrate clearly the adverse flood starting progressively earlier down river. Unlike the upriver passage, boats with limited power will be motoring for several hours with the tide against them.

At a modest 5kn, a single passage to the sea can be completed in about 14 hours (Honfleur 12½ hours) provided the adverse flood is met well upriver, avoiding the strong tides downstream of Quillebeuf-sur-Seine (PK332), when a spring flood could bring modestly powered boats to a virtual standstill for several hours.

For such boats, the best time to leave Rouen is at LW Le Havre. The contrary flood will be met after about 5 hours, but should not be more than 2kn against, leaving sufficient time to complete the passage to Honfleur and the sea on the new ebb. The navigator should plot the boat's progress regularly to make certain that they will not get caught by the changing tide in the lower reaches. In these parts, each kilometre is marked on the river bank so speed made good can be rapidly calculated.

The tides and restrictions have been described in some detail to demonstrate that a Seine cruise is a practical proposition for small craft of, say, 8m with a 10bhp inboard engine.

The tidal passage between Le Havre/Honfleur and the first lock ———

Leaving Le Havre's Port de Plaisance, boats have to head out to sea in the main shipping channel for almost 2nm to reach No 11 channel buoy before turning to cross the mouth of the estuary. On arriving at the beginning of the Chanal de Rouen around LW, the training walls, marked with poles, will be clearly visible. The channel from the first of the buoys (Ratier NW) to just downriver of the Tancarville bridge (distance 12nm) is well marked with red and green buoys. Pleasure craft must not enter the shipping channel, keeping just outside the red buoys.

The surroundings in the estuary are bleak, with mile after mile of refineries upriver from Le Havre, and vast stretches of marshland beyond. The scenery soon changes as the marshes give way to steep chalk cliffs, and the river sweeps round through the hilly Parc Naturel Regional de Brotonne which is a vast area of forest, much of which runs right down to the water's edge. Apart from Norman farmsteads, there are few signs of civilisation until Caudebec and Duclair.

The quays, some sadly neglected, extend for miles downriver from the centre of Rouen. If height does not preclude passing beneath Rouen's bridges, most boats will make for the Port de Plaisance on Île Lacroix. The alternative is to secure alongside the pontoon in Bassin St Gervais, well downriver of the bridges in Rouen's docklands.

The 40km of the Seine between Rouen and the Amfreville lock is unremarkable scenery with the occasional riverside factory, and two industrial towns Oissel and Elbeuf. Most skippers on passage over this section would not be looking for stopping places, unless it is a for a short stay alongside Elbeuf's quay for provisions. There is also a Port de Plaisance at Elbeuf in an old basin accessible around high water.

Stopping at Duclair or Caudebec?

As indicated above, this might be a necessity for small craft passage-making downriver from Rouen. They are not ideal and should only be considered if the hours of daylight and tidal calculations dictate two passages. The pontoon at Caudebec and the barge at Duclair are used by tourist boats and their skippers do not take kindly to their berths being occupied. The local tourist office can usually advise whether a boat is due to land or pick up passengers. If there is space, it will be a worryingly uncomfortable berth due to the wash of passing ships that can be underway all through the night. The wash is less at Caudebec because ships slow down in this part of the river to change pilots from the local pilot station. There are also mooring buoys off Caudebec, suitable for craft up to 10m, but with a strong current it will be a noisy, bumpy night at times.

Notification of passage plan

Boat owners starting a passage from the sea to Rouen should call up Rouen Port Control on Ch 73 (the prominent radar tower just upriver of the entrance channel to Honfleur), to advise them that the vessel is on passage to Rouen, giving an estimated time of arrival. On the outskirts of Rouen, the harbour master's office (Rouen Port) should be advised of your boat's arrival on Ch 73. Making the passage downriver, Rouen Port and Rouen Port Control should likewise be notified. English is used for ship/shore communication.

Refuelling

It is strongly recommended that you top up with fuel at Le Havre. The next opportunity is at Amfreville, 3km upstream from the centre of Rouen. Thereafter, with nothing in Paris, there is no alongside refuelling for pleasure craft (white diesel) on the Seine until St-Mammès, 80km upriver south of the capital.

It is advisable to carry a spare fuel can on board.

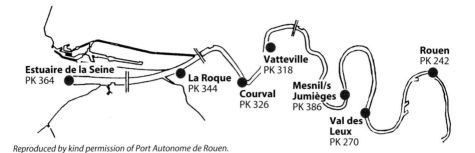

Reproduced by kind permission of Port Autonome de Rouen.

Tidal Seine

Based on hours after LW Le Havre (bottom scales on the graphs), the following seven graphs show the strength of the tide in knots at springs (Coef 90), mid-way (Coef 70) and neaps (Coef 45).

PK (Pointe Kilometrique) denotes position (see above).

From the graphs it will be seen that at springs around PK 326, the flood reaches almost 5 knots.

In Rouen, flood and ebb rarely exceed 2 knots.

Estuaire de la Seine   PK 364

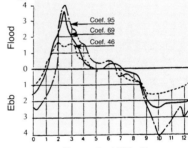

Hours after LW Le Havre

La Roque   PK 344

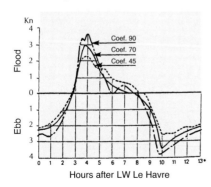

Hours after LW Le Havre

Courval   PK 326

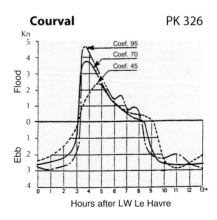

Hours after LW Le Havre

Vatteville la Rue   PK 318

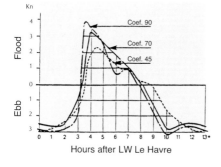

Hours after LW Le Havre

Mesnil/s/Jumièges   PK 386

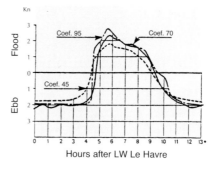

Hours after LW Le Havre

Val des Leux   PK 270

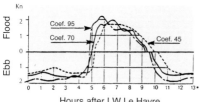

Hours after LW Le Havre

Rouen   PK 242

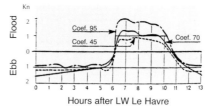

Hours after LW Le Havre

Plenty of company of all shapes and sizes. *Photo: David Jefferson*

The Lower Seine

WATERWAY	PK ref	Town/*village*/≪ lock	Total km ▼ ▲
SEINE ESTUARY	PK 378	**Le Havre** The second largest seaport in France. It suffered greater damage in World War II than any other port. Priority was given to rebuilding the town after the war in the shortest time possible. The new town was designed by architect Auguste Perret who pioneered the use of reinforced concrete. Visitors' pontoon, outermost, is in the first of the two marinas. Masts can be unstepped here (see page 32). Fuel pontoon. Access to Tancarville canal – see below.	0 379
RIVER SEINE	PK 356	**Honfleur** Artists and photographers compete to capture the *Vieux Bassin* where visiting boats secure. Packed with art galleries, souvenir shops and tourists. Church of St Catherine built of wood by local shipbuilders. Lock operates round the clock: entry on the hour, exit on the half hour (around low water springs, deep-keeled craft may have to delay entry for an hour or so until there is sufficient water in the approach channel). *Vieux Bassin* accessed through opening road bridge. Very crowded in high season. ⌑	22 357
	PK 353	*Pont de Normandie* Built between 1988 and 1995, with a span of 856m, suspended by steel stays from two vast 200m towers, It is the largest single-stayed bridge in the world.	
LEFT end of 25km Tancarville canal from Le Havre	PK 338.5	*Tancarville canal* is rarely used by pleasure craft. Involves two locks in Le Havre and six lifting bridges in canal. Le Hode bridge with 7m headroom requires 24 hours notice. Access to the Seine at Tancarville is restricted to the lock working times HW −4 to HW +3¼. Seek advice from ⌑ *Capitainerie* at Le Havre. Much quicker by sea.	

Vieux Bassin, Honfleur. *Photo: David Jefferson*

WATERWAY	PK ref	Town/*village*/≪*lock*	Total km
			▼ ▲
RIVER SEINE	PK 338	*Pont de Tancarville* was the longest suspension bridge in Europe when it was completed in 1959.	
	PK 313.5	*Villequier* 15 minutes' walk downstream of Caudebec. Victor Hugo's daughter, Leopoldine, and her husband Charles Vacquerie, drowned here by the *Mascaret*. This tidal wave is no more, the estuarial tides having been tamed by the training walls off Honfleur. The Vacquerie family house is now the Victor Hugo Museum.	
	PK 310	**Caudebec** Picturesque small town with interesting Musée de la Marine de Seine which features old film footage of the notorious *Mascaret*. The substantial landing stage can be used if not required by tourist boats (check with Tourist Office in Hôtel de Ville – tel: 02 35 96 20 65) or secure to a mooring (see page 71).	68 311

WATERWAY	PK ref	Town/*village*/≪ *lock*	Total km
			▼ ▲
RIVER SEINE	PK 308	*Pont de Brotonne* built between 1974 and 1977 when it was the largest stayed bridge in the world.	
	PK 278	**Duclair** Attractive small town with sailing club. Possible to stop alongside landing stage (one-time barge) if not required by tourist boats. Check with Hôtel de Ville – tel: 02 35 37 50 06, and beware of wash (See page 71.)	100 279
	PK 245	*Bassin St Gervais* ♒ in docks area in outskirts of Rouen. Lack of security, so no yacht should be left here unattended. Self-operated crane (1.5 ton) for lowering light masts (no more than 7m). 20min walk to city centre.	
	PK 241.5	**Rouen** Impressive run-in to centre of Rouen, dominated by the cathedral. Having passed beneath three bridges, pleasure craft take the spur to port where, just beyond the fourth bridge, are the pontoons of the municipal ⚑ on Île Lacroix. Called the City of a Hundred Spires, many of Rouen's historic buildings survived the last war. Jeanne d'Arc burnt at the stake by the English in Place du Vieux-Marché. Rue du Gros-Horloge in the old quarter spanned by vast 14th century clock tower and flanked by half-timbered houses with many shops, restaurants and bars at ground level.	136.5 242.5
	PK 239	*Amfreville* Fuelling barge.	
	PK 220–218	**Elbeuf** Industrial town. No protection from wash alongside town quay. ⚑ on N side just upstream of quay. Deep water pontoon berths in old basin with access around high water. Fuel available.	
	PK 202	≪ *Amfreville* VHF Ch 18	176 203

Halte de Plaisance, Rouen. *Photo: David Jefferson*

Non-tidal Seine: First lock (Amfreville) ↔ Paris

Maximum boat dimensions: *Height above waterline* **5.5m** (in average height of river) reducing to **3.7m** if river abnormally swollen.
Length **180m**   *Beam* **11.4m**   *Draught* **3m**

Speed limits: From first lock (Amfreville) to outskirts of Paris (PK 12): **20km/h (10.8kn)**
Through Paris: **18km/h (9.7kn)**
Less than 20m off riverside facilities (moored boats, pontoons etc.) and backwaters: **12km/h (6.5kn)** or as indicated by speed restriction signs (see page 41)

Distance: First lock Amfreville (PK 202) to Port de Plaisance Paris-Arsenal (PK 168): **203km**

Locks: 6 Operate daily except for some national holidays 0700–1900 (the alternative Bougival lock's hours are Mon–Sat 0700–1900; Sun 0800–1200 & 1330–1830).

The locks have chambers large enough to accommodate a single shunting barge, pushing along two strings each of four dumb barges. With the decline in commercial traffic, the Seine lock keepers undertake to limit the waiting time for pleasure craft to no more than 30 minutes.

VHF communication with the lock keepers is not obligatory, but can save time. Boat owners without handheld VHF who have dropped their masts along with the VHF aerial might consider a temporary aerial on the deck which will be more than adequate for communicating at close range. Advise the lock keeper when you are 10 minutes away indicating whether you are on passage upstream (*montant*) or downstream (*avalant*).

Navigation

Watch out for traffic crossover signs directing all traffic from one side of the Seine to the other (see river signs, page 41). There are many islands in the Seine, most of them with an arrow indicating which side of the island to pass, but this sign can sometimes be difficult to spot amongst the greenery.

The short section (1km) one-way system in the middle of Paris past Île de la Cité and Notre-Dame must be strictly observed. Traffic lights on Pont au Change allow passage upstream on the hour to 20 minutes past the hour. Downstream traffic is controlled by lights on Pont Sully, allowing passage between 35 minutes and 50 minutes past the hour.

Between the first lock (Amfreville) and Paris

The constraints of the tide are gone (in the summer months, the downstream current rarely exceeds 0.5kn), and there is a delightfully varied choice of places to moor up ranging from sleepy backwaters to well-established yacht harbours. Many islands are to be found in this section of the Seine, ranging from the small and uninhabited to the Île de la Cité, with perhaps the second most famous of the Parisian landmarks – Notre-Dame Cathedral. The backwaters behind many of the islands provide pleasure craft with an alternative route, leaving the main channel for a while and free of the wash of passing barges, but you should keep a lookout for rowers and fishermen. The depth of these backwaters naturally varies, and anyone wanting to explore them should have the *Navicarte* of the Seine which shows the 'TE' (*tirant d'eau*) – see page 306.

The scenery varies enormously from forests to great cliffs where, around La Roche Guyon, caves and doorways cut into the chalk can be seen. Nearer to Paris, there are more sailing clubs, centres for waterskiing, rowing clubs and waterside restaurants. There are inevitably some stretches of river bordered by industry and other sections flanked by elegant houses, with beautifully kept lawns running down to the water where there may be a speedboat waiting to be launched from davits.

The final approach to the capital is very impressive, but expect it to be hectic on the water with barge traffic joined by a huge number of tourist *bateaux mouches* underway at any one time. There is only one place to moor up in the centre of Paris and this is the Port de Plaisance de Paris-Arsenal – the excellent marina in the basin at the Seine end of the Canal St Martin. The cost of an overnight stop here is very reasonable, particularly considering it is only 20 minutes' walk from Notre Dame and there are two Metro stations conveniently close by.

Port de Plaisance de Paris-Arsenal. *Photo: David Jefferson*

The Lower Seine

WATERWAY	PK ref	Town/*village*/≪*lock*	Total km
			▼　▲
RIVER SEINE	PK 202	≪ *Amfreville* VHF Ch 18.	176　203
	PK 202	*Amfreville* ⛴.	
	PK 201	*Poses* Quay through cut behind islands.	
	PK 176	*Val St Martin* Small ⚓. Narrow entrance with only one berth for a visitor.	
	PK 174	**Les Andelys** Community dates back to the Romans. Overlooked by Château Gaillard built in 12th century by Richard the Lionheart, King of England and Duke of Normandy. ⚓ which is prone to silting up. Most water in berths nearest to the entrance.	204　175
	PK 161	≪ Notre-Dame-de-la-Garenne VHF Ch22.	
	PK 150	**Vernon** Old quarter around 12th century collegiate church of Notre-Dame.	228　151

View from Château Gaillard, Les Andelys. *Photo: David Jefferson*

WATERWAY	PK ref	Town/*village*/≪*lock*	Total km
			▼ ▲
RIVER SEINE	PK 150	*Vernonnet* On right bank, opposite Vernon. ⚑ pontoon off grounds of a manor house now used as a children's activity centre. Covered shoal marked by pole to be avoided in approaches. Close pontoons with caution if more than 1m draught. This is the nearest stopping place to visit Claude Monet's house, his famous gardens, the Hôtel Baudry and the Musée Américain showing the expatriate American Impressionists all in the village of Giverny (10 minutes by taxi or 50 minutes' walk from the pontoons at Vernonnet. Try to get there early to avoid the queues.	
	PK 139	*Gloton* ⚑ (Port Saint-Nicolas) behind Grande Île – approach with caution from upstream because of shallows.	
	PK 121	≪ Méricourt VHF Ch 18.	
	PK 120	⚑ (*Port de l'Ilon*). Reached through a cut on the weir side of the river. Developed around sandpits. Full range of boatyard facilites, including travel lift. Shops in village of *Guernes* (1.8km). Fuel.	
	PK 109.5	**Mantes-la-Jolie** Much industrial development in the suburbs, but still dominated by magnificent Gothic collegiate church of Notre-Dame in the centre.	268.5 110.5
	PK 109.5	**Limay** Municipal ⚓ (no charge, maximum stay 48 hours). In deepwater behind Île de Limay.	
	PK 93	**Meulan** Municipal ⚓ (no charge, maximum stay 48 hours). Accessed through cut between Belle Île and le Fort. Pontoon off parkland. Excellent market Monday and Friday mornings.	284 94
	PK 81	⚑ (*Port Saint-Louis*) Bleak surroundings in old gravel pit.	

The Lower Seine

WATERWAY	PK ref	Town/*village*/≪*lock*	Total km
			▼ ▲
RIVER SEINE	PK 79	**Poissy** ⌐ behind Île des Migneaux accessed upstream end of island.	298 80
	PK 72.5	≪ *Andrésy* VHF Ch 22.	
	PK 73	**Andrésy** Municipal ⌂ (no charge, maximum stay 48 hours) in deep water, behind Île de Nancy (through lock, round the upstream end of the island, and then head back for 1km).	304 74
LEFT River Oise (Route 8)	PK 71.5		
	PK 71	**Conflans-Ste-Honorine** Barge capital of France – almost all permanently moored up. The barge *Je Sers* moored alongside the town quay is the community's chapel. Difficult to land in the town where there is a VNF office in Cours de Chimay (downstream end of the town where the Oise meets the Seine). ⌐ 2.5km upriver of road bridge on left bank.	306 72
	PK 62.5	*La Frette* Municipal ⌂ (no charge, maximum stay 48 hours). On right bank, remote, no shops nearby.	
	PK 48.5	≪ *Bougival* VHF Ch 22. Traffic uses either *Bougival* lock off the left bank or continues 4km upstream to *Chatou* lock. If stopping off at Bougival's Municipal ⌂ or Chatou's Municipal ⌂ use *Bougival's* triple lock.	
	PK 48	**Bougival** 19th century playground for the Parisian younger set and also a centre for the Impressionists. Municipal ⌂ 500m upstream of lock off right bank (no charge, maximum stay 48 hours).	329 49
	PK 45.5	**Chatou** La Maison Fournaise (19th century inn) was a meeting place for the Impressionists. Renoir painted *The Luncheon of the Boating Party* here and Monet captured many local scenes on	331.5 46.5

Conflans-Ste-Honorine. *Photo: David Jefferson*

WATERWAY	PK ref	Town/*village*/≪ lock	Total km
			▼ ▲
RIVER SEINE		canvas. Municipal ⚓ 3km upstream of *Bougival* lock off south side of Île de Chatou. (no charge, maximum stay 48 hours).	
	PK 44.5	≪ *Chatou* VHF Ch 18. Alternative single-chamber lock to ≪ *Bougival* (PK 48.5).	
	PK 35	Port de Genneviliers – the largest of 3 commercial ports administered by the Port Autonome de Paris.	
LEFT Canal St Denis (see Route 9B)	PK 29		
	PK 24	Port Van Gogh – yacht harbour primarily for large motor boats with permanent berths.	
	PK 19.5	**La Défense** World-famous town-planning project. Vast skyscrapers, including *La Grande Arche*, housing head offices of many international companies.	357.5 20.5
	PK 17	≪ *Suresnes* VHF Ch 22.	

The Lower Seine

The Eiffel Tower marks the start of the impressive entry into France's capital. *Photo: David Jefferson*

WATERWAY	PK ref	Town/*village*/≪ *lock*	Total km
			▼ ▲
RIVER SEINE	PK 5.5–PK 1	**Central Paris** *Left Bank*: Eiffel Tower, Hôtel des Invalides, Esplanade des Invalides, Quai d'Orsay (Foreign Office), Palais Bourbon (National Assembly). *Right Bank*: Grand Palais, Place de la Concorde, Jardin des Tuileries, Palais du Louvre.	
	PK 1–0	Île de Cité and Île St-Louis with Palais de Justice and Notre-Dame cathedral.	
	PK 1	Traffic lights controlling upstream traffic through Bras de la Cité and Bras St-Louis.	

WATERWAY	PK ref	Town/*village*/≪*lock*	Total km	
			▼	▲
RIVER SEINE	PK 0	Traffic lights controlling downstream traffic through Bras St-Louis and Bras de la Cité.	377	1
			▼	▲
1km upstream of PK 0		≪ **Port de Paris-Arsenal** VHF Ch 9 and Canal St Martin. Holding pontoon outside entrance to lock. Intercom connection with *Capitainerie* who operate lock remotely from the office. See page 115 for gaining access to marina after *Capitainerie* closed. 65 berths reserved for overnight stops. Accommodates craft from 6 to 25m. Restaurant overlooking basin. Attractively landscaped gardens. Only 20 minutes' walk along the Seine's right bank to Notre-Dame.	378	0
Continues as Seine *amont* (upper) (Route 2)				

Pont St Michel, Paris. *Photo: David Jefferson*

The Lower Seine

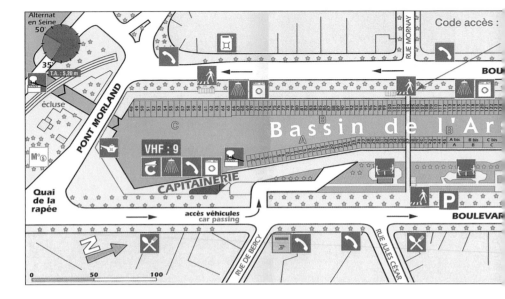

Approaching Île Saint Louis, Paris. *Photo: David Jefferson*

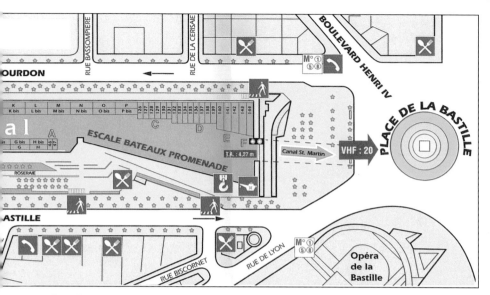

ABOVE Plan of Port de Plaisance de Paris-Arsenal. BELOW Plan showing entry to Port de l'Arsenal from the Seine. © *Chambre de Commerce et d'Industrie de Paris /Marie de Paris*

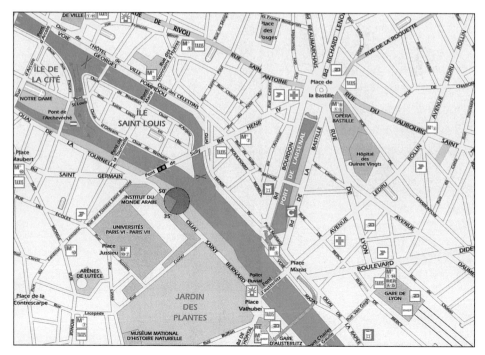

Bassin de la Seine

Le bassin de la Seine covers a huge area extending northwards into Picardy, to the east into the Champagne region and southwards to the start of the Bourgogne and Bourbonnais routes to the south of France and the Mediterranean. The Canals of Paris are also featured.

The *bassin* also includes the Seine between Paris and Rouen, but, for ease of reference, this is in Section One which covers the popular Seine passage from the sea to Paris as a single route.

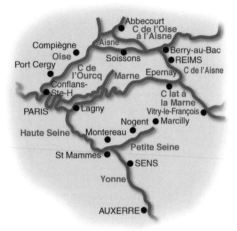

Route 2

The Upper Seine (*la Seine amont*):
Paris ←→ Montereau

The Seine is classified in three sections:

- Basse-Seine or Seine *aval* (lower) between the sea and Paris (**Route 1**)
- Haute-Seine or Seine *amont* (upper) between Paris and Montereau – where the Seine meets the Yonne River (**Route 2**)
- Petite-Seine from Montereau to Marcilly (**Route 3**).

From the sea to Marcilly is a distance of 546km with 25 locks.

Maximum boat dimensions: *Height above waterline* 5.5m   *Draught* 2.8m

Speed limits: Central Paris to Port à l'Anglais lock (PK 161): **18km/h (9.7kn)**
   Port à l'Anglais lock (PK 161) to Montereau (PK 68): **20km/h (10.8kn)**

Locks: **8** (180m long x 11.40m wide) Operate Mon–Sat 0700–1900; Sun 0800–1230 & 1330–1830

Distance: Port de Plaisance Paris-Arsenal to junction with canalised Yonne river: **100km**

Boat owners who have berthed in the Port de Paris-Arsenal, and plan to continue southwards towards the Mediterranean will motor the full length of the Haute-Seine (100km and 8 locks) if taking the Bourgogne route to the Med. Those opting for the quicker Bourbonnais route will leave the Haute-Seine at St-Mammès, 13km downriver of Montereau. For comparisons of routes to the Mediterranean see pages 5 and 122–3. Another alternative is to leave Paris to explore the Champagne region to the east by way of the Marne which would mean leaving the Seine a mere 5km upriver of Port de Paris-Arsenal (**Route 5**).

   The first part of the Haute-Seine, upriver of the yacht harbour, is exceptionally wide and spanned by interesting bridges, including the stone Pont de Bercy built in the second half of the 19th century. Fifty years later a many-arched viaduct was added to carry the Métro above the road traffic. Beyond the junction with the Marne, you are cruising in the predominantly industrial suburbs of Paris but after a couple of hours the surroundings become more countrified with the Forest of Sénart monopolising the right bank and then Fontainbleu's forest on the other. The villages are still within commuting distance of the capital, and there are many fine houses by the river. Sailing clubs have been established along the banks of the Upper Seine, no doubt busy at weekends when there will be a reduction in the barge activity on the water.

WATERWAY	PK ref	Town/*village*/≪*lock*	Total km	
			▼	▲
UPPER SEINE	PK 168	**Paris** ⊓ Paris-Arsenal see page 85.	0	100
LEFT Marne (Route 5)	PK 163.5			
	PK 161	≪ No 10 *Port-à-l'Anglais* VHF Ch 18.		
	PK 154.5	**Paris suburbs Villeneuve Triage** ⊓.	13.5	86.5
	PK 150	≪ No 9 *Ablon* VHF Ch 22.		
	PK 148	**Paris suburbs Vigneux-sur-Seine** ⊓.	20	80
	PK 146.5	**Paris suburbs Draveil** ⊓.		
	PK 145	**Paris suburbs Viry Châtillon** ⏛.	23	77
	PK 139	≪ No 8 *Evry* VHF Ch 18.		
	PK 132	*Saintry-sur-Seine* ⊓.		
	PK 129.5	≪ No 7 *Le Coudray* VHF Ch 22.		
	PK 129	*Morsang-sur-Seine* ⊓.		
	PK 123.5	*Seine-Port* ⊓.		
	PK 116	≪ No 4 *Vives Eaux* VHF Ch 18.		
	PK 112	*Boissettes* ⊓.		
	PK 109	**Melun** Industrial and agricultural market town. Old capital of Brie Française region ⊓.	59	41
	PK 101	≪ No 3 *La Cave* VHF Ch 22.		
	PK 101	*Chartrettes* ⊓.		
	PK 93	**Samois-sur-Seine** ⏛.		
	PK 90	**Avon** ⊓.	78	22
	PK 84	**Champagne-sur-Seine** ⏛.		
	PK 83.5	≪ No 2 *Champagne* VHF Ch 18.		

WATERWAY	PK ref	Town/*village*/≪lock	Total km	
			▼	▲
UPPER SEINE				
RIGHT Canal du Loing & Bourbonnais route (Route 10)	PK 81.5			
	PK 81	**St-Mammès** Barge town at an important Seine junction ⚑. Fuel.	87	13
	PK 71.5	≪ No 1 *Varennes* VHF Ch 22.	▼	▲
RIGHT Yonne River & Bourgogne route (Route 12)	PK 68	**Montereau** Industrial barge town at end of the Haute-Seine where most craft enter the Yonne river if making for the Med by way of the Canal de Bourgogne or, if draught permits, the Canal du Nivernais (Route 11). Moorings off the left bank just upstream of the junction and the bridge in Petite Seine.	100	0
AHEAD continues as Petite Seine (Route 3)				

Samois-sur-Seine. *Photo: Maison Départmentale du Tourisme de Seine et Marne*

Route 3

Petite Seine: *Montereau* ↔ *Marcilly*

The Seine rises on the plateau of Langres at St-Germain-Source-Seine, 29km NW of Dijon in the Côte d'Or. It is 776km from the source to the sea, and the third longest in France. Navigable for 535km, Route 1 covers the Lower Seine; Route 2 the Upper Seine and Route 3 below the Petite Seine.

Maximum boat dimensions: *Height above waterline* Montereau (PK 68) – Nogent (PK 20) **5.2m**. Nogent (PK 20) – Marcilly (PK 1) **3.15m**

Draught Montereau (PK 68) – barrage de la Grande Bosse (PK 49) **2.8m**
Barrage de la Grande Bosse (PK 49) – Bray (PK 46) **2.2m**
Bray (PK 46) – Nogent (PK 20) **1.8m**
Nogent (PK 20) – Marcilly (PK 1) **1.2m**

Speed limit: 15km/h (8kn)

Locks: 11 Apart from the electrified Marolles lock which is 7km above Montereau and La Grande Bosse (PK 49) both of which can take 180m length of barge traffic, the remaining 9 are manual and small by comparison (38.50m long x 7.50m wide).
Operate Mon–Sat 0700–1900; Sun 0800–1230 & 1330–1830 except for La Grande Bosse, Jaulnes and Vezoult operate Mon–Fri 0800–1230 & 1330–1800; weekend by arrangement only.

Distances: Montereau – Nogent **48km**   Nogent – Marcilly **20km**

Most yachts navigating the Upper Seine from Paris will be heading south, leaving the Seine at St-Mammès (Route 10) or Montereau (Route 4) and heading south via the Bourbonnais or Bourgogne waterways. Those who choose to continue along the Seine will be able to reach Nogent-sur-Seine (48km) but continuing on up river to Marcilly, which is the end of the navigation, will depend on the boat's dimensions. As indicated above, both headroom and draught are considerably reduced for this final section, and it would be prudent to enquire about depth at Nogent-sur-Seine before tackling the last 19km of the navigable Seine to Marcilly.

The scenery is not particularly remarkable, and between Montereau and the industrial surroundings at Bray-sur-Seine, the two locks (Marolles and Grande Bosse) still handle the larger barges. A substantial part of the navigation between Montereau and Marcilly is dead straight man-made canal bypassing shallows in the Seine river.

WATERWAY	PK ref	Town/*village*/≪ *lock*	Total km	
			▼	▲
PETITE SEINE				
RIGHT Yonne River (Route 4)	PK 68			
	PK 68	**Montereau** (see page 91).	0	68
	PK 61	≪ No 13 *Marolles* VHF Ch 18.		
	PK 61	**Marolles-sur-Seine** 🛏.		
LEFT **PETITE SEINE**	PK 56.5			
AHEAD Bray–La Tombe Canal (closed)				
	PK 49	≪ *La Grande Bosse* VHF Ch 22.		
RIGHT Bray–La Tombe Canal (closed)	PK 46.5			
	PK 45.5	**Bray-sur-Seine** Small town with waterside parkland with various attractions for visitors ⚑.	22.5	45.5
	PK 43	≪ No 9 *Jaulnes.*		
	PK 37	≪ No 8 *Vezoult.*		
AHEAD canal bypass	PK 32.5			
RIGHT closed river				
	PK 32	≪ No 7 *Villiers.*		
	PK 27	≪ No 6 *Metz.*		
AHEAD **PETITE SEINE**	PK 23.5	≪ No 5 *Beaulieu.*		

Bassin de la Seine: Petite Seine

WATERWAY	PK ref	Town/*village*/≪*lock*	Total km	
			▼	▲
PETITE SEINE				
RIGHT closed river	PK 19.5	≪ No 4 *Nogent.*		
	PK 20	**Nogent-sur-Seine** Industrial town ♨.	48	20
ABOVE Nogent reduced head-room and draught				
AHEAD canal bypass	PK 16.5			
LEFT closed river				
	PK 16.5	≪ No 3 *Bernières.*		
	PK 14	*Marnay-sur-Seine* ♨.		
	PK 14	≪ No 2 *Marnay.*		
	PK 3.5	*Conflans-sur-Seine* ♨.		
AHEAD	PK 3.5	≪ No 1 *Conflans.*		
PETITE SEINE				
LEFT closed river				
	PK 1	*Marcilly-sur-Seine* Pleasant village with camping site and 'beach' ♨.	▼	▲
End of navigation	PK 0		68	0

Route 4

River Yonne: *Montereau ↔ Auxerre*

Maximum boat dimensions: *Height above waterline* 4.4m   *Draught* 1.8m

Speed limit: 15km/h (8kn)

Locks: 26 (all over 90m long x 8m wide) First three locks Nos 17, 16, 15 Operate Mon–Fri 0700–1900; weekends 0800–1230 & 1330–1830; Nos 14–5 Mon–Fri 0800–1230 & 1330–1800; weekends by arrangement only; Nos 4–1 & 9–1 end Mar– early Nov daily 0900–1230 & 1330–1900; early Nov– late Mar by arrangement only

Distance: 108km

Commercial traffic on the Yonne is light, with ever-growing numbers of pleasure craft using the waterway. The latter consist of chartered boats, hotel barges and those Med-bound or making their way back to Northern France. A few boat owners heading for the warmer climate in the South of France, who have joined the Yonne from the Upper Seine, have a choice of reaching the Saône and Rhône via the Canal de Bourgogne (Route 12) or the Canal de Nivernais (Route 11). The beautiful Nivernais may look tempting, but
many sea-going boats will have to opt for the Bourgogne route when leaving the Yonne because of their craft's draught and/or height above waterline. This is hardly a sacrifice, as parts of the Bourgogne route are equally stunning.

Having reached the Yonne, a boat owner will have completed roughly a third of the passage from Le Havre to the Mediterranean, and will be nudging into Burgundy and sampling a flavour of the delights of the region to come. The canalised river meanders through small colourful villages and a string of interesting towns steeped in history.

The only reservation about the river is the unique shape of the locks. In most of them, one or both sides of the lock are sloping which can be a problem for down-stream traffic particularly with twin-props. Most locks have a pontoon in the chamber to enable the crew to land with the head rope as the ladders inset into the sloping walls are too slippery to use. Sometimes it may be prudent to land the crew before entering the lock. Having secured, the boat must then be kept clear of the sloping side, fending off with a heavy boathook and fendered along the waterline (fenders half-filled with water and strung horizontally are a good precaution).

WATERWAY	PK ref	Town/*village*/≪*lock*	Total km	
			▼	▲
T-junction Upper Seine (Route 2) & Petite Seine (Route 3)	PK 68			
YONNE	PK 108	**Montereau** (see page 91) ⚑.	0	108
	PK 105	≪ No 17 *Cannes* VHF Ch 8.		
	PK 100.5	≪ No 16 *Labrosse* VHF Ch 8.		
	PK 96	≪ No 15 *Barbey* VHF Ch 8.		
Canal *dérivation* bypassing river	PK 91.5	≪ No 14 *Port-Renard* VHF Ch 8.		
	PK 90	≪ No 13 *Vinneuf* VHF Ch 8.		
End of canal *dérivation*	PK 87			
YONNE	PK 80	≪ No 12 *Champfleury* VHF Ch 8.		
	PK 79	**Pont-sur-Yonne** Pleasant small town. Old bridge and historical remains. 12th century church.	29	79
	PK 74.5	≪ No 11 *Villeperrot* VHF Ch 8.		
	PK 69.5	≪ No 10 *St Martin* VHF Ch 8.		
	PK 66.5	**Sens** 12th century St-Étienne cathedral. Treasury collection among the best known in Europe. Tree-lined boulevards ⚓.	41.5	66.5
	PK 65	≪ No 9 *St Bond* VHF Ch 8.		
	PK 60.5	≪ No 8 *Rosoy* VHF Ch 8.		
	PK 56	≪ No 7 *Étigny* VHF Ch 8.		
	PK 50.5	≪ No 6 *Villeneuve*.		

WATERWAY	PK ref	Town/village/≪lock	Total km
			▼ ▲
YONNE	PK 50	**Villeneuve-sur-Yonne** Interesting old town. One-time Royal residence. Quays on both sides of the river ⚓. Cruiser hire.	58 50
	PK 45	≪ No 5 *Armeau.*	
	PK 42	*Villevallier* ⚓.	
	PK 40	≪ No 4 *Villevallier.*	
Canal *dérivation* bypassing river	PK 36	2 pontoons in first km of river for shallow draught boats.	
	PK 35.5	≪ No 3 *St-Aubin* ⚓ beyond.	
End of canal *dérivation*	PK 32.5		
	PK 31.5	**Joigny** Pleasant medieval town with narrow streets and attractive half-timbered houses ⚑. Fuel. Cruiser hire.	76.5 31.5
	PK 28.5	≪ No 2 *Pêchoir.*	
	PK 25	≪ No 1 *Épineau.*	
	PK 24	*La Roche-Saint-Cydroine* ⚓.	

Villeneuve-sur-Yonne. *Photo: Keith Harris*

Bassin de la Seine: River Yonne

WATERWAY	PK ref	Town/*village*/≪*lock*		Total km
			▼	▲
YONNE				
LEFT Canal de Bourgogne (Route 12)	PK 23			
	PK 22.5	**Migennes** ⌓ through lock in entrance to Canal de Bourgogne. Cruiser hire	85.5	22.5
	PK 21	≪ No 9 *la Gravière* ⌂ beyond.		
	PK 18	*Bassou* ⌂. Showers at camp site.		
	PK 17	≪ No 8 *Bassou*.		
Canal *dérivation* bypassing river	PK 15.5			
	PK 15	≪ No 7 *Reveuse*.		
	PK 14	≪ No 6 *Néron*.		
End of canal *dérivation*	PK 10.5			
	PK 10	*Gurgy* ⌂.		
	PK 7.5	≪ No 5 *Monéteau*.		
	PK 6.5	*Monéteau* ⌂.		
	PK 6	≪ No 4 *Boisseaux*.		
	PK 4	≪ No 3 *Dumonts*.		
	PK 2.5	≪ No 2 *L'Ile Brûlée*.		
	PK 1	≪ No 1 *la Chaînette*.	▼	▲
	PK 0	**Auxerre** Capital of the Yonne *département*. Centre of wine and beautiful district of vineyards and orchards. An old town built on a hill, a most attractive sight from the river. Old churches and a cathedral ⌓. Fuel. Cruiser hire.	108	0
Continues as Canal du Nivernais (Route 11)				

Route 5

The Marne and Canal latéral à la Marne: *Paris (Port de Plaisance de Paris-Arsenal)* ←→ *Vitry-le-François*

Maximum boat dimensions: *Height above waterline* 3.4m   *Draught* 1.8m

Speed limit: Marne 15km/h (8kn); Canal latéral à la Marne 8km/h (4.3kn)

Locks: 33 Marne locks operate No 18, 17: Mon–Fri 0700–1900; weekend 0800–1230 & 1330–1830. No 16–10: Mon–Fri 0800–1800; weekend 0800–1230 & 1300–1800. No 9 & 8: April–Oct daily 0800–1230 & 1330–1800; Nov–Mar by arrangement only. No 7–1: April–Oct daily 0800–1800; Nov–Mar, Mon–Sat 0800–1800

Canal latéral à la Marne locks No 15–12: April–Oct daily 0800–1800; Nov–Mar, Mon–Sat 0800–1800. No 11–1: April–Oct daily 0700–1800; Nov–Mar daily 0730–1730

Distances: Seine 4.5km   Marne 178km   Canal latéral à la Marne 66km

It may come as a surprise to some boat owners to discover just how close the champagne region is to Paris. Nanteuil-sur-Marne, the first of many riverside villages harvesting the distinctive *pinot meunier* grape which gives the fruity taste to champagne, is only 100km by waterway from the centre of Paris.

Those who have moored up in Port de Plaisance de Paris-Arsenal, will mostly be *en route* to the Mediterranean or stopping over for a few days sightseeing before the return trip downriver. Either way, having reached the capital, it is certainly worth considering extending the trip to explore the Marne valley and sampling the champagne. Med-bound, this Marne diversion to the east adds only 68km compared with the Bourgogne route from Le Havre to Port St Louis.

An earlyish departure from the Port de Plaisance de Paris-Arsenal allows plenty of time to reach the cathedral city of Meaux before the locks close at the end of the first day. Those who set off later, have a good choice of stop-overs in the outskirts of Paris. The entrance to the canalised Marne river is just 4km up the Seine from the Paris-Arsenal marina. After 3km on the Marne, there is a

600m tunnel which bypasses a great loop in the river. Beyond the tunnel, and a yacht is in exclusive Parisian outskirts where elegant houses with beautifully kept lawns line the banks of the river. This part of the Marne is famous for its *guinguettes* where a certain class of Parisians dined, drank and waltzed in the afternoons, sometimes accom-panied by accommodating *filles aguicheuses* (good-time girls). These days there is an association promoting these tea dances in several of the waterside restaurants in these parts.

Just 2.5km upstream of the tunnel is one of the most exclusive yacht harbours in the Paris suburbs at Nogent-sur-Marne. Beyond Nogent and a yacht is already in the countryside with two short sections of canal to negotiate to bypass parts of the river closed to navigation. Once through these canals there is a great choice of stopping places including Meaux, the largest town in the Seine-et-Marne *département*, Poincy with a Port de Plaisance and the once fortified town of La Ferté-sous-Jouarre.

Still less than 100km by waterway from the centre of Paris, east-bound traffic is now entering the Champagne region proper where the vines cover the gentle slopes of the Marne valley all the way to Épernay and beyond, often stretching from the river to the distant skyline.

The first opportunity to visit the cellars of a champagne house is when you are moored up in the old town of Château-Thierry. The champagne villages then come thick and fast. Each producer offers an individual tour and tasting ranging from a formal pre-arranged visit with an English-speaking guide to a wander round the premises escorted personally by the proprietor.

Cumières, which has a long pontoon for visiting boats, is almost an obligatory stop. Surrounded by *premier crus* vineyards, the village has 18 champagne houses

LEFT Nogent-sur-Marne.
Photo: David Jefferson

RIGHT Meaux.
Photo: David Jefferson

including the cellars of Maître-Geoffroy which were established in 1878. From Cumières, the pilgrimage to the birthplace of champagne can be made on foot. Hautvillers is 3km to the north, high up on the hillside above Cumières. It was here in the 17th century that Dom Pierre Pérignon, cellar master of the local abbey, perfected the process of blending local wines to make champagne.

A kilometre upriver of Cumières, the waterway divides. Straight on is the Canal Latéral à la Marne; to the right, the Embranchement d'Épernay is the final 5km of navigable Marne river leading to the hospitable Société Nautique d'Épernay.

Épernay vies with Reims to be considered the champagne capital of France. Many of the great champagne names are located in Épernay, majestically lining the first mile of the Avenue de Champagne.

The 66km of the Canal latéral à la Marne curving round to the south follows the direction of the non-navigable Marne River until Vitry-le-François. At the beginning of the canal are the villages of Ay and Mareuil-sur-Ay, with their renowned Grand Crus vineyards on the eastern boundary of the Champagne region.

Although partly industrial, the largest of the two towns on the canal and the capital of the Marne *département*, Châlons-en-Champagne has some fine old buildings ranging from half-timbered houses in the back streets to the 13th century St-Etienne cathedral and 12th century Romanesque-gothic Notre-Dame en Vaux church.

At the end of the canal is the barge town of Vitry-le-François, built by François 1 in the 16th century as a fortress but almost totally destroyed in WWII. It is a significant waterway crossroads with its canal access to Paris to the west, Alsace-Lorraine to the east and the Saône and Rhône to the south.

Bassin de la Seine: River Marne

WATERWAY	PK ref	Town/*village*/≪ lock	Total km	
			▼	▲
RIVER SEINE	PK 168	**Paris** Port de Plaisance de Paris-Arsenal (see page 85).	0	249
4.5km upstream then left into **MARNE**	PK 178		4.5	244.5
	PK 177	≪ No 18 *St-Maurice* VHF Ch 22.		
LEFT Lock & tunnel 600m	PK 174.5	≪ No 17 *St-Maur* VHF Ch 18.		
STRAIGHT ON (end of navigation beyond)		*Créteil* (3km) ≪ and ♋		
End of tunnel	PK 173.5			
RIGHT *Joinville* ⚑ .				
LEFT **MARNE**				
	PK 171	**Nogent-sur-Marne** ⚑ in parkland with several other leisure facilities.	11.5	237.5
	PK 168.5	**Le Perreux-sur-Mer** ♋.		
CHELLES CANAL	PK 165	Entrance to Chelles canal and ≪ No 16. *Neuilly-sur-Marne* ⚑ in Marne just upstream of canal entrance off an island accommodating a vast camp site with bar/restaurant and showers.		
MARNE	PK 156	End of Chelles canal and ≪ No 15 *Vaires*. ♋ and cruiser hire in Marne just downstream of canal entrance.		
	PK 151	**Lagny** ⚑ and long quay.	31.5	217.5
	PK 145.5	*Chalifert* ⚑ just upstream of canal entrance.		
RIGHT tunnel 300m	PK 145.5	≪ No 14 *Chalifert* VHF Ch 11 and 300m tunnel.		
& **CANAL DE CHALIFERT**	PK 145	≪ No 13 *Lesches* VHF Ch 11		
End of canal rejoin **MARNE**	PK 133.5	**Meaux** ≪ No 12 *Meaux* VHF Ch 14. Cathedral town with all facilities. Public ♋ to port after lock between town bridges.	49	200

WATERWAY	PK ref	Town/*village*/≪*lock*	Total km
			▼ ▲
MARNE		⛿/Cruiser hire on quayside opposite lock.	
	PK 128.5	*Fublaines* ♨.	
	PK 127	**Trilport** ♨.	
	PK 125	*Poincy* ⛿ with nearby restaurant.	
	PK 121	*Germigny l'Evêque* Restaurant.	
	PK 113	≪ No 11 *Isles-les-Meldeuses.*	
	PK 105.5	≪ No 10 *St-Jean-les-Deux-Jumeaux.*	
	PK 99.5	*Changis-sur-Marne* ♨.	
	PK 90.5	**La Ferté-sous-Jouarre** Once fortified town where old walls still dominate the right bank of the river. Town quay on left bank between bridges. Public ♨ in parkland inside island above second bridge (1.2m water).	92 157
	PK 87	≪ No 9 *Courtaron* VHF Ch 14.	
	PK 76	≪ No 8 *Méry.*	
	PK 74	*Nanteuil-sur-Marne* Start of the champagne region. ♨.	
	PK 66.5	≪ No 7 *Charly.* ♨ upriver of lock.	

River Marne. *Photo: David Jefferson*

Bassin de la Seine: River Marne

WATERWAY	PK ref	Town/*village*/≪*lock*	Total km
			▼ ▲
MARNE	PK 63	*Nogent-l'Artaud*. Museum *Centre de l'Automobile Ancienne.* ♒.	
	PK 56	≪ No 6 *Azy*.	
	PK 50.5	**Château-Thierry** Tour the medieval cellars of Champagne Pannier hewn out of the hillside. Castle and pedestrian ways with market stalls. ♒ alongside town quay.	132 117
	PK 42.5	≪ No 5 *Mt St-Père*.	
	PK 37	*Jaulgonne* Shops and restaurants ♒.	
	PK 30.5	≪ No 4 *Courcelles*.	
	PK 26	**Dormans** Small market town by railway. Camp site with swimming pools. Castle and park ♒.	156.5 92.5
	PK 18	≪ No 3 *Vandières*.	
	PK 12	*Reuil* Champagne houses in village and nearby *Oeuilly* where a 17th century grower's house has been turned into a champagne museum ♒.	
	PK 8	≪ No 2 *Damery*.	
	PK 5	*Damery* Champagne houses ♒.	
	PK 3	≪ No 1 *Cumières*.	
	PK 1.5	*Cumières* 18 champagne houses. *Hautvillers*, 3km to the north, is the much-visited birthplace of champagne in the 17th century ♒.	
RIGHT last 5km of navigable Marne and Épernay	PK 0		182.5 66.5
	PK 4	**Épernay** Champagne capital. Famous champagne houses line the Avenue de Champagne beneath which are over 100km of tunnels and cellars with 200 million bottles. *Musée du Vin de Champagne* in	186.5 70.5
End of navigation		Château Perrier ⚑ .(Yacht Club).	
Continues as **CANAL LATÉRAL À LA MARNE**	PK 0/66.5	≪ No 15 *Dizy*.	

WATERWAY	PK ref	Town/*village*/≪lock	Total km
			▼ ▲
CANAL LATÉRAL	PK 62	≪ No 14 *Ay*.	
À LA MARNE	PK 59	*Mareuil-sur-Ay*. The last and best of the region's vineyards ⚐. Cruiser hire.	
	PK 58	≪ No 13 *Mareuil*.	
	PK 53	≪ No 12 *Tours* ⚓ upstream of lock.	
LEFT Canal de l'Aisne à la Marne (Route 7)	PK 48.5		
	PK 48.5	*Condé-sur-Marne* ⚓.	
	PK 44.5	≪ No 11 *Vraux*.	
	PK 39	≪ No 10 *Juvigny*.	
	PK 32	**Châlons-en-Champagne** ≪No 9 *Châlons*. Many fine old buildings including Gothic 13th century cathedral and museum in cloisters of Notre- Dame-en-Vaux church. ⚓ upstream of lock.	217 32
	PK 26	≪ No 8 *Sarry*.	
	PK 21.5	≪ No 7 *St-Germain*.	
	PK 15	≪ No 6 *la Chaussée* ⚓ upstream of lock.	
	PK 11.5	≪ No 5 *Ablancourt*.	
	PK 9	≪ No 4 *Soulanges* ⚓ upstream of lock.	
	PK 5	≪ No 3 *Couvrot*.	
	PK 3.5	≪ No 2 *Lermite*.	
	PK 2	≪ No 1 *Vitry-le-François*.	▼ ▲
T-junction	PK 0	**Vitry-le-François** Barge town rebuilt after WWII. Waterway crossroads where three canals meet. ⚐ at the start of Canal de la Marne à la Saône.	249 0
LEFT Canal de la Marne au Rhin (Route 39)	PK 0		
RIGHT Canal de la Marne à la Saône (Route 36)			

Route 6

Canal latéral à l'Aisne:
Vieux-lès-Asfeld ↔ Celles
Canalised River Aisne:
Celles ↔ Compiègne

Maximum boat dimensions:
Height above waterline 3.7m
Draught Canal latéral à l'Aisne 1.8m
    Canalised Aisne 2m

Speed limits: Canal latéral à l'Aisne **8km/h (4.3kn)**   Canalised Aisne **15km/h (8kn)**

Locks: **15** (min 38.50m long x 5.20m wide) Operate April–Oct Canal latéral à l'Aisne: Mon–Fri 0700–1800; weekends 0700–1230 & 1330–1800; Canalised Aisne: daily 0700–1230 & 1330–1800. Nov–Mar Canal latéral à l'Aisne: Mon–Sat 0800–1800 (except Nos 1 & 2 daily 0730–1730); Canalised Aisne: Mon–Sat 0800–1230 & 1330–1700

Distance: 108km

These two short canals provide the connection between the Canal des Ardennes and the canalised Oise.

WATERWAY	PK ref	Town/*village*/≪*lock*	Total km	
			▼	▲
Junction with Canal des Ardennes (Route 32)	PK 0		0	108
CANAL LATÉRAL À L'AISNE	PK 7	≪ No 1 *Pignicourt*.		
	PK 10.5	*Variscourt* ⊔.		
	PK 14	≪ No 2 *Condé-sur-Suippe*.		
Junction with Canal de l'Aisne à la Marne to Reims (Route 7)	PK 18.5			

WATERWAY	PK ref	Town/*village*/≪*lock*	Total km	
			▼	▲
CANAL LATÉRAL	PK 18.5	*Berry-au-Bac* ♺.		
À L'AISNE	PK 32.5	*Maizy* ♺.		
	PK 38	*Bourg-et-Comin* ♺.		
RIGHT Canal de l'Oise à l'Aisne (Route 7)	PK 38.5			
	PK 38.5	≪ No 4 *Cendrière*.		
	PK 44.5	≪ No 5 *Cys*.		
	PK 46.5	≪ No 6 *St-Audebert*.		
	PK 49	**Vailly-sur-Aisne** ♺ in branch of R Aisne.	49	59
	PK 51	≪ Nos 7 & 8 (double) *Celles*.		
Continues as **CANALISED AISNE RIVER**	PK 51.5			
	PK 64.5	≪ No 9 *Villeneuve-St-Germain* ♺.		
	PK 67	**Soissons** 12th century St-Gervais-et-St-Protais cathedral. Even more impressive remains of the ancient twin-spired Abbaye de St-Jean-des-Vignes founded in 1076 ♺.	67	41
	PK 68.5	≪ No 10 *Vauxrot*.		
	PK 79	≪ No 11 *Fontenoy* ♺.		
	PK 85	*Vic-sur-Aisne* ♺.		
	PK 85.5	≪ No 12 *Vic-sur-Aisne*.		
	PK 92	≪ No 13 *Couloisy*.		
	PK 97.5	≪ No 14 *Hérant*.		
	PK 104.5	≪ No 15 *Carandeau*.	▼	▲
T-junction LEFT direction Paris; RIGHT direction Canal du Nord (Route 8)	PK 108/99		108	0

Canal de l'Oise à l'Aisne:
Abbécourt ←→ Bourg-et-Comin   48km 13 locks

Part Canal latéral à l'Aisne:
Bourg-et-Comin ←→ Berry-au-Bac   20km 1 lock

Canal de l'Aisne à la Marne:
Berry-au-Bac ←→ Condé-sur-Marne   58km 24 locks

These three short lengths of different canals are used by boats coming from the northern entry ports via the Canal du Nord or Canal St-Quentin and then making for the Saône/Rhône via the extensions to the Marne waterway, well to the east of Paris. The route takes a boat through the champagne region and the champagne city of Reims which vies with nearby Épernay to be considered the world centre for champagne where many of the famous champagne houses have been established for many years.

Maximum boat dimensions: *Height above waterline* 3.5m *Draught* 1.8m

Speed limit: 8km/h (4.3kn)

Locks: 38 (min 38.50m long x 5.20m wide) Operate Canal de l'Oise à l'Aisne No 1–13: daily 0700–1800
Canal latéral à l'Aisne, Berry-au-Bac lock: Mon–Fri 0700–1800; weekends 0700–1230 & 1330–1800
Canal de l'Aisne à la Marne No 1–12: daily 0700–1800; No 13–24: April–Oct daily 0700–1800; Nov–Mar daily 0730–1730

Distance: 126km

WATERWAY	PK ref	Town/*village*/≪*lock*	Total km
			▼ ▲
T-junction with Canal latéral à l'Oise (Route 8)			
CANAL DE L'OISE À L'AISNE	PK 0		0 125.5
	PK 0.5–17	≪ Nos 1-4.	
	PK 25.5	*Pinon* ⟐.	
	PK 26–35	≪ Nos 6-9.	
	PK 35	*Pargny-Filain* ⟐.	
Braye tunnel (2365m)	PK 38		
End of tunnel	PK 40.5		
	PK 42.5–45	≪ Nos 10-13.	
T-junction **CANAL LATÉRAL À L'AISNE**	PK 48/38	*Bourg-et-Comin* ⟐.	
RIGHT direction Soissons/ Compiègne (Route 6)			
LEFT Berry-au-Bac			
	PK 32.5	*Maizy* ⟐.	
	PK 18.5	≪ No 3 *Berry*.	
AHEAD continues as Canal latéral à l'Aisne (Route 6)	PK 18.5		
	PK 18.5	*Berry-au-Bac* ⟐.	
RIGHT **CANAL DE L'AINSE À LA MARNE**	PK 0-2	≪ Nos 1, 2 & 3.	
	PK 4	*Cormicy* ⟐.	
	PK 4.5–12	≪ Nos 4-9.	
	PK 12.5	*Courcy* ⟐.	

WATERWAY	PK ref	Town/*village*/≪*lock*	Total km
			▼ ▲
CANAL DE L'AINSE À LA MARNE	PK 23.5	**Reims** Modern city, rebuilt after damage of two world wars. Many kings of France were crowned here. Centre of champagne producing region. Germans surrendered in Reims in May 1945. Notre Dame cathedral (13th century). Visits to champagne cellars of many of the leading producers ⌓. Cruiser hire.	91 34.5
	PK 24.5–33.5	≪ Nos 10, 11, 12 & 13.	
	PK 33.5	*Sillery* ⌓.	
	PK 35.5–39.5	≪ Nos 14, 15 & 16.	
Mont de Billy tunnel (2302m)	PK 46.5		
End of tunnel	PK 49		
	PK 51	*Vaudemanges* ⌂.	
	PK 51.5–57.5	≪ Nos 17-24.	▼ ▲
	PK 58		125.5 0
T-junction Canal latéral à la Marne RIGHT Épernay LEFT Vitry-le-François (Route 5)			

Route 8

Canal latéral à l'Oise and River l'Oise:
Chauny ↔ Conflans-Ste-Honorine

Maximum boat dimensions: *Height above waterline* Canal latéral à l'Oise **3.5m** l'Oise **5.0m** *Draught* Canal latéral à l'Oise **2.2m** l'Oise **2.5m**

Speed limits: Canal latéral à l'Oise **10km/h** l'Oise **15km/h**

Locks: 11 (min 39m long x 6.50m wide) Operate Canal latéral à l'Oise No 1 & 2: Mon–Fri 0700–1900; Sat 0700–1800; Sun 0800–1230 & 1330–1830. No 3 & 4: Mon–Sat 0700–1900; Sun 0800–1230 & 1330–1830; l'Oise No 1–5: Mon–Fri 0700–2000; weekend 0700–1900. No 6 & 7: Mon–Sat 0600–2000; Sun 0800–1230 & 1330–1830

Distance: 138km

Much of the flat countryside around the Canal latéral à l'Oise and the Oise river is forest. The modest drop of 10.45m in the canalised Oise is achieved with 7 locks, and in the first section from Chauny to Janville the drop is 13.1m achieved with 4 locks. There is one large town – Compiègne – on a commercial route which has a reasonable selection of stopping places specifically for pleasure craft. Half-way along the route, the surroundings become more industrialised. Barge traffic is heavy along the entire length, and boat owners heading for Paris will often choose to cover this waterway as quickly as possible. With relatively few locks (each with two chambers), and speed limits of 15km/h on the canalised Oise and 10km/h on the Canal latéral à l'Oise, the passage from the end of the St-Quentin canal to the Seine will still take 2 – 3 days.

Bassin de la Seine: Canal latéral à l'Oise

WATERWAY	PK ref	Town/*village*/≪lock	Total km	
			▼	▲
From Canal de St-Quentin (Route 29)				
CANAL LATÉRAL À L'OISE	PK 0	**Chauny** ⊡.	0	138
LEFT Canal de l'Oise à l'Aisne (Route 7)	PK 3			
	PK 3	*Abbécourt* ⊓.		
	PK 9	≪ *No1 St Hubert* (double) VHF Ch 18.		
	PK 18	*Pont l'Evêque* ⊓.		
	PK 18	≪ *No 2 Sempigny* (double)VHF Ch 22.		
RIGHT Canal du Nord (Route 28)	PK 18.5	Direction Péronne.		
	PK 28	≪ *No 3 Bellerive* (double) VHF Ch 18.		
	PK 33	**Longueil-Annel** 13th century church ⊡. Cruiser hire.	33	105
	PK 34	≪ *No 4 Janville* (double) VHF Ch 22.		
Continues as **L'OISE**	PK 103.5	*Janville.*		
LEFT River Aisne (Route 6)	PK 99	Direction Soissons.		
	PK 98	**Compiègne** Royal residence of several kings of France who hunted in nearby forest. Louis XV rebuilt the royal château which now houses three museums – the Royal Apartments, Second Empire and National Automobile Museum (cars, carriages and coaches) ⊡.	40	98
	PK 96	≪ *No 1 Venette* (double – chamber each side of island) VHF Ch 18.		
	PK 91.5	*Jaux* ⊡.		
	PK 82.5	≪ *No 2 Verberie* (double) VHF Ch 22.		
	PK 82	**Verberie** Small town with 12th century church and 19th century	56	82

WATERWAY	PK ref	Town/*village*/≪*lock*	Total km	
			▼	▲
L'OISE		château. ⚓ (private sailing club).		
	PK 72.5	≪ No 3 *Sarron* (double) VHF Ch 18.		
	PK 70.5	**Pont-Ste-Maxence** 14th century Abaye Royal du Moncel.		
	PK 62	*Verneuil-en-Halatte* ⚓.		
	PK 59	**Nogent-sur-Oise** Industrial town.	79	59
	PK 59	**Creil** Industrial town. Maison Gallé-Juillet (Creil pottery museum) ⚓.		
	PK 56	≪ No 4 *Creil* (double) VHF Ch 22.		
	PK 41	≪ No 5 *Boran* (double) VHF Ch 18.		
	PK 39	*Noisy-sur-Oise* ⚓ in first entrance to back-water on left. Depth 1m.		
	PK 34	**Persan** ⚓.		
	PK 34	**Beaumont-sur-Oise** Ancient fortified market town (opposite Persan ⚓).	104	34
	PK 30.5	*Champagne-sur-Oise* ⚓ (sailing club).		
	PK 28	≪ No 6 *l'Isle-Adam* (double) VHF Ch 22.		
	PK 27	**L'Isle-Adam** Water sports playground with extensive beach. ⚓.	111	27
	PK 22	*Auvers-sur-Oise* ⚓.		
	PK 15	**Pontoise** Old walled town with 12th century cathedral. Painted by Cézanne and Pissarro ⚓.	123	15
	PK 13.5	≪ No 7 *Pontoise* (double) VHF Ch 18.		
	PK 11.5	*Eragny* ⚑.		
	PK 9	**Cergy** ⚑ Port Cergy. Well protected and all facilities.	129	9
T-junction where l'Oise meets the Seine (Route 1)	PK 0			
	PK 0	**Conflans-Ste-Honorine** Barge capital of France, almost all permanently moored up. Difficult for pleasure craft to find a berth. See page 82.	138	0

CANALS OF PARIS
9A: Canal Saint-Martin
9B: Canal Saint-Denis
9C: Canal de l'Ourcq (Grande Section)
9D: Canal de l'Ourcq & canalised River Ourcq (Petite Section)

Canal Saint-Martin, Canal Saint-Denis and Canal de l'Ourcq together make up the 'Canals of Paris', administered by the city since 1802. You enter Canal Saint-Martin when you go into the Port de Plaisance de Paris-Arsenal, the only major harbour for pleasure craft in the centre of the capital.

Anyone planning to spend a few days in the Port de Plaisance de Paris-Arsenal should consider taking the boat for an evening or day trip on the Paris canals. For those who have tired of trudging round the tourist sites on foot, faces buried in guide books, this can provide a delightful opportunity for sampling something different.

At the other end of the Canal Saint-Martin, which is only 4.5km long, is the Bassin de la Villette. You can cruise between the Port de Plaisance and the Bassin or set out on a day's sightseeing tour, taking in the tunnel at the top end of the Port de Plaisance, Canal Saint-Martin, Bassin de la Villette and Canal Saint-Denis, returning up the Seine in the evening to the same berth in the Port de Plaisance, having sampled the magnificent river sights between the Eiffel Tower and Notre-Dame.

Whether you plan an excursion to the Bassin de la Villette or the 40km circular tour via the two canals and the Seine, it is essential to discuss your proposed itinerary with the Port de Plaisance *Capitainerie* who will advise on a departure time for entering the tunnel on the first leg of your passage. There have been one or two accidents in the tunnel in recent years, so navigation is one-way only, with a stream of tourist *vedettes* plying between Bassin de la Villette and the Port de Plaisance de Paris-Arsenal. These *vedettes* have priority, so the opportunities for pleasure craft to slip through the 2km tunnel are strictly limited which is why it is essential to consult with the *Capitainerie*.

If making the circular canal trip and returning via the Seine in the evening to the berth in the Port de Plaisance, then the *Capitainerie* will obviously arrange an early departure time for the passage through the tunnel. When planning this excursion, remember that you must be through Suresnes lock in the Seine by 1900 when it closes for the night. The *Capitainerie* will make arrangements for you to be locked back into the basin of the Port de Plaisance if you intend arriving here after the *Capitainerie* has closed (2000 in high season). You gain access between 2000 and 2300 by contacting the lock keeper at the first of Canal Saint-Martin's locks by intercom on the waiting pontoon outside the entrance to the marina. He should have seen you on his closed-circuit TV, and will open up the lock into the basin remotely, but only if he has been given advance notice of your intentions by the *Capitainerie* earlier in the day.

Summary of the circular sight-seeing tour of Paris

Passage	Waterway	Distance	Locks
P de P Paris-Arsenal ↔ Bassin de la Villette	Canal St-Martin	4.5km	5* (Route 9A)
Bassin de la Villette ↔ St-Denis	Canal St-Denis	6.6km	7** (Route 9B)
St-Denis ↔ P de P Paris-Arsenal	Seine	28.9km	1*** (Part Route 1)

*1 single and 4 double (operate 0800–2345). Although only 4.5km in length, allow 2½ hours for the Canal St-Martin passage.

**Each with two chambers alongside each other, reducing waiting time at locks (operate 0630–2130)

***Operates 0700–1900

For circuit: *Maximum height above waterline* **4.27m**   *Draught* **1.9m**

Port-aux-Perches at the end of the canalised Ourcq. *Photo: David Jefferson*

Route 9A

Canal Saint-Martin: *Port de Plaisance de Paris-Arsenal* ↔ *Bassin de la Villette*

Maximum boat dimensions: *Height above waterline* 4.27m   *Draught* 1.9m

Speed limit: 6km/h (3.24kn)

Locks: 5 (min 42m long x 7.7m wide) Operate 0800–2345 (Port de Plaisance de Paris-Arsenal lock only opened by prior arrangement after 1900/2000 when *Capitainerie* closed)

Distance: 4.5km

The 4.5km passage from Port de Plaisance de Paris-Arsenal to Bassin de la Villette involves passing through the 2km vault or tunnel, and then negotiating four double locks to climb 28m (2m more than the climb between the sea and Paris via the Seine). Allow around 2½ hours for the passage through the tunnel and the locks in a canal that takes you through a fascinating upmarket residential area of Paris. Lined with chestnut trees and spanned by attractive iron footbridges, the canal has been much used for locations for film and TV productions like *Maigret, Last Tango in Paris* and *Hôtel du Nord*.

By day, the only illumination of the tunnel is from shafts of sunlight through ventilation holes in the roof, beneath the Boulevards Richard Lenoir and Jules Ferry. After dark, some form of light from the boat is necessary to illuminate the roof and pick out the long bend in the tunnel. Towards the northern end of the tunnel, there may appear alarming flashing red lights, which will turn out to be friendly messages (in English if an English boat is expected), saying 'Welcome to the Canals of Paris' or 'Have a Good Journey'.

Emerging from the tunnel, the first of the four double locks (Temple) will almost certainly be open for immediate entry. If planning to return to the Port de Plaisance de Paris-Arsenal in the evening either from the Seine or back down Canal Saint-Martin, it can be prudent to talk to the Temple lock keeper about your planned return passage. If coming back down from Bassin de la Villette, you should leave no later than 2100.

Entering the vast Bassin de la Villette, on the left are the waterway offices and a cruiser hire base; on the right is the embarkation point for a fleet of *vedettes*. Ahead is the raising Pont de Crimée. A light beam on the right-hand side of the basin, when broken by a passing boat brings down the road traffic barriers and starts the lift wheels of this remarkable ancient bridge which dates back to 1885.

At the top end of the basin, on one side there is parkland and a long stretch of quayside for mooring, and on the other side is the exhibition centre Cité des Sciences et de l'Industrie occupying 10 acres. The main attraction here is Explora which consists of four permanent exhibitions: The Adventure of Life, From the Earth to the Universe, Matter and the Work of Man and Language and Communication. Anyone could easily spend a day in one section and still not see everything. For those with only an hour or two to spare, the Cité staff suggest viewing the orbital space station, the Ariane rocket and a Nautilus submarine, all located in the hall From the Earth to the Universe.

WATERWAY	PK ref	Town/village/≪lock	Total km	
			▼	▲
FROM Route 1 Entry from Seine	PK 4.5	≪ Arsenal.		
CANAL SAINT-MARTIN	PK 4.5	**Paris** Port de Plaisance de Paris-Arsenal. (page 85).	0	4.5
TUNNEL 1971m	PK 3.8			
End of tunnel	PK 1.8	≪ Nos 8 & 7 (double) Temple.		
	PK 1.3	≪ Nos 6 & 5 (double) Récollets.		
	PK 0.7	≪ Nos 4 & 3 (double) Morts.		
	PK 0	≪ Nos 2 & 1 (double) Villette.	▼	▲
	PK 0	Bassin de la Villette. Quays. Cruiser hire. Fuel.	4.5	0

At end basin
LEFT Canal Saint-Denis (Route 9B)
AHEAD Canal de l'Ourcq (Route 9C)

Vedette, leaving for the Canals of Paris, approaching the 2km tunnel at the top end of the Port de Plaisance de Paris-Arsenal. *Photo: David Jefferson*

Canal Saint-Denis: *(Bassin de la Villette ↔ Saint-Denis)*

Maximum boat dimensions: *Height above waterline* **4.44m** *Draught* **2.6m**

Speed limit: 6km/h (3.24kn)

Locks: 7 (min 38.9m long x 5.2m wide) All remotely controlled from centres at each end of the canal. Operate daily 0630–1915

Distance: 6.6km

The canal carries considerable barge traffic loaded with building materials, but as each lock has two chambers side-by-side, there should be little delay passing through the locks. A small charge is levied at the last lock. Allow about 1½ hours to cover Canal Saint-Denis, and the passage must be planned to lock out into the Seine in good time to complete the next 12km along the Seine, between Saint-Denis and the lock at Suresnes (Route 1) which closes at 1900.

Much of the town of Saint-Denis is industrial, but it also has one of the finest examples of a Gothic basilica in France, where most of the nation's monarchs are buried.

WATERWAY	PK ref	**Town**/*village*/≪*lock*	Total km	
			▼	▲
CANAL SAINT-DENIS	PK 0	**Paris** – Bassin de la Villette (see page 114).	0	6.5
	PK 0	≪ No 1 *Flandre.*		
	PK 1.3	≪ No 2 *Quatre Chemins.*		
	PK 2.2	≪ No 3 *Aubervilliers.*		
	PK 3.2	≪ No 4 *Vertues.*		
	PK 4.6	≪ No 5 *Porte de Paris.*		
	PK 5.7	≪ No 6 *Saint-Denis.*	▼	▲
T-junction LEFT & RIGHT River Seine (Route 1)	PK 6.5	≪ No 7 *la Briche.*	6.5	0

Route 9C

Canal de l'Ourcq (Grande Section):
Bassin de la Villette ↔ outskirts of Sevran

Maximum boat dimensions: *Height above waterline* 4.04m   *Draught* 2.6m

Speed limit: 6km/h (3.24kn)

Locks: none

Distance: 11km

Having reached Bassin de la Villette by way of Canal Saint-Martin, instead of turning left along Canal Saint-Denis towards the Seine, boats can continue ahead at least for another 11km along the Grande Section of the Canal de l'Ourcq. For this section, the height above waterline should be less than 4.0m and the draught no more than 2.6m. These dimension restrictions will be no problem for most boats that have already reached Bassin de la Villette, but unfortunately this Grande Section has few stopping places and is mostly unremarkable industrial suburbs.

WATERWAY	PK ref	Town/*village*/≪*lock*	Total km	
			▼	▲
CANAL DE L'OURCQ	PK 0	**Paris** – Bassin de la Villette (see page 114).	0	11
(Grande Section)	PK 5	**Bobigny.**		
	PK 8	**Bondy.**		
	PK 10	**Pavillons-sous-Bois.**	▼	▲
End of Grande Section	PK 11		11	0
Continues as Petite Section (Route 9D)				

Route 9D

Canal de l'Ourcq and canalised River Ourcq (Petite Section): *Outskirts of Sevran ↔ Port aux Perches*

Maximum boat dimensions: *Height above waterline* 2.6m   *Draught* 0.8m (1.1m at owner's risk)
Speed limit: 6km/h (3.24kn)
Locks: 10 (min 40m long x 3.1m wide) Lock No 1 Sevran operates 0900–1700; the remainder are self-operated
Distance: 97km

It is the Petite Section of the Ourcq (navigable only by shallow draught boats for the entire 97km) that provides a marvellous escape to the countryside with the occasional town or village with an *halte nautique* for the night or you can close the canal/river bank and secure to a couple of trees for peace and tranquillity in delightful surroundings. Sadly, this excursion is precluded to most passage-making boat owners as the height above waterline must be no more than 2.6m and the draught should not exceed 0.8m.

One possibility of seeing something of the Upper Ourcq is to join one of the fare-paying boat trips. Canauxrama transport passengers from Bassin de la Villette to one of their boats out in the countryside for a return passage back to the Bassin by water, stopping off for lunch and maybe a tour of the Usine Élévatoire de Trilbardou, the remarkable pumping station built in 1869, and still lifting water 12m from the nearby River Marne to the Canal de l'Ourcq. The end of the Ourcq navigation is at the Port-aux-Perches in the village of Silly-la-Poterie where the passenger-boat operator Un Canal… Deux Canaux have a base for their boats which ply between Port-aux-Perches and Meaux.

WATERWAY	PK ref	Town/*village*/≪*lock*		Total km
			▼	▲
CANAL DE L'OURCQ Start of Petite Section	PK 11		0	97
	PK 13.5	≪ No 1 *Sevran.*		
	PK 27	**Claye-Souilly** ♒. Fuel. Cruiser hire.	16	81
	PK 32	*Fresnes-sur-Marne* ♒.		
	PK 33	≪ *Fresnes-sur-Marne.*		
	PK 38	*Trilbardou* ♒ to visit Usine Élévatoire.		
	PK 40.5	≪ *Vignely.*		
	PK 47.5	≪ *Villenoy.*		
	PK 48	**Meaux – Saint-Rémy** ♒. Cruiser hire.	37	60
	PK 55	≪ *St-Lazare.*		
	PK 64.5	*Varreddes* ♒.		
	PK 65	≪ *Varreddes.*		
	PK 73	*Villers-les-Rigault* ♒ to visit Usine Élévatoire.		
	PK 77	*Lizy-sur-Ourcq* ♒.		
RIGHT Canal de Clignon 1.2km long draught 0.8m headroom 3.1m	PK 93			
	PK 97	*Mareuil-sur-Ourcq* ♒. Cruiser hire.		
CANALISED OURCQ	PK 97	≪ *Mareuil.*		
	PK 99.5	≪ *Queue d'Ham.*		
	PK 102.5	≪ *Marolles.*		
	PK 104	**La Ferté-Millon** 14th century château ♒.	93	4
	PK 104	≪ *la Ferté-Milon.*		
End of navigation	PK 108	*Silly-la-Poterie/Port-aux-Perches* ♒. No shops but restaurant run by Un Canal... Deux Canaux.	▼ 97	▲ 0

Bassin du Centre-Est

The Bassin du Centre-Est covers the three central routes from the Seine to the Saône. Crews of those Med-bound boats who have left Paris many kilometres astern and reached the junction of the Haute Seine and the Canal du Loing at St-Mammès will by then have rigged the bimini or a large umbrella and stowed any warm clothing.

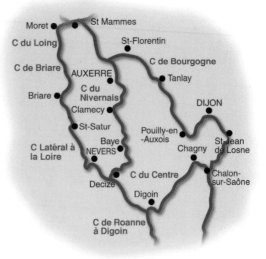

Many who are crossing France by waterway, find the canals in the Bassin du Centre-Est the most attractive. This is not to denigrate the beauty of parts of the Seine or the broad waters of the Saône and Rhône, but these rivers lack a certain intimacy that you can only experience on the smaller canals where, in some parts, you will be assigned your own *éclusier itinerant* instead of communicating over the VHF with a remote lock keeper high up above in his control tower.

Summarising the differences between the Bourgogne and Bourbonnais routes, the Burgundy canal rates three stars for its beauty; against this, for anyone in a hurry, the Bourbonnais route has 40 fewer locks. Another consideration is the water level after a long dry spring and summer. In recent years, the Canal du Centre has had to be closed in the summer months due to lack of water, blocking off the Bourbonnais route from the Seine and St-Mammès to the Saône.

ABOVE The fuel base at St-Mammès. This is the first fuel berth on the Seine after Rouen. *Photo: Keith Harris*

RIGHT This *éclusier itinerant* (left) travelled between locks all day on her mobilette. *Photo: Keith Harris*

The Nivernais too is prone to a shortage of water in the summer, when a boat with a draught of 1.4m will struggle to get through some sections of the river.

If height above waterline is critical, the much quoted maximum for the Bourgogne is 3.4m, but the limit to pass through the Pouilly tunnel is only 3.1m across a beam of 3m, whereas the maximum height above the waterline on the Bourbonnais route is 3.5m with no tunnels.

The Bourbonnais route: *St-Mammès* ↔ *Chalon-sur-Saône*

For Med-bound boats coming from Paris, the Bourbonnais is the most southerly and quickest route down to the Saône and Rhône. Having arrived at the barge terminal of St-Mammès, 83km south of Paris on the Haute Seine, the boat owner has a choice of three routes to the Med. Time available may eliminate the slower Bourgogne route, and the boat's dimensions may well preclude the Nivernais.

Maximum boat dimensions: *Height above waterline* 3.5m   *Draught* 1.8m

Speed limit: 6km/h (3.2kn)

Locks: 149 (38.50m long x 5.20m wide) Operate mid Mar–Oct daily 0900–1200 & 1300–1900 (except Canal du Centre 0830–1830). Nov–mid Mar daily 0900–1200 & 1300–1800 (except Canal du Centre – by arrangement only).

Distance: 414km

Four canals make up the popular Bourbonnais route:

	km	locks
Canal du Loing (St-Mammès to Montargis outskirts):	49	18
Canal de Briare (Montargis outskirts to Briare):	55	32
Canal lateral à la Loire (Briare to Digoin):	196	38
Canal du Centre (Digoin to Chalon-sur-Saône):	114	61

The Canal du Loing, man-made for the most part, was opened in 1723 running for most of its length alongside the Loing river. The canal still carries some commercial traffic transporting cereals through the wooded countryside. The Briare canal is the oldest in France. Work started here in 1604 on what would be adopted as the prototype for future canal construction. Of particular interest are the ancient locks which, until 1880, formed the original 7-lock staircase at Rogny, which lifted barges more than 30m to the summit of the canal.

The Canal latéral à la Loire is famous for its canal bridges, particularly 662m 'pont-canal' at Briare carrying the canal over the River Loire. Gustave Eiffel worked on this engineering project with its ornate lighting. Nearly 200km long, the canal passes through vast areas of vineyards, by towns and villages associated with the best of the region's wines. Progress along this waterway should improve because the frequency of locks is less than the other three canals.

Of the four canals that make up the Borbonnais route, the Canal du Centre carries the most commercial traffic particularly between Montceau-les-Mines and Chalon-sur-Saône. Although this is a more industrial part of the region, there is little evidence of this from the canal which also takes in the southern parts of the Burgundy vineyards and the plains of the Charollais.

WATERWAY	PK ref	Town/village/≪lock	Total km	
			▼	▲
T-junction with the Haute Seine (Route 2)				
CANAL DE LOING	PK 49	**St-Mammès** Barge town with several quayside moorings for pleasure boats in the Seine.	0	411
	PK 47	**Moret-sur-Loing** Fortified town much painted by the Impressionists including Sisley who lived here. Summer residence of French royalty ♨.	2	409
	PK 47–36.5	≪ Nos 19, 18, 17, 16, 15 & 14.		
	PK 30	**Nemours** Pleasant town in wooded setting. Museum ♨.	19	392
	PK 30–21	≪ Nos 13, 12, 11, 10 & 9.		
	PK 21	*La Madeleine-sur-Loing* ♨.		
	PK 19	*Souppes-sur-Loing* Large activity centre including swimming pool and water slides ♨.		
	PK 17–16	≪ Nos 8 & 7.		

Moret-sur-Loing. *Photo: Keith Harris*

WATERWAY	PK ref	Town/*village*/≪*lock*	Total km ▼	▲
CANAL DE LOING	PK 15.5	*Néronville* ♨. Small town of **Château-Landon** 2km.	33.5	377.5
	PK 11–5	≪ Nos 6, 5, 4, 3 & 2.		
	PK 3	*Cepoy* ♨.		
	PK 2	≪ No 1.		
CANAL DE BRIARE	PK 0/57		49	362
	PK 57–52	≪ Nos 36, 35, 34 & 33.		
	PK 52	**Montargis** With a network of smaller canals and at the junction of three rivers, the town with its many bridges has been compared with Venice ⚐. Cruiser hire.	54	357
	PK 48–43	≪ Nos 32, 31, 30, 29, 28 & 27.		
	PK 35	*Montbouy* ♨.		
	PK 34.5–32	≪ Nos 26 & 25.		
	PK 29	*Châtillon-Coligny* 12th century castle ♨. Showers at campsite.		
	PK 29–23.5	≪ Nos 24, 23, 22, 21, 20 & 19.		

WATERWAY	PK ref	Town/*village*/≪lock	Total km
			▼ ▲
CANAL DE BRIARE	PK 19	*Rogny-les-Sept-Écluses* 2 ⌶ (Quai Sully & Port des Lancières). Cruiser hire.	
	PK 19–17	≪ Nos 18-13 (chain).	
	PK 12.5–10	≪ Nos 12-8 (chain).	
	PK 8	≪ No7.	
	PK 8	*Ouzouer-sur-Trézée* ♒.	
	PK 6–5	≪ Nos 6 & 5.	
RIGHT to Briare	PK 3/200		
	PK 3–1	≪ Nos 4, 3 & 2.	
	PK 1	**Briare** Principal claim to fame is the Pont Canal, 640m long, built by Eiffel in 1890 to carry the Briare Canal over the River Loire. ⌶. Cruiser hire.	103 308
LEFT continues as **CANAL LATÉRAL À LA LOIRE**	PK 3/200		103 308
	PK 198	**Briare** alternative ⌶ (in Port de Commerce).	105 306
	PK 198	The famous canal bridge.	
	PK 192	**Châtillon-sur-Loire** ♒.	111 300
LEFT Châtillon branch canal (4km 3 locks) giving access to River Loire (local boats only)	PK 187		
	PK 184	*Beaulieu-sur-Loire* ♒. Showers at campsite.	
	PK 182.5	≪ No 38.	
	PK 180	*Belleville-sur-Loire* ♒.	
	PK 180	≪ No 37.	
	PK 175	*Léré* ♒.	
	PK 173.5–166	≪ Nos 36, 35 & 34.	
	PK 159.5	**St-Satur** Quayside mooring or **St-Thibault** ⌶ in short cutting to lock giving access to Loire (local boats only).	143.5 267.5

Bassin du Centre-Est: The Bourbonnais route

WATERWAY	PK ref	Town/village/≪lock	Total km	
			▼	▲
CANAL	PK 157	_Ménétréol sous Sancerre_ ⌂.		
LATERAL	PK 156–146	≪ Nos 33, 32 & 31.		
À LA LOIRE	PK 143	_Herry_ ⌂.		
	PK 143–125.5	≪ Nos 30, 29, 28, 27, 26 & 25.		
	PK 125	**Marseilles-lès-Aubigny** ⌂.	178	233
	PK 120	_Cours-les-Barres_ ⌂.		
	PK 116	≪ No 24.		
Sampanges bridge controlled by lights	PK 110	≪ Nos 22/21 (double).		
	PK 103	_Plagny-Semoise_ Private moorings.		
LEFT canal branch to Nevers (3km 2 locks 1.2m draught)	PK 100	**Nevers** Principal town of the Nièvre département. Medieval streets. Well known for pottery.11th century St Cyr cathedral. ⚑ (Port de la Jonction in basin. City is a short walk across Loire bridge.	203	208
	PK 89.5–80.5	≪ Nos 20, 19 & 18.		
	PK 80	_Fleury-sur-Loire_ ⌂.		
	PK 76.5	_Avril-sur-Loire_ ⌂.		
	PK 76	≪ Nos 17 & 16.		
LEFT canal branch to Decize and Canal du Nivernais (Route 11)	PK 68.5	**Decize** ⚑ (Port de la Jonction) in basin through lock. Continue along basin, through another lock to town quays. Cruiser hire.	234.5	176.5
	PK 67–58	≪ Nos 15, 14 & 13.		
	PK 53	_Gannay-sur-Loire_ ⌂.		
	PK 52.5–45	≪ Nos 12, 11 & 10.		
	PK 41	_Garnat-sur-Engièvre_ ⌂.		
	PK 39.5	≪ No 9.		
	PK 37.5	_Beaulon_ ⌂.		
	PK 37.5–33	≪ Nos 8 & 7.		

WATERWAY	PK ref	Town/*village*/≪*lock*	Total km
			▼ ▲
RIGHT canal branch to Dompierre-sur-Besbre (2km)	PK 29	**Dompierre-sur-Besbre** ♌.	274 137
CANAL LATERAL À LA LOIRE	PK 29	≪ No 6.	
	PK 26	*Diou* ♌.	
	PK 22.5–20.5	≪ Nos 5 & 4.	
	PK 19	*Pierrefitte-sur-Loire* ♌.	
	PK 17	≪ No 3.	
	PK 15	*Coulanges* ♌.	
	PK 8	*Molinet* ♌.	
RIGHT Canal de Roanne à Digoin (55km 10 locks) max dimensions: height above waterline 3.45m draught 1.8m	PK 6	Attractive 55km stretch of canal now monopolised by pleasure craft. ⌓ at *Briennon* (PK 15) and **Roanne** (PK 0). ♌ at *Chassenard* (PK 49), *Luneau* (PK 42), *Avrilly* (PK 40), *Chambilly* (PK 33), *Artaix* (PK 30), *Melay* (PK 26) and *Iguerande* (PK 21).	
	PK 5	≪ No 1.	
	PK 4	**Digoin** Industrial town, well known for pottery. Pont Canal with eleven arches connects Canal latéral à la Loire with Canal du Centre ⌓. Cruiser hire.	299 112
Continues as **CANAL DU CENTRE**	PK 108–104	≪ Nos 26, 25 & 24.	
	PK 102	**Paray-le-Monial** ♌.	309 102
	PK 101.5–82	≪ Nos 23, 22, 21, 20, 19, 18, 17 & 16.	
	PK 81	*Génelard* ♌.	
	PK 79–67	≪ Nos 15, 14, 13, 12, 11 & 10.	
	PK 65	**Montceau-les-Mines** One-time mining town ♌.	346 65
	PK 64–62.5	≪ Nos 9 & 8.	
	PK 61	*Blanzy* ♌.	
	PK 59.5–52.5	≪ Nos 7, 6, 5, 4, 3, 2 & 1.	

Bassin du Centre-Est: The Bourbonnais route

WATERWAY	PK ref	Town/*village*/≪ lock	Total km ▼	▲
CANAL DU CENTRE	PK 52	**Montchanin** ⏸.	359	52
	PK 49–45	≪ Nos 1, 2, 3, 4, 5, 6, 7 & 8.		
	PK 45	*St-Julien-sur-Dheune* ⏸.		
	PK 44–34	≪ Nos 9, 10, 11, 12, 13, 14, 15, 16, 17, 18 & 19.		
	PK 33	**St-Léger-sur-Dheune** ⏸.	378	33
	PK 32–29	≪ Nos 20, 21, 22 & 23.		
	PK 24.5	*Santenay* ⏸.		
	PK 19	**Chagny** Thriving town between River Dheune and the canal. Surrounded by famous Burgundy vineyards. ⏸. Cruiser hire.	392	19
	PK 18–17	≪ Nos 24, 25 & 26.		
	PK 17	*Rully* ⏸.		
	PK 16.5–8.5	≪ Nos 27, 28, 29, 30, 31, 32, 33 & 34.		
	PK 8	*Fragnes* ⏸.		
	PK 3.5	≪ No 34b.	▼	▲
T-junction with Saône (Route 15)	PK 0	**Chalon-sur-Saône** (⏸ in Saône see page 154).	411	0

Châlon-sur-Saône. *Photo: Crown Blue Line*

Route 11

Canal du Nivernais: *Auxerre ↔ Decize*

Maximum boat dimensions: *Height above waterline* 2.7m   *Draught* 1.4m

Speed limit: 6km/h (3.2kn)

Locks: 110 (min 30m long x 5.05m wide) Operate end Mar to early Nov daily 0900–1200 and 1300–1900. Closed early Nov to end Mar

Distance: 174km

This lovely canal is, as will be seen from the above, only available to those boats with a shallow draught and a height above the waterline that can be reduced sufficiently to pass beneath the numerous low bridges spanning the Nivernais. This may well preclude the majority of those Med-bound boats that have reached St-Mammès, south of Paris, and then have to choose between the Bourgogne or Bourbonnais routes, assuming their dimensions are too great to leave the Yonne to sample the delights of the Canal du Nivernais. It  should also be mentioned that the 1.4m draught referred to above is in normal conditions; in recent years, after prolonged periods of drought, the water level in sections of the canal has dropped to below 1m.

Most of the Nivernais canal traffic consists of hire cruisers. Aquafibre, who make the mouldings at Norwich for many of the cruisers operated in France by the charter companies, build an 11m hull with a 3.86m beam and an all-important draught of 0.9m with an air draught of 2.64m. When fitted out it can comfortably accommodate four in two cabins and is ideal for the Nivernais.

The idea of connecting Paris with the Loire basin was conceived in the 18th century primarily to maintain a constant supply of firewood to the capital. Trees from the Bazois and Morvan forests could be cut down and then rafted along a new waterway into the Yonne and Haute Seine.

Work started in 1784 and the canal was finally completed in 1843. Between conception and the first boat navigating the full length of the new waterway, there

Auxerre. *Photo: Keith Harris*

were long periods of inactivity when politicians and engineers argued over the primary use of the canal. Many wanted the transport of firewood to be the main objective; others, with an eye to the future, considered navigation should be the priority. This wrangling explains why there is a 58km section that cannot take the normal length of barge because the locks are shorter in length than the standard Freycinet gauge by 8m.

Coal replaced firewood, and barge traffic took over for a time, but this traffic slowly declined as did general canal maintenance, and closure was muted. Fortunately for the pleasure boat fraternity, in the 1970s a Monsieur PP Zivy, who had experienced canal cruising in England, had the vision to establish hire cruisers on the French waterways, and successfully campaigned for considerable restoration work on the Nivernais to be undertaken. Cruiser hire operators have now established themselves along the whole length of this canal, and many stopping places have been provided for hungry, thirsty crews seeking a shower, a meal and a mooring for the night.

Care has been taken to avoid spoiling the environment as the Nivernais threads its way through woodland and forest in the Yonne valley and then enters the lush pastures of the Alnain and Aron valleys. Features include 3 tunnels, a 16-lock staircase, 3 aquaducts and 2 canal bridges. Many consider the Nivernais to be one of the most beautiful canals in Europe.

WATERWAY	PK ref	Town/*village*/≪*lock*	Total km ▼ ▲
Continues from the Yonne (Route 4)			
CANAL DU NIVERNAIS	PK 174	**Auxerre** Principal town in the Yonne *département* in the heart of the Auxerrois wine-growing region. Old town built on a hill, a most attractive sight from the river. Carolingian church with 9th century frescoes (the oldest mural paintings in France). St-Étienne cathedral (11th–16th century), St-Germain museum (Prehistoric and Gallo-Roman archaeology) ⌐.	0 174
	PK 173–169	≪ Nos 81, 80, 79 & 78.	
	PK 168	*Vaux* Auxerrois wine-tasting. ♌.	
	PK 166–161	≪ Nos 77, 76, 75 & 74.	
	PK 159.5	**Vincelles** ⌐. Cruiser hire.	14.5 159.5
	PK 159.5–158	≪ Nos 73 & 72.	
	PK 156	*Cravant* ♌.	
	PK 155	≪ No 71.	
LEFT Vermenton branch canal (4km 2 locks)	PK 154	*Accolay* ♌. Showers at camp site. **Vermenton** Delightful small town on River Cure. One-time centre for wine-growing and log-floating industries ♌. Cruiser hire.	20 154
	PK 154	≪ No 70.	20 154
	PK 153	*Bazarnes* ♌.	
	PK 152.5–148	≪ Nos 69, 67, 66 & 65.	
	PK 145.5	**Mailly-la-Ville** ⌐.	28.5 145.5
	PK 145–143	≪ Nos 63 & 62.	
	PK 142	*Mailly-le-Château.* Fortified village by Yonne ♌.	
	PK 139–136.5	≪ Nos 60 & 59.	

Bassin du Centre-Est: Canal du Nivernais

WATERWAY	PK ref	Town/*village*/≪*lock*	Total km	
			▼	▲
CANAL DU NIVERNAIS	PK 136.5	*Merry-sur-Yonne* Shallow ♒. Showers at camp site.		
	PK 134–132.5	≪ Nos 58 & 57.		
	PK 132.5	*Châtel-Censoir* ⚑.		
	PK 130–123	≪ Nos 56, 55, 54, 53b/53 & 52.		
	PK 123	*Coulanges-sur-Yonne* ⚑.		
	PK 121	*Pousseaux* ⚑.		
	PK 118–117	≪ Nos 50 & 49.		
1.5km canal section to Clamecy with locks at either end closed to navigation	PK 116–114.5			
	PK 114	≪ No 47.		
	PK 113.5	**Clamecy** Mediaeval town. One-time centre for log-floating industry ⚑. Cruiser hire.	60.5	113.5
	PK 111–110.5	≪ Nos 46 & 45.		
	PK 110	*Chevroches* ♒.		
	PK 109–104.5	≪ Nos 44, 43 & 42.		
	PK 104.5	*Villiers-sur-Yonne* ♒.		
	PK 102.5–98	≪ Nos 41, 40 & 39/38.		
	PK 96	**Tannay** Surrounded by vineyards. Sample excellent local dry white wines. 14th century church. Superb views of the Morvan hills ⚑. Cruiser hire.	78	96
	PK 93.5–89	≪ Nos 37, 36, 35 & 34.		
	PK 89	*Dirol* ♒.		
	PK 88.5–86	≪ Nos 33 & 32.		
	PK 85	*Marigny-sur-Yonne* ♒.		

WATERWAY	PK ref	Town/*village*/≪*lock*	Total km
			▼ ▲
CANAL DU	PK 84.5–83.5	≪ Nos 31, 30 & 29.	
NIVERNAIS	83.5		
	PK 82	*Chaumont* ⌐. Fuel.	
	PK 81.5–79.5	≪ Nos 28, 27 & 26/25.	
	PK 79	*Pazy* ♨.	
	PK 77.5–74.5	≪ Nos 24, 23, 22, 21, 20, 19, 18 & 17.	
	PK 74	*Sardy-les-Epiry* ♨.	
16-lock staircase	PK 74–70	≪ Nos 16–1.	
in 4km leading			
to summit and			
3 tunnels –			
Breuilles 212m,			
Mouas 268m and			
la Collancelle			
758m.			
Traffic lights.			
	PK 67	*Baye* Port des Poujeats (⌐) Cruiser Hire.	
	PK 66–59	≪ Nos 1, 2, 3, 4/5/6 & 7/8.	
	PK 59	*Chevance* ♨.	
	PK 57	≪ Nos 9/10. Mont-et-Marré ♨.	
	PK 56–51	≪ Nos 11, 12, 13, 14 & 15.	
	PK 50.5	**Châtillon-en-Bazois** Dominated by castle. Popular stopover ⌐. Showers at camp site.	123.5 50.5
	PK 48–38	≪ Nos 16, 17, 18, 19, 20 & 21.	
	PK 37.5	*Fleury* ♨.	
	PK 36.5–31	≪ Nos 22, 23 & 24.	
	PK 30.5	*Panneçot* 16th century Anizy Castle. Bellevaux Abbey. ⌐ by campsite.	
	PK 28–18.5	≪ Nos 26, 27, 28 & 29.	
	PK 16.5–15.5	**Cercy-la-Tour** Fortified town from the Middle Ages. ♨ above ≪ No 30. ⌐ between ≪ Nos 30 & 31 (*garde*).	157.5 16.5
	PK 16	≪ No 30.	

WATERWAY	PK ref	Town/*village*/≪ lock	Total km
			▼ ▲
CANAL DU NIVERNAIS	PK 10	*Verneuil* 13th century Romanesque church and 15th century castle ♌.	
	PK 8–5	≪ Nos 32 & 33.	
	PK 5	*Champvert* ♌.	
	PK 2–0.5	≪ Nos 34 & 35.	▼ ▲
AHEAD La Loire (closed to navigation) LEFT ⚑ and 2 locks to Canal Lateral à la Loire (see Route 10)	PK 0	**Decize** Old town at the junction of several waterways. Promenade des Halles leads to beach and sports stadium. Several town quays and Port de la Jonction (⚑). Cruiser hire.	174 0

Decize. *Photo: Crown Blue Line*

Route 12

Canal de Bourgogne: *Laroche-Migennes ↔ St-Jean-de-Losne*

Maximum boat dimensions: *Height above waterline* 3.4m*   *Draught* 1.8m**

Speed limit: 6km/h (3.25kn)

Locks: 189 (40m long x 5.2m wide) Operate end Mar to early Nov daily 0900–1200 & 1300–1900. Early Nov to late Mar by arrangement only

Distance: 242km

* Except for Pouilly tunnel with only 3.1m at sides 1.5m from centre line

** In recent years, the Yonne side of the summit has suffered from a lack of water in the summer with depths reducing to 1.4m

For those boat crews that have entered the waterways in Northern France and chosen the Burgundy route to reach the Saône and Rhône and Mediterranean, the Canal de Bourgogne will be the highlight of the inland cruise across France.

Linking the valleys of the Yonne and the Saône, the canalised river meanders through the valley of the Armançon and through regions of outstanding scenery and of particular historical interest. There are the castles around Tonnerre and the magnificent Cistercian Fontenay Abbey in the Auxois region. The 50km between the summit, dropping down through the Ouche valley to Dijon, the old capital of the Dukes of Burgundy, is considered to be one of the most beautiful stretches of waterway in France.

This lovely route is not for anyone in a hurry. Over a distance of 12km before reaching the summit (motoring in the direction of the Saône), there are 34 locks divided into 3 chains or ladders. Individual boats or those travelling in company will be allocated an 'itinerant' lock keeper. Usually a student; he or she will accompany you on a moped or something similar, to work the locks ahead of you. The 12km will take about one and a half days to cover, so it will be necessary to arrange a start time on the second day with your *éclusier itinerant*.

It should be noted that the maximum height above waterline to clear the Pouilly tunnel is 3.10m Before entering the 3,300m long Pouilly-en-Auxois tunnel at the summit of the canal, the lock keeper nearest to the entrance to the tunnel should be consulted. The lock keeper will issue a pass authorising passage through the tunnel and indicating the time you should enter. He will then inspect the boat to make certain you have lifejackets and adequate lighting to illuminate the tunnel. When you finally emerge at the other end, the pass must be surrendered to the lock keeper at the first lock beyond the end of the tunnel. Make the best of the scenery between the tunnel and Dijon (50km) because between Dijon and St-Jean-de-Losne and the Saône, the canal is dead straight and the countryside, compared with what has been before, is unremarkable.

WATERWAY	PK ref	Town/*village*/≪lock	Total km ▼	▲
CANAL DE	PK 0	≪ Nos 115/114.		
BOURGOGNE	PK 0	**Laroche-Migennes** ⌷.	0	242
	PK 2–8	≪ Nos 113–112.		
	PK 9	*Brienon-sur-Armançon* ⟅.		
	PK 10–18	≪ Nos 111–108.		
	PK 19	**St-Florentin** ⌷.	19	223
	PK 22–31	≪ Nos 107–100.		
	PK 31	*Flogny la Chapelle* ⟅.		
	PK 35–45	≪ Nos 99–95.		
	PK 45	**Tonnerre** Old town. Wine centre. 13th century hospital with arched wooden roof contains 15th century Holy Sepulchre, one of the best Burgundian statues to survive. 13th century Notre-Dame church. ⌷. Cruiser hire.	45	197
	PK 46.5–53	≪ Nos 94–90.		
	PK 53	*Tanlay* Castle. ⟅.		
	PK 55.5–63	≪ Nos 89–85.		
	PK 63	*Lezinnes* ⟅.		
	PK 65–71.5	≪ Nos 84–81.		
	PK 74	**Ancy-le-Franc** 16th century château ⟅.	74	168

WATERWAY	PK ref	Town/*village*/≪*lock*	Total km
			▼ ▲
CANAL DE BOURGOGNE	PK 74.5–82	≪ Nos 80-76.	
	PK 83	*Ravières* ⚓.	
	PK 84–86.5	≪ Nos 75-74.	
	PK 87	*Cry sur Armançon* ⚓.	
	PK 87–91.5	≪ Nos 73-71.	
	PK 93	*Aisy-sur-Armançon* ⚓.	
	PK 94–102	≪ Nos 70-64.	
	PK 102	**Montbard** ⚑.	102 140
	PK 105–114.5	≪ Nos 63-56.	
	PK 115	**Vénarey les Laumes** ⚑.	115 127
	PK 116–120	≪ Nos 55-44.	
	PK 120	*Pouillenay* ⚓.	
	PK 120–125	≪ Nos 43-28.	
	PK 126	*Marigny le Cahouet* ⚓.	
	PK 126–135	≪ Nos 27-14.	

The Canal de Bourgogne passes through vineyards and lush, gently rolling farmland.
Photo: Keith Harris

Pouilly-en-Auxois tunnel. *Photo: Keith Harris*

WATERWAY	PK ref	**Town**/*village*/≪ *lock*	Total km ▼	▲
CANAL DE BOURGOGNE	PK 137	*Pont-Royal* ⚐.		
	PK 137.5–155	≪ Nos 13–1.		
	PK 155	**Pouilley-en-Auxois** ⚐.	155	87
Tunnel (3345m)	PK 156–159.5			
	PK 161	*Escommes* Ω.		
	PK 161–163	≪ Nos 2–8.		
	PK 163	*Vandenesse en Auxois* Ω.		
	PK 163.5–169	≪ Nos 9–16.		
	PK 169	*Crugey* Halte Ω.		
	PK 170–172	≪ Nos 17–19.		
	PK 173	*Pont D'Ouche* ⚐.		
	PK 173–175	≪ Nos 20–22.		

WATERWAY	PK ref	Town/*village*/≪*lock*	Total km
			▼ ▲
CANAL DE	PK 176	*Veuvey sur Ouche* ♌.	
BOURGOGNE	PK 176.5– 180	≪ Nos 23–26.	
	PK 180	*La Bussiere sur Ouche* ♌.	
	PK 180.5– 186	≪ Nos 27–32.	
	PK 187	*Gissey sur Ouche* ♌.	
	PK 187.5– 206	≪ Nos 33–49.	
	PK 208	*Plombieres les Dijon* ♌.	
	PK 207–211	≪ Nos 50–54.	
	PK 213	**Dijon** Medieval, industrial and wine trading city. Flourishing commercial and art centre. Many reminders that in the 15th century Dijon was a chief centre of European civilisation. St Benigne cathedral. Palais de Justice was the former seat of the Burgundy parliament. One of the oldest and best art galleries in France ⌅. Cruiser hire.	213 29
	PK 213–217	≪ Nos 55–58.	
	PK 217	*Longvic* ♌.	
	PK 217.5– 239	≪ Nos 59–75.	
	PK 241	*Saint-Usage* ♌.	▼ ▲
	PK 242	**St-Jean-de-Losne** Important in view of its position as the junction of four major waterways ⌅. Cruiser hire.	242 0
	PK 242	≪ No 76.	
T-junction with the Saône (Route 15)			

Rhône – Saône Basin

This section features both the Rhône and all the navigable canalised rivers feeding into this mighty waterway. These include, to the north of Lyon, the Saône with the Petite Saône and the southern arm of the Canal du Rhône au Rhin and, just a few kilometres from the Mediterranean, the Petite Rhône and the Rhône à Sète Canal. The section will be of interest to anyone con-sidering moving their boat down to the Mediterranean by the waterways because ultimately the choice is limited to navigating the Rhône or a seaward passage down the Bay of Biscay and taking the Canal des Deux Mers (Route 49). The Rhône is the more popular choice.

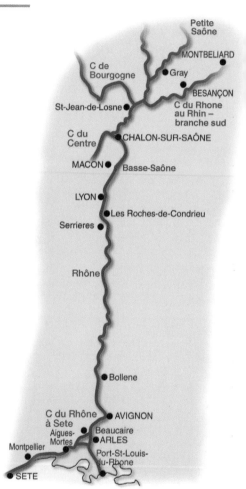

Particularly for smaller craft, the Rhône comes as something of a challenge after days spent progressing at a leisurely walking pace along the Bourgogne or Bourgonnais routes, stopping for lunch and mooring up in the early evening near a promising restaurant. In the space of a few days, the skipper is suddenly having to cope with a strong current and pay some attention to the weather as the boat is piloted down the broad waters of the fast-moving Rhône, sweeping her towards the giant locks that are a feature of the waterway.

The rivers that feed into the Rhône are peaceful enough during the summer months. There is little current to cope with on the Saône (Routes 13 & 15) which is particularly popular with those who choose to charter boats on the French waterways. Those who are bringing their boats through France to the Mediterranean from the Strasbourg region or from Germany may well be motoring along the southern arm of the Canal du Rhône au Rhin (Route 14) and experiencing mile after mile of spectacular scenery along the Doubs valley.

At the Mediterranean end of the Rhône, the skipper has the choice of either continuing almost to the end and branching off at Port St Louis or joining the Petit Rhône (Route 17) which enables a boat to tranfer to the Rhône à Sète Canal (Route 18) and motor through the Camargue to reach a more westerly Mediterranean port.

River Saône. *Photo: Keith Harris*

Route 13

Petite Saône: *Corre* ↔ *St-Jean-de-Losne*

Maximum boat dimensions: *Height above waterline* 3.5m   *Draught* 1.8m

Speed limits: Upstream of Auxonne: River 15km/h (8kn) Canal sections (river bypasses) 6km/h (3.2kn) Downstream of Auxonne: 30km/h (16kn) Canal sections (river bypasses) 15km/h (8kn) Around St-Jean-de-Losne: 12km/h (6.5kn)

Locks: 21 (40m long x 5.10m wide) Operate late Mar–Oct daily 0900–1230 and 1330–1900. Nov–mid Mar by arrangement only

Distance: 192km

The source of the Saône is in the Vosges mountains at Viomesnil. It is navigable below Corre for 363km down to Lyon where it meets the Rhône. Between Corre and St-Jean-de-Losne, the river is known as the Petite Saône. A gentle river during the season, with only 21 locks, it is the second most popular waterway in France, carrying 7000 boats annually. A large proportion of the river traffic is cruiser hire with the major charter companies operating large fleets of motor boats from their Saône bases. During the winter months flooding in recent years has resulted in rapid changes in the water level and a less tranquil current.

There are many '*dérivations*' to look out for. These are short lengths (usually 2–3km) of man-made bypasses of short shallow sections of the river, parts of which are no longer navigable. Around these *dérivations* the PK numbering references look strange because they still relate to the old river route.

WATERWAY	PK ref	Town/*village*/≪*lock*	Total km	
			▼	▲
PETITE SAÔNE	PK 407	*Corre* ◨.	0	192
	PK 407	≪ No 46 *Corre.*		
	PK 400.5	≪ No 1 *Ormoy.*		
	PK 392	≪ No 2 *Cendrecourt* ♨ just downstream of lock.		
	PK 383	≪ No 3 *Montureux.*		
	PK 381	*Fouchécourt* ◨.		
	PK 380	*Baulay* ♨.		
	PK 372.5	≪ No 4 *Conflandey* ◨ just downriver of lock.		
	PK 365	**Port-sur-Saône** ◨.	42	150
	PK 364	≪ No 5 *Port-sur-Saône.*		
	PK 360	≪ No 6 *Chemilly.* 13th century castle ♨.		
STRAIGHT ON Scey-sur-Saône ♨ (1.5km) end of navigation	PK 357			
LEFT lock & tunnel		≪ No 7 *Scey-sur-Mer* ◨ just upstream of lock.		
Tunnel 680m	PK 353			
	PK 343.5	≪ No 8 *Rupt-sur-Saône.*		
	PK 340	≪ No 9 *Chantes.*		
	PK 329	≪ No 10 *Soing* Just downstream of lock round up to port and backtrack 3km up the river to *Soing* ◨ (end of navigation).		
	PK 324	≪ No 11 *Charentenay* Just downstream of the lock round up to starboard and backtrack 1km up the river to *Ray-sur-Saône.* Fortified with castle (end of navigation).		
	PK 314	*Seveux/Savoyeux* Château ◨. Cruiser hire.		
Tunnel 640m				
	PK 307	≪ No 13 *Savoyeux.*		
	PK 296	≪ No 14 *Vereux.*		
	PK 288	≪ No 15 *Rigny* ♨.		

Rhône – Saône Basin: Petite Saône

WATERWAY	PK ref	Town/village/≪lock	Total km
			▼ ▲
PETITE SAÔNE	PK 283.5	**Gray** One-time flourishing port. The old town has a castle housing the Baron Martin Museum, a 15th century Basilica and an impressive Hôtel de Ville. ⊓ upstream of lock, quay downstream.	123.5 68.5
	PK 283	≪ No 16 *Gray*.	
	PK 276	*Mantoche* ⊓.	
	PK 270	≪ No 17 *Apremont*.	
RIGHT Canal de la Marne à la Saône (see Route 36)	PK 255		
	PK 255	≪ No 18 *Heuilley*.	
	PK 251.5	*Pontailler-sur-Saône* ⊓ above bridge. Quayside ⬭ downstream of bridge.	
	PK 239.5	≪ No 19 *Poncey-lès-Athée*.	
	PK 233	**Auxonne** Fortified town, associated with Napoleon Bonaparte who served here. Bonaparte museum. ⬭ – pontoon above bridge, quay below.	174 18
LEFT Canal du Rhône au Rhin (Route 14)	PK 219		
RIGHT Canal de Bourgogne (Route 12)	PK 214.5		
			▼ ▲
	PK 214.5	**St-Jean-de-Losne** All facilities including fuel. One time barge town with barge museum. Crown Blue Line base in basin off entrance to Canal de Bourgogne (before lock) or quayside moorings either side of Saône bridge.	192 0
Continues Route 15 St-Jean-de-Losne to Lyon			

Route 14

Canal du Rhône au Rhin (Branche Sud): *Niffer/Mulhouse* ←→ *St-Symphorien/St-Jean-De-Losne*

Maximum boat dimensions: *Height above waterline* 3.5m   *Draught* 1.8m

Speed limits: Niffer-Mulhouse and locks 41–2 and 3–7 (S of Bourgogne) **8km/h (4.3kn)**; remainder (Saône side of summit) **10km/h (5.4kn)** Canal sections (river bypasses) **6km/h (3.2kn)**

Locks: 112 (min 38.50 long x 5.20m wide) Operate Niffer–Mulhouse section: Mon–Fri 0500–2100; Sat 0500–2000; Sun 0800–2000; remainder: daily late Mar–Oct 0900–1230 & 1330–1900; Nov–late Mar by arrangement only

Distance: 237km

There have been plans to develop the waterway between Alsace and Burgundy by restoring the canal between the northern and southern branches of the Canal du Rhône au Rhin and upgrading much of the existing waterway to take the larger barges. Although some work has started on linking the two branches, the overall grandiose plans involving a huge investment to upgrade the entire length of the Rhône au Rhin to make it more commercially viable seem to be on hold.

At present, the only access to the Alsace end of the *branche sud* of the Canal du Rhône au Rhin is from the busy commercial Grand Canal d'Alsace which links up with the canalised Rhine (Route 40).

Having locked in at Niffer, the passage to the summit of the Rhône au Rhin canal and then on to Montbéliard (73km) involves a heavy density of locks and a tunnel, and mostly industrial surroundings.

Once south of Montbéliard, a boat is heading for the valley of the Doubs and for the best part of 150km crews can relish the spectacular surroundings of forests and steep cliffs and two magnificently situated towns – Besançon and Dole both of which have served as the capital of the Franche-Compté region. By the end of the route, the boat is just a few hours motoring from Burgundy.

WATERWAY	PK ref	Town/*village*/≪*lock*	Total km	
			▼	▲
Lock providing access to Kembs/Niffer branch canal from Grand Canal d'Alsace (Route 40)	PK 0	≪ *Kembs-Niffer*. Sharp left after lock into Canal de Huningue for *Kembs*. ⌐ – 2km (end of navigation).	0	237
	PK 1	*Niffer* ⌐.		
KEMBS/NIFFER BRANCH CANAL	PK 1	≪ *Niffer* (alternative to lock at PK 0).		
LEFT **CANAL DU RHÔNE AU RHIN – BRANCHE SUD**	PK 13.5/37.5			
RIGHT closed Branche Nord of Canal du Rhône au Rhin				
	PK 35	≪ No 41.		
Tunnel (140m)	PK 33	**Mulhouse** ⌐.	18	219
	PK 32–10	≪ Nos 39–33, 31–17.		
	PK 10	**Dannemarie** ⌐.	41	196
	PK 9.5–5	≪ Nos 16–2.		
Summit	PK 5–0/186			
	PK 185.5–174	≪ Nos 3–8.		
AHEAD branch canal to Belfort (9.5km 5 locks) air draught 3.5m draught 1.6m.	PK 172/0			
	PK 6	*Trévenans* ⌐ **Châtenois-les-Forges** (2km).		
End of navigation	PK 9.5	*Botans* ⏛.		
LEFT lock and **CANAL DU RHÔNE AU RHIN**	PK 171.5	≪ No 9.		

WATERWAY	PK ref	Town/*village*/≪*lock*	Total km
			▼ ▲
RIGHT lock and **CANAL DU RHÔNE AU RHIN**	PK 171	≪ No 10	
	PK 169.5–165	≪ Nos 11, 12 & 14.	
	PK 164.5	**Montbéliard** Prés la Rose 25-acre park. Pavillon des Sciences. 18th century Château des Princes, now a museum, overlooks the town. Quaint old houses. Peugeot Adventure Museum (2km) ⚐. Cruiser hire.	72.5 164.5
	PK 164–150	≪ Nos 15–22.	
	PK 148	*St-Maurice-Colombier* ♨.	
	PK 147.5–141	≪ Nos 23–26.	
	PK 140.5	**l'Isle-sur-le-Doubs** ♨.	96.5 140.5
	PK 139.5–127	≪ Nos 27–32.	
	PK 127	*Clerval* ♨.	
	PK 123–112	≪ Nos 33–39.	
	PK 109.5	**Baume-les-Dames** Ancient town, named after a nunnery that was once on the site. Many 18th century houses. ♨ some distance from town.	127.5 109.5
	PK 107–97	≪ Nos 40–44	
	PK 96	*Laissey* ♨.	
	PK 94.5	≪ No 45.	
	PK 92.5	*Deluz* ♨.	
	PK 90	≪ Nos 46/47 (double).	
	PK 86.5	*Novillars* ♨.	
	PK 83–76	≪ Nos 48 & 49.	
LEFT optional tunnel & lock No 50N *Tarragnoz* to	PK 74		

WATERWAY	PK ref	Town/*village*/≪ lock	Total km	
			▼	▲
bypass Besançon or continue to alt. lock No 50B *St-Paul* and through town **CANAL DU RHÔNE AU RHIN**	(PK 74)	**Besançon** Principal town of the Franche-Compté region. Surrounded by seven hills and dominated by the Vauban Citadel. Buildings include the cathedral and a palace housing the Time Museum ⌂. Cruiser hire.	163	74
	PK 73.5–63	≪ Nos 51–54/55 (double).		
LEFT tunnel (185m)	PK 60			
	PK 59.5	*Thoraise* ⌕.		
	PK 59–40.5	≪ Nos 56, 57, 58, 58A, 59 & 60.		
	PK 39.5	*Ranchot* ⌕.		
	PK 38.5–27.5	≪ Nos 61, 62, 63 & 64.		
	PK 26	*Rochefort-sur-Nenon* ⌕.		
	PK 22–19	≪ Nos 65 & 66.		
	PK 18.5	**Dole** One-time capital of Burgundy. Old tanners district where Louis Pasteur was born. Scientific museum. ⌂. Cruiser hire.	218.5	18.5
	PK 18–10.5	≪ Nos 67, 68, 69 & 70.		
	PK 10.5	**Damparis** ⌕ in industrial surroundings.	226.5	10.5
	PK 8.5	≪ Nos 71, 72 & 73.		
	PK 0.5	*St-Symphorien-sur-Saône* ⌕.		
	PK 0.5	≪ No 74.	▼	▲
T-junction with Saône (Route 15) LEFT ⌂ at St-Jean-de-Losne (5km)	PK 0	≪ No 75 *Saône*.	237	0

Route 15

Saône: *St-Jean-de-Losne* ←→ *Lyon*

Maximum boat dimensions: *Height above waterline* 4.7m *Draught* 3.5m

Speed limits: on river **30km/h (16kn)** Canal sections (river bypasses) **15km/h (8kn)** through St-Jean-de-Losne, Chalon-sur-Saône, Mâcon (bypass), Lyon **12km/h (6.5kn)**

Locks: **5** (185m long x 12m wide) Operate late Mar–Oct 0600–2100 (Couzon 0500–2100); Nov– late Mar 0700–1900 (Couzon 0600–2000)

Distance: **170km** The detailed route shows a distance of 214km based on the PK numbering system of the old route which has been shortened to 170km by bypasses (*dérivations*) short sections of canal bypassing the river

Yachts bound for the Mediterranean by way of the northern waterways will eventually reach the important junction at St-Jean-de-Losne. On the way there, some will have sampled the considerable attractions of the Canal de Bourgogne, others will have chosen the Marne route through the Champagne region. Boats passage-making from Strasbourg and the north east will have emerged from the Canal du Rhône au Rhin and others may have experienced the delights of the Petite Saône. Only those who have taken the most 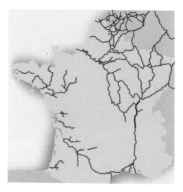 westerly Bourbonnais route will miss St-Jean-de-Losne, meeting the Saône 57km downriver at Chalon-sur-Saône.

Having arrived at St-Jean-de-Losne, via the various routes from the north, west or east, crews should anticipate a marked contrast in their surroundings once through the first of the Saône's massive locks (*Seurre*). The channel widens from a modest 12-15m in the Petite Saône to a minimum of 40m and at times the river is 200m across from one bank to the other. There are numerous shoals, shallows and man-made submerged training walls to be avoided, with red and green channel buoys much in evidence.

Watch out for the *dérivations* on the Saône. These are canal sections bypassing parts of the river that are no longer navigable. Sometimes a portion of what is being bypassed can be navigated and provides a peaceful night's stop free from

St-Jean-de-Losne marina. *Photo: Keith Harris*

the wash of passing barges. There is still commercial traffic on the Saône, with pushing tugs connected to several dumb barges creating considerable wash as they speed by at 15 knots. When considering the day's passage, the crew will appreciate an itinerary that makes provision for a quiet berth for the night, undisturbed by the wash of passing traffic.

During the season, there is little current unless, due to exceptional weather conditions, the water level is markedly heightened with local flooding. If navigating the river early or late in the year, and you are concerned about the height/current, contact *direction interrégionale Rhône-Saône*, 2, rue de la Quarantaine, 69321 Lyon cedex 5. Tel: 04 72 56 59 00. Fax 04 72 56 59 01. e-mail sn-rhone-saone@vnf.fr www.vnf.fr

Between St-Jean-de-Losne and Lyon, much of the countryside is rich meadowland dotted with farmhouses with their distinctive red tiled roofs associated with the south of France. Arriving in Mâcon brings you into a famous wine-growing area. Then the scenery changes to woodland and cliffs. All along the route, there are plenty of stopping places including *ports de plaisance* in most of the riverside towns. With only 5 locks to cope with a very modest fall, you can reckon on 20–25 hours to cover the 170km to Lyon, unless you are tempted to dawdle awhile and perhaps explore a short length of the beautiful Doubs river.

The Saône at St-Jean-de-Losne. *Photo: Alain Dore CRT Bourgogne*

WATERWAY	PK ref	Town/*village*/≪ lock	Total km
			▼ ▲
SAÔNE	PK 214.5	**St-Jean-de-Losne** see page 146.	0 214.5
AHEAD *dérivation* de Seure	PK 208		
RIGHT river closed to navigation			
Re-join **SAÔNE**	PK 188	≪ No 7 *Seurrre*. ♒ just downstream of lock, and quayside moorings at ♒ (Lechâtelet), 10km up S end of bypassed river.	
	PK 176	≪ No 6 *Écuelles*.	
LEFT Le Doubs River and Verdun-sur-le-Doubs. River navigable for 8km to *Navilly*	PK 167.5	**Verdun-sur-le-Duobs** Pretty town, partly on an island ⚑. Cruiser hire.	47 167.5
	PK159	*Gergy* Leisure centre pontoon. Shops.	

The Pont de Bourgogne at Chalon-sur-Saône. *Photo: Alain Dore CRT Bourgogne*

WATERWAY	PK ref	Town/*village*/≪lock	Total km ▼ ▲
SAÔNE			
RIGHT Canal du Centre (Route 10)	PK 145		
	PK 142	**Chalon-sur-Saône** One time capital of Burgundy and centre of shipbuilding. Musée Nicéphore Niépce (History of Photography) ⚑ with fuel on the far side of Ile St-Laurent.	72.5 142
	PK 123	*Gigny* ⚑ in chamber of old lock. Cruiser hire.	
	PK 119	≪ No 4 *Ormes* over the weir.	
	PK 111.5	**Tournus** Ancient town with superb example of Romanesque abbey ♫. Cruiser hire. Hotel pontoon on left bank.	103 111.5

WATERWAY	PK ref	Town/*village*/≪*lock*	Total km
			▼ ▲
SAÔNE			
LEFT Seille river 39km 4 locks air draught 3.05m draught 1.3m	PK 106	*la Truchère* (PK 1) ⌂ through first lock. Pontoons at *Cuisery* (PK 13.5), *Branges* (PK 35.5– arm before lock) and *Louhans* (PK 38) end of navigation.	
LEFT Canal de Pont de Vaux. 3.7 km 1 lock air draught 3.5m draught 1.2m	PK 97.5	*Pont-de-Vaux* (3.7km) end of navigation. Large ⌷ Fuel.	
	PK 90	*Asnières-sur-Saône* ⌂.	
	PK 87.5	*Vésines* ⌂.	
	PK 83	**Mâcon** Large ⌷ in outskirts of town.	131.5 83
LEFT *dérivation* bypassing Mâcon	PK 82		
	PK 81–80	**Mâcon** Ancient city and centre of the wine trade. The Mâconnais white grapes (Pinot and Chardonnay) give Mâcon Blanc and the Pouillys (especially Pouilly-Fuisse) the characteristic nutty flavour. The black Gamay grape produces the sprightly Mâcon Rouge and Mâcon Rosé. Quayside mooring.	
LEFT southern end of city bypass	PK 79		
	PK 72.5	*Port Arciat* ⌷ for Crêches (1km).	142 72.5
	PK 66.5	*St-Symphorien-d'Ancelles* ⌂ just downstream of bridge.	
	PK 62	≪ No 3 *Dracé.*	
	PK 43	*Fareins* ⌂. Fuel.	
	PK 40	*Jassans-Riottier* ⌂. Fuel.	
	PK 31	**Trévoux** ⌂.	183.5 31
	PK 26	*Parcieux* ⌷ in old lock.	
	PK 23.5	*Genay* ⌂. Crane.	

WATERWAY	PK ref	Town/*village*/≪*lock*	Total km
			▼ ▲
SAÔNE	PK 22.5	*St-Germain* Large ⌂.	
	PK 20.5	*Neuville-sur-Saône* ♘.	
	PK 19	*Albigny* Choice of several ♘, but no nearby shops.	
	PK 17	≪ No 9 *Couzon*.	
	PK 16.5	*Rochetaillée-sur-Saône.* Musée de l'automobile (15 minutes' walk from pontoons) ♘.	
	PK 14.5	*Fontaines-sur-Saône* ♘.	
	PK 12	*Collonges-au-Mont-d'Or* ♘.	▼ ▲
	PK 10–0	**Lyon** Third largest city in France. Most important buildings and shops are in the area between the Saône and the Rhône conveniently near to quayside moorings. The hill of Fourvière with Notre-Dame Basilique at its summit may be ascended by funicular railway. Old city is a maze of narrow streets lined with houses from the Gothic and Renaissance periods. ♘ in ancient lock at PK 10 or moor up alongside more central quays (*Pêcherie* PK 4.5, *Maréchel Joffre* PK 3, *Rambaud* PK 0.5, and, in the Rhône, *Avenue Leclerc* PK 0.5 where fuel is available). Boats should not be left unattended alongside Lyon's quays.	214.5 0

Confluence of the Saône and Rhône.
Continues Lyon to Port St Louis (Route 16) Upper (Haut) Rhône, upstream of Lyon, see page 159

On the Saône at Montureux-les-Baulay.
Photo: Crown Blue Line

Route 16

Rhône: *Lyon* ↔ *Port-St-Louis*

Max Boat Dimensions: *Height above waterline* **6.3m** *Draught* **3m**
Speed limit: 30km/h (16kn)
Locks: **13** (190m long x 12m wide) Daily 0500–2100 except Port-St-Louis (0600–2000)
Distance: 323km

Having reached Lyon by the Saône, most boat owners will then have stocked up and re-fuelled in preparation for their descent of the mighty River Rhône. On this passage there will be no backwaters to escape from the current and passing wash of other traffic or provide shelter from the *mistral* or *scirocco*. Boats setting off southwards from Lyon will either be making for the sea at Port-St-Louis or planning to enter the Petit Rhône at Arles and use St-Gilles lock to access the Canal du Rhône à Sète which connects with the Mediterranean ports to the west of Port-St-Louis.

In the 19th century, this descent of the Rhône would almost certainly have been a challenging one-way journey carried downriver by a fierce current, avoiding the midstream rocks, shifting sands and banks of mud and gravel swept into the waterway by non-navigable fast-flowing feeder rivers. Some of this early barge traffic did attempt to make the return trip back to Lyon, but it required a team of 30 – 40 horses to haul them upriver. Other cargo was simply floated downriver on collapsible rafts which could then be either destroyed or returned to Lyon overland. The introduction of steam accounted for some increase in river traffic, although all the navigational hazards remained.

It was not until the realisation that the Rhône could be harnessed to generate electricity on a vast scale that consideration would be given to taming the waterway for both commercial and pleasure use. To this end, the government decided that the profits from generating electricity would benefit river navigation and agriculture. The gargantuan scheme has encompassed the construction of barrages, reservoirs and hydro-electric power stations that contribute about

10 per cent of the country's requirements. On the river there has been the development of a large new commercial port on the outskirts of Lyon and the construction of 13 vast locks.

Considerable work on the bed of the river has removed many of the navigational hazards with a minimum of 3m in the 60m-wide channel. Much of the river is much wider than the channel, sometimes opening out to almost half a mile from one bank to the other. The Rhône still has to be treated with considerable respect, more so than any other commercial waterway in France. That said, 8m yachts with a modest 10bhp engine do make the downriver trip from Lyon to the sea. Returning is another matter – some will plan to stay in the Mediterranean, others will seek overland transport or pay to be motored upstream roped alongside a barge. There will nearly always be a minimum of two knots of current, and progress upriver in some sections against this would be painfully slow with a 10bhp engine.

If you are considering returning from the Mediterranean to Lyon roped up alongside a barge, you should start making enquiries at Port-St-Louis. If you have entered from one of the other nearby ports and plan to use the Petit Rhône to gain access to the Rhône proper, you should enquire at the St-Gilles lock or at Arles. It is all informal; negotiate the cost direct with the bargee. Irrespective of the size of your craft, it is likely to cost around €600 to be motored all the way up to Lyon.

You may be unlucky when attempting to motor back to Lyon under your own steam, and encounter the *mistral*, a strong wind (sometimes over 50mph) from the north rushing down the Rhône valley. It can last for several days and coming downriver, with the wind behind you, the boat will fly along, but berthing and approaching locks and bridges can sometimes be alarming if you only have modest power to manoeuvre. The *scirocco* is from the south and is usually for a shorter duration, but this wind against the current can quickly whip up a disturbed surface in the more exposed stretches of river.

The Rhône rises in the Alps, and when the Alpine snows melt there is an increase in the height of the river and the current can build up to 7 or 8 knots. Passages early in the season should therefore be avoided. With the totally unpredictable climate changes, it is difficult to advise on the best time to navigate the Rhône, which is at least unaffected by long periods of drought. In July 1996, with exceptionally heavy rainfall over Central Europe, the rapid rise in water level caused considerable damage to moored boats, pontoons and bridges on the Rhône. The river was closed, and remained impassable to boats with limited power for several weeks after it had reopened. One of the additional hazards to pleasure boats, after flooding, is the dangerous debris in the river.

The locks are controlled by traffic lights; buzzers aquaint you with the lock operation, that is the raising and lowering of the safety barriers in the front of the upper gates, the opening and closing of the gates/ shutters and the movement of the water. Floating bollards, set in the lock walls, carry your warps up or down with you so that no adjustment is necessary. In Bollène lock there is an astonishing 26m drop which is achieved with hardly a ripple on the water, and coming the other way the water level in the lock rises with an almost eerie silence.

For almost 200km, the Côtes-du-Rhône vineyards line either side of the river, some perched on terraces high up above the waterway and others stretching over plains to the distant horizon. Great wines are produced in these parts like Châteauneuf-du-Pape and Condrieu.

Exiting the Bolléne lock. *Photo: Keith Harris*

Haut-Rhône

At the northern end of the Rhône, above Lyon, the river is called the Haut-Rhône which climbs up to its source in the Swiss Alps. For the most part, the waters of the Haut-Rhône serve as a playground for waterskiers, fishermen, rowers and shallow-draught motor boats. With a depth as shallow as 0.2m in some patches, the Haut-Rhône comes outside the scope of this guide.

Petit Rhône

The Petit Rhône (Route 17) is the western arm of the Rhône delta. It is 55km in length from Arles to the sea at Port l'Amarée but with just one lock at St-Gilles, giving boats access from the Petit Rhône to the Canal du Rhône à Sète (the only access from the Rhône until the lock at Beaucaire is restored). The channel in the Petit Rhône is well marked between Arles and the St-Gilles lock with 2.5m of water and clearance beneath the bridges of 5.24m. However, downstream of the lock between St- Gilles and the sea, the bridge clearance is only 3m and the water depth can be less than 1m so this lower part of the Petit Rhône is exclusively used by shallow draught local boats.

The Mediterranean end of this great river comes as something of an anti-climax, because navigation virtually ceases beyond the entrance to Port-St-Louis where the Rhône fans out into several trickling shallow rivers making their way to the sea across desolate mudflats.

WATERWAY	PK ref	Town/*village*/≪ *lock*	Total km	
			▼	▲
RHÔNE	PK 0	**Lyon** see page 156.	0	323
	PK 3	Port Edouard-Herriot – large commercial port.		
	PK 3.5	**St-Fons** ♒.	3.5	319.5
11km *dérivation* bypassing river.	PK 4	≪ *Pierre-Bénite* VHF Ch 22.		
End of canal *dérivation*	PK 15			
	PK 18	**Givors** ♒.	18	305
	PK 26.5	*St-Romain-en-Gal* ♒.		
	PK 29	**Vienne** Ancient town important in Roman times. Developed industrially, particularly textiles. Roman Temple of Augustus and Livia, 25 BC Roman theatre and many other Roman remains. Almost opposite Vienne, on the other bank of the river, one of the most famous and oldest of all the Côtes-du-Rhône red wines is produced, the Côte Rôtie, which has been appreciated since Roman times for its richness ♒.	29	294

WATERWAY	PK ref	Town/*village*/≪*lock*	Total km	
			▼	▲
RHÔNE	PK 34	≪ *Vaugris* VHF Ch 20.		
	PK 40	*Les-Roches-de-Condrieu* Large ⊳ with fuel. Wine-tasting in nearby town of **Condrieu**.	40	283
12km *dérivation* bypassing river	PK 51			
	PK 61	≪ *Sablons* VHF Ch 22.		
End of canal *dérivation*	PK 63			
	PK 69`	*Andance* ⬮.		
	PK 69	*Andancette* ⬮.		
3.5km *dérivation* bypassing river	PK 82.5			
End of canal *dérivation*	PK 86	≪ *Gervans* VHF Ch 20.		
	PK 91	**Tournon** Busy old town. Near here, on the west bank, are produced the full-flavoured red and white St Joseph wines, the red Cornas, and the sparkling white St Peray. On the opposite bank are the districts of Crozes Hermitage, producing the full-bodied red and delicate white Hermitage wines ⬮.	91	232
	PK 99.5	*La Roche de Glun* ⬮.		
10km *dérivation* bypassing river	PK 98			
	PK 106	≪ *Bourg-les-Valence* VHF Ch 22.		
End of canal *dérivation*	PK 108			
	PK 110	**Valence** Important ancient town with many historical associations. 17th century cathedral. Town quay just downriver of bridge but better protection in 290-berth marina Valence-L'Epervière another 2km downriver	110	213
	PK 112	*Valence-L'Epervière* Large ⊳. Fuel.		

WATERWAY	PK ref	Town/*village*/≪ *lock*	Total km
			▼ ▲
RHÔNE			
6.5km *dérivation* bypassing river	PK 119.5		
	PK 124	≪ *Beauchastel* VHF Ch 20.	
End of canal *dérivation*	PK 126		
8.5km *dérivation*	PK 135.5		
	PK 142.5	≪ *Logis-Neuf* VHF Ch 22.	
End of canal *dérivation*	PK 144		
13.5km *dérivation* bypassing river	PK 152.5		
	PK 164	≪ *Châteauneuf* VHF Ch 20.	
End of canal *dérivation*	PK 166	**Viviers** Fascinating old town with public quay. Harbour tends to get silted up. Possible to back-track a little way up bypassed river, and then anchor.	166 157
30km *dérivation* bypassing river	PK 170.5	Donzère gorge – dramatic scenery.	
	PK 190	≪ *Bollène* VHF Ch 22.	
End of canal *dérivation*	PK 200.5		
6km *dérivation* bypassing river	PK 212.5		
	PK 216	≪ *Caderousse* VHF Ch 20.	
End of canal *dérivation*	PK 218.5	Possible to backtrack up bypassed river 4km to 40-berth L'Ardoise marina (no nearby shops).	
14km *dérivation* bypassing river and Avignon	PK 230		
	`PK 234	≪ *Villeneuve-les-Avignon* VHF Ch 22.	
End of canal *dérivation*	PK 244	**Avignon** Walled town with grand Papal palace. To reach the town, round up at the downstream end of Ile Piot, before the	244 79

WATERWAY	PK ref	Town/*village*/≪*lock*	Total km
			▼ ▲
RHÔNE		railway viaduct, and motor for 2km up the *Bras d'Avignon*, beneath two bridges and the marina is just upriver of the remains of the famous *balad* bridge.	
LEFT Durance river (extensive silting)	PK 247		
	PK 261	*Vallabrègues* ⌂.	
6.5km *dérivation* bypassing river	PK 262.5		
	PK 265	≪ *Vallabregues Beaucaire* VHF Ch 20.	
End of canal *dérivation*	PK 269		
RIGHT Petit Rhône 23km to lock *St-Gilles* and access to Canal du Rhône à Sète (Route 18)	PK 279	Petit Rhône see Route 17.	
	PK 282	**Arles** Remains of Roman occupation include magnificent amphitheatre, public baths and *alyscamps* ⌂.	282 41
LEFT entrance (lock) to Canal d'Arles à Fos (industrial)	PK 283.5	Commercial interest only.	
LEFT entrance to Liaison Rhône-Fos (no pleasure boats)		PK 316.5.	
			▼ ▲
End of Rhône navigation	PK 323	≪ *Port-Saint-Louis* VHF Ch 12 **Port-Saint-Louis** Small town with all supplies. Large marina. Fuel.	323 0
LEFT lock from marina Canal Saint-Louis (3km)		**The Mediterranean**	

Route 17

Petit Rhône *(navigable section between Arles and St-Gilles lock)*

Maximum boat dimensions: *Height above waterline* 5.24m   *Draught* 2.5m
Speed limit: 15km/h (8kn)
Lock: 1 (195m long x 12m wide) Operates all year 0700–1900, but advance notice required (VHF Ch 18 or Tel: 04 66 87 75 30)
Distance: 20km

The Petit Rhône is the western arm of the Rhône delta. The river's total length is 57km starting from just above Arles on the Rhône proper and eventually trickling out into the sea at Grau d'Orgon. It is only the first 20km that concerns most of the river traffic, because on the Petit Rhône between St-Gilles lock and the sea (37km), the bridge clearance is only 3m and the water depth less than 1m, so these wild bleak surroundings are for local shallow-draught boats and fishermen only.

The first section of the river provides the only link between the Rhône and the Canal du Rhône à Sète for those boats who have chosen to finish their waterway passage in one of the Mediterranean ports to the west of Port-Saint-Louis. Years ago, it was possible to leave the Rhône and gain direct access to the canal via the lock at Beaucaire, but this is currently out of commission.

The navigable 20km of Petit Rhône is dense vegetation with no signs of civilisation from the water. Boats must stick to the channel, which is well marked up to the turning off for the lock, but beyond this turning there is nothing to guide the navigator through the shallows of the Petit Rhône.

WATERWAY	PK ref	Town/*village*/≪*lock*	Total km	
			▼	▲
RHÔNE	PK 279.5		0	10
RIGHT into **PETIT RHÔNE**				
RIGHT into **CANAL DE ST-GILLES**	PK 299.5		10	0
	PK 300	≪ St-Gilles VHF Ch 18		
Junction with Canal du Rhône à Sète (Route 18)	PK 300.5 (28.5)			
RIGHT St-Gilles (4km) & Beaucaire (28km)				
LEFT Sète (71km)				

Camargue horses. *Photo: France Afloat*

Route 18

Canal du Rhône à Sète: *Beaucaire* ←→ *Sète*

Maximum boat dimensions: *Height above waterline* 4.7m   *Draught* 1.8m
Speed limit: 10km/h (5.4kn)
Lock: 1 (Nourrigier – PK 7.5*) (80m x 12m) Self-operated 0700–1900
Distance: 100km

*Nourrigier lock, between Bellegarde and Beaucaire is upstream of St-Gilles, towards the Rhône end of the canal. Boats joining the canal from the Petit Rhône, passing through St-Gilles lock and then making for Sète (giving Beaucaire a miss), have no more locks in the 71km pound between St-Gilles and Sète.

The Rhône à Sète canal takes you through parts of the Camargue where you really can see pink flamingoes, half-wild bulls and the famous Camargue horses. The canal is used by those Med-bound boat owners who have opted to leave the Rhône just above Arles and take the Petit Rhône instead of continuing on downriver to Port-St-Louis (see page 163). There are also many hire boats on the canal, with Crown Blue Line operating a large fleet from St-Gilles.

The Carmargue scenery, viewed from the boat, is mostly low-lying wild and sometimes desolate marshland and *étangs* or lakes, some of which are occupied by large flocks of flamingoes. Trees rarely line the banks of the canal, so there is little protection from the sun and the bimini is essential. Much of the time the Mediterranean beaches are less than 500m from the canal, but you would hardly know it except perhaps when motoring by the sea-facing Grande Motte development, unmistakeable with its great pyramidal towers blotting out the horizon.

Those who have spent weeks on the waterways, working their boats towards the Mediterranean, now have a choice of achieving their goal by making for the fishing port of Grau-du-Roi or continuing on to the end of the canal to Sète, one of the largest ports on the Mediterranean catering for industry, fishing and pleasure boats.

Le Grau de Roi and the Mediterranean. *Photo: David Jefferson*

All the towns *en route* between Beaucaire and Sète, and those reached by way of detours from the main canal, have something to tempt passage-making crews to stop off for a while and explore. There is the remarkable walled-town of Aigues-Mortes and beyond, along 5km of Canal Maritime, the Mediterranean port and resort of Le Grau du Roi. The yacht harbour and resort of Palavas provides a pleasant sample of Mediterranean beaches and, near the harbour, an *étang* which nearly always provides the magnificent sight of hundreds of flamingoes. Boats can motor 5km 'inland' up the Lez river to Port Ariane. Sète, at the westward end of the canal, is called *L'île bleue*, with the great expanse of water of the Étang de Thau on one side and the Mediterranean on the other with waterways criss-crossing the town. There are moorings in the town centre and a large marina on the Mediterranean coastline, which is a popular alternative to Port-St-Louis for those entering or leaving the waterways.

Beaucaire, at the other end of the canal, is a deadend since the closure of the town's lock which gave direct access to the Rhône. Apart from the town's industrial outskirts, it is a pleasant day's outing from St-Gilles (25km – 1 lock – 3 hours) or an overnight stop for those with the time to spare.

WATERWAY	PK ref	Town/*village*/≪ *lock*	Total km
			▼ ▲
CANAL DU RHÔNE À SÈTE	PK 0/1	**Beaucaire**. One-time important trading port from which wine was shipped. Basin in town centre now used as ⏛ and a base for Connoisseur Cruisers. Ruins of 11th century castle with fine views over Rhône from remaining tower.	0 100
	PK 7.5	≪ *Nourriguier* – self-operated at user's risk according to notice	
	PK 13.5	**Bellegarde** Town 1km ⚑. Fuel. Restaurant.	13.5 86.5
	PK 24.5	**St-Gilles** Called the Gate of the Camargue and City of Roman Art. World-famous 12th century Abbey ⚑. Cruiser hire.	24.5 75.5
LEFT access to *St-Gilles* lock and Petit Rhône (Route 17)	PK 28.5		
	PK 39.5	*Gallician* ⏛.	
RIGHT Canal du Rhône à Sète bypassing Aigues-Mortes and Le Grau-du-Roi	PK 48		
STRAIGHT ON to Aigues-Mortes and Le Grau-du-Roi	PK 48		
	PK 51	**Aigues-Mortes** Walled town with 17 towers and 10 gates, in the middle of saline marshes and lagoons from which gets its name (*aquae mortuae*, dead waters). Surrounded by mountains of salt. Was an important port, now 5km inland. Large ⏛ but does get very crowded. Easier to park boat at **le Grau-du-Roi**, then taxi, train or bus to explore Aigues-Mortes.	

WATERWAY	PK ref	Town/*village*/≪*lock*	Total km
			▼ ▲
CANAL DU RHÔNE À SÈTE			
Western arm leading back to main canal from Aigues-Mortes is one-way, regulated by time-table displayed on prominent bankside notice	PK 51		
Canal maritime (5km) between Aigues-Mortes and le Grau-du-Roi		**le Grau-du-Roi** Large fishing port. Pontoons for pleasure boats opposite. Le Vidourle river, north of harbour, silted up. Access to sea through swing bridge (VHF Ch 12). Quaysides packed with restaurants. Port-Camargue (1nm S), the largest marina in the south of France, and two miles the other way is **Grande-Motte** with its marina flanked by pyramid-shaped buildings.	

Aigues-Mortes. *Photo: David Jefferson*

WATERWAY	PK ref	Town/*village*/≪ lock	Total km	
			▼	▲
CANAL DU RHÔNE À SÈTE				
LEFT western arm to Le Grau-du-Roi (one-way, regulated by time-table on bankside notice)	PK 53.5			
LEFT and RIGHT le Vidourle river silted up and barrage	PK 55.5			
	PK 61.5	⌂ by transformer (2km from **Grande Motte**)	61.5	38.5
RIGHT	PK 70.5	**Pérols** ⌂.		
LEFT		Large maritime marina and seaside resort of Carnon to seaward of fixed very low bridge (1.2m headroom).		
RIGHT	PK 75.5	Le Lez river and Port-Ariane (6km – 1 lock) 3.5m headroom restriction beneath cable		
LEFT	PK 75.5	**Palavas-les-Flots** 3.5m headroom restriction beneath bridge. Two more bridges between ⚑ and sea (headroom 5m and 2m). Maritime marina. Popular holiday resort with casino, revolving restaurant with many more restaurants packing the quaysides. Flamingoes on nearest *étang*.	75.5	24.5
	PK 79	⌂ for **Villeneuve-lès-Maguelonne**. Old town 2.5km from mooring.	79	21
LEFT arm to sea and fishing harbour – commercial craft only	PK 91.5			

WATERWAY	PK ref	Town/*village*/≪*lock*	Total km
			▼ ▲
CANAL DU RHÔNE À SÈTE	PK 92 – 93	**Frontignan** Boats moor either side of lifting railway bridge (3 daily openings on weekdays, 2 at weekends). Noisy berths. Interesting old town with large quayside wine cellar.	92 8
	PK 98-100	Buoyed entrance channel to **Sète**. Once through pierhead harbour entrance, quayside berths to port. Inner harbour in town centre for pleasure boats through 2 large bridges (headroom 2.5m), opened twice daily. *Capitainerie* in quayside building in basin, opposite railway station. More opening bridges over maritime canal giving access to Port de Commerce, Port de Pèche and Maritime ⚑.	100 0
Continues as Canal des Deux Mers (Royan – Sète). See Route 49			

Palavas-les-Flots and the Mediterranean. *Photo: David Jefferson*

The Northern Region

Nord-Pas de Calais, the most northerly of France's regions, is bordered by Belgium and, to the south, Picardy. The region's two major ports (Dunkerque and Calais) giving access to the waterways, are of particular interest to boat owners with craft based around the Thames estuary or on the UK's east coast. Two smaller ports – Gravelines, between Dunkerque and Calais, and St-Valery-sur-Somme in Picardy,

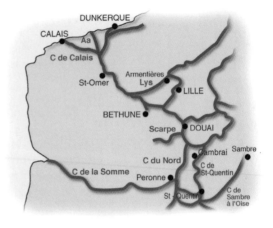

also provide access to the waterways (see page 182 and 202–3). Those that do make for Gravelines or St-Valery-sur-Somme will find the entrances more challenging, but much of interest *en route*, particularly along Picardy's Canal de la Somme. The other option for yachts based in the south-east is to continue down the coast to Le Havre and the Seine estuary, but this adds about 100 miles to the sea passage.

Like many cross-channel motorists seeking the warmer climate in the south of France, the temptation for Med-bound boat owners and crews, once having sorted out the necessary paperwork to use the waterways, will be to press on as quickly as possible making for the Mediterranean via Paris or Reims. True, the Nord-Pas de Calais is a densely populated region, with much heavy industry and a landscape of former coal mines, but those with the time to explore will find a network of canals in this northern part of France, where there has been considerable development in recent years to promote water tourism.

There is a network of 680km of canals within the Nord-Pas de Calais region linking up with Belgium's waterways in the provinces of Hainaut and Western Flanders. Nord-Pas de Calais has 10 per cent of the national waterways carrying 20 per cent of the commercial traffic. The most heavily used is the Liaison Dunkerque-Escaut, consisting of several enlarged canals providing a route through to Belgium from Dunkerque for great convoys of barges.

This northern region is ideal for those boat owners who want to sample the French waterways, perhaps with a view to a long-distance cruise in the future. The waterbourne visitor can soon depart from the busy 'liaison' and take to the smaller canals to tour fortified towns such as Bergues, Gravelines and Saint-Omer or to sample the countryside bordering the canalised Lys as it meanders across the French/Belgian border, taking in Armentières and then perhaps heading for Lille, the capital of the French Flanders region on the Deûle canal. Arras, capital of the Artois region, can be reached at the top end of the Scarpe river, or you can sample the national park around the Sambre river.

Liaison Dunkerque-Escaut: *Dunkerque ↔ Valenciennes ↔ Tournai (Doornik, Belgium)*

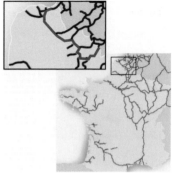

The route below covers the predominantly commercial waterway between Dunkerque and the Belgian border. What is generally referred to as the 'liaison' was achieved by widening the existing network of seven canals and canalised rivers to take huge vessels up to 3000 tonnes. Pleasure craft making for Paris, having entered at Dunkerque or Calais, will mostly use the first section of the 'liaison' to the junction with the Canal de St Quentin, unless desperate to save time by opting for the quicker route, leaving the 'liaison' earlier at the junction with the Canal du Nord, and joining the heavy Nord traffic (see Route 28)

A boat arriving in Dunkerque will either be berthed in one of the two tidal marinas (Port du Grand Large or Yacht Club Mer du Nord) or will have negotiated the Trystram lock and four bridges to berth in the Bassin du Commerce. From a pontoon berth in one of the tidal marinas (where masts can be lowered/raised), yachts can reach the waterways via the Bassin Maritime which runs westwards just inside the seawall into the great Bassin de Mardyck and then through the Mardyck lock into the Liaison Dunkerque Escaut.

Alternatively, boats already in the Bassin du Commerce can proceed into the Canal de Bourbourg through Jeu-de-Mail lock and continue along this waterway for 10 kms until reaching the junction with the Dunkerque–Escaut waterway. The advantage of this route for those who have not yet obtained their VNF licence (see page 34–5) is that the licence can be issued at the local VNF office which is just by Jeu-de-Mail lock.

Maximum boat dimensions: *Height above waterline* **4.5m**   *Draught* **2.5m**

Speed limit: **12km/h (6.4kn)** in France; **8km/h (4.3kn)** in Belgium

Locks: **14** (min 110m long x 10.5m wide) Operate Mon–Sat 0630–2030 or later by arrangement; Sun 0830–1800.

Distance: **202km**

Dunkerque ↔ Valenciennes ↔ Tournai (Doornik, Belgium)

With 140km and 8 locks to cover between Dunkerque and the turning off to the Canal de St Quentin (and a speed limit of 12km/h or 6.4kn), one or two overnight stops will be necessary, and these may not be in the most salubrious surroundings. The wash from passing traffic can be a problem when secured alongside the canal bank. Monday to Saturday, the locks operate from 0630 to 2030 or later (by arrangement, commercial traffic can continue until midnight). Over this period, the only way of avoiding the wash from the stream of barges, is to slip into one of several smaller canals feeding into the 'liaison' (see below). The widening process has reduced the number of stopping places, with one-time quaysides being replaced with great slabs of concrete which now form much of the banks of the waterway.

WATERWAY	PK ref	Town/*village*/≪*lock*	Total km
			▼ ▲
		Dunkerque Third largest port in France. Holiday resort at neighbouring Malo-Les-Bains with a fine beach, promenade and casino to the east of the port. The beach between Malo-Les-Bains and Bray-Dunes is forever associated with the evacuation of 350,000 troops in 1940. Musée Portaire, overlooking the Bassin du Commerce in an old tobacco warehouse, is devoted to the history of the port. In the basin is the splendid three-masted *Duchesse Anne* and the old *Sandettie* lightship.	0 202
Departing from tidal marinas, enter **BASSIN MARITIME**			
LEFT into **BASSIN DE MARDYCK**			
	PK 143.5	≪ *Mardyck* VHF Ch 18.	
LEFT Canal de Bourbourg (back to Dunkerque)	PK 137.5		

Dunkerque – Bassin du Commerce. *Photo: Réseau Plaisance Côte d'Opale*

WATERWAY	PK ref	Town/*village*/≪ lock	Total km ▼ ▲
Departing from *Bassin du Commerce* through bridges into **CANAL DE BOURBOURG**		≪ *Jeu de Mail* VHF Ch 22.VNF office.	
Junction with **LIAISON DUNKERQUE-ESCAUT**	PK 137.5		
RIGHT Canal de Bourbourg (9.3km 2 locks to junction with River Aa)	PK 135	Useful stopping place in Canal de Bourbourg clear of the traffic in the 'Liaison'.	
LEFT Canal de la Colme (closed)	PK 128		
	PK 121.5	≪ *Watten/Holques* VHF Ch 22.	

WATERWAY	PK ref	Town/*village*/≪ *lock*	Total km
			▼ ▲
LIAISON DUNKERQUE-ESCAUT			
RIGHT canalised River Aa to Gravelines (17km 1 lock – see Route 21) also provides access to Canal de Calais (see Route 20)	PK 121		
	PK 120	*Watten* ⚓.	
RIGHT la Houlle River, navigable for 4km to Houlle	PK 118		
RIGHT northern branch to St-Omer (closed)	PK 112.5		
	PK 108.5	**Arques** ⚑ in basin just before lock.	35 167
	PK 108	≪ *Flandre* VHF Ch 18.	
RIGHT southern branch to St-Omer (3km 1 lock)	PK 107.5	**St-Omer** The northern branch to St-Omer off the 'Liaison' at PK 112.5, is closed. The southern branch (which includes 1 lock) is accessed just after *Flandre* lock. Elegant St-Omer has many 17th and 18th century buildings and a magnificent 13th century basilica. Can be difficult to organise bridge and lock opening in St-Omer.	
	PK 106	≪ *Fontinettes* VHF Ch 22. Remarkable nearby boat lift constructed in 1888. Closed in 1967, but refurbished as a tourist attraction.	
	PK 94	**Aire-sur-la Lys** ⚓.	49.5 152.5
LEFT canalised Lys (65km 7 locks) to Belgium. Prettiest river in the region	PK 93	(see Route 24)	

WATERWAY	PK ref	Town/village/≪lock	Total km	
			▼	▲
LIAISON	PK 72.5	**Béthune** ♎.	71	131
DUNKERQUE-	PK 63.5	≪ Cuinchy. VHF Ch 18.		
ESCAUT				
LEFT	PK 60.5	**La Bassée** ♎.	83	119
T-junction	PK 54			
LEFT Deûle canal				
to Lille and River				
Lys (see Route 25)				
RIGHT **LIAISON**				
DUNKERQUE-				
ESCAUT	PK 50	Pont à Vendin ♎.		
RIGHT Canal de	PK 44	Courrières ♎ (just inside Canal de Lens).		
Lens 8km to				
Harnes ♎				
LIAISON	PK 36	**Courcelles-les-Lens** ⚑.	107.5	94.5
DUNKERQUE-				
ESCAUT				
LEFT Scarpe	PK 30			
Inférieure				
(37.5km 6 locks				
to Mortagne du				
Nord). See				
Route 26				
LIAISON	PK 28	≪ Douai VHF Ch 22.		
DUNKERQUE-	PK 28/27	**Douai** Mostly industrial. ♎ on Quai	115.5	86.5
ESCAUT		d'Alsace and Quai des Augustins.		
	PK 24	≪ Courchelettes VHF Ch 18.		
	PK 24	**Courchelettes** ♎.	119.5	82.5
RIGHT Scarpe	PK 23.5			
supérieure				
(22.5km 9 locks to				
Arras see Route 27)				
LEFT alternative				
access to Scarpe				
inférieure (small				
boats only)				

WATERWAY	PK ref	Town/village/≪lock	Total km
			▼ ▲
LIAISON DUNKERQUE-ESCAUT	PK 20	≪ *Goeulzin* VHF Ch 22.	
RIGHT Canal du Nord (Route 28)	PK15		
RIGHT direction Canal St-Quentin (Route 29)	PK 3		
RIGHT direction Canal St-Quentin (Route 29)	PK 0.5		
Liaison continues as **CANALISED RIVER ESCAUT**	PK 0	≪ *Pont Malin* VHF Ch 18.	143.5 58.5
	PK 2.5	*Bouchain* Ⴔ.	
	PK 9	≪ *Denain* VHF Ch 22.	
	PK 15.5	≪ Trith St-Léger VHF Ch 18.	
	PK 22	**Valenciennes** Ⴔ.	165.5 36.5
	PK 22	≪ Folien VHF Ch 22.	
	PK 25	≪ Bruay VHF Ch 18.	
	PK 30	Fresnes-sur-Escaut Ⴔ.	
	PK 31	≪ Fresnes VHF Ch 22.	
RIGHT closed Canal Pommeroeul-Condé	PK 31.5		
	PK 44	Mortagne-du-Nord Ⴔ.	
LEFT Scarpe inférieure (Route 26)	PK 44.5		
	PK 45.5(0)	Border with Belgium	189 13
	PK 7.5	*Antoing* Ⴔ.	▼ ▲
	PK 13	**Tournai (Doornik)** Commercial and artistic centre. Roman occupation. Notre-Dame cathedral.	202 0

Route 20

Canal de Calais: *Calais* ←→ *Watten*

Maximum boat dimensions: *Height above waterline* **3.6m**   *Draught* **2m**
Speed limit: 8km/h (4.3kn)
Lock: 1 (92m long x 8m wide) Operates April–Sept: Mon–Sat 0830–1230 & 1330–1730; Sun 0930–1230 & 1330–1830; Oct–Mar: Mon–Sat 0830–1230 & 1330–1730; Sun by arrangement only.

Note: this refers to the canal lock (Hennuin), not the maritime lock giving access to the Bassin Carnot which operates HW -1½ to HW+¾ or Batellerie non-tidal lock from Bassin Carnot into the canal (operated 0800–1200 & 1400–1800 Mon–Fri but closed Sat afternoon and all day Sun).

Distance: 35km

Being only 22 miles from Dover, Calais is the shortest Channel-crossing to a port giving access to the waterways. There is an excellent yacht harbour in the Bassin de l'Ouest with all facilities including a hospitable yacht club. Being a major cross-channel ferry port, Calais is a convenient harbour for crew change. Arrangements for the mast to be lowered/raised can be made with the *Capitainerie*.

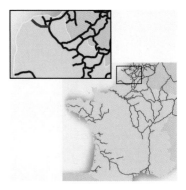

WATERWAY	PK ref	Town/*village*/≪*lock*	Total km	
			▼	▲
CANAL DE CALAIS	PK 30	**Calais** Distinctive neo-Flemish style Hôtel de Ville fronted by Rodin's famous bronze statue 'Burghers of Calais'. Occupied by the English for 200 years. Notre Dame Church built around 1400 by the occupying English. WWII museum in German *blockhaus*. Good bathing beach near yacht harbour. ≪ *la Batellerie* VHF Ch 10.	0	35

Calais.
Photo: Réseau Plaisance Côte d'Opale

WATERWAY	PK ref	Town/*village*/≪*lock*	Total km
			▼ ▲
CANAL DE CALAIS			
RIGHT Canal de Guines (closed)	PK 26		
RIGHT Canal d'Ardres (closed)	PK 18.5		
RIGHT Canal d'Audruicq (closed)	PK 8		
	PK 6	≪ *Hennuin* VHF Ch 18.	
T-junction **RIVER AA** LEFT Gravelines RIGHT Watten (Route 21)	PK 0/15		
T-junction **LIAISON DUNKERQUE-ESCAUT** LEFT Dunkerque RIGHT Watten (Route 19)	PK 11		▼ ▲
	PK10/120	*Watten* ♨.	35 0

Route 21

River Aa: *Gravelines* ←→ *Watten*

Maximum boat dimensions: *Height above waterline* 3.5m   *Draught* 1.8m
Speed limit: 8km/h (4.3kn)
Lock: 1 (38.50m long x 5.05m wide) Operates April–Sept: daily 0830–1230 & 1330–1730; Oct–Mar: Mon–Sat 0830–1230 & 1330–1730.
 Note: this refers to the lock giving access to the waterways from the Bassin Vauban and not the maritime lock and bridge which operate HW -3 to HW +3 except at weekends.
Distance: 18km

Gravelines provides an interesting alternative to Dunkerque and Calais as a port of entry providing access to the canal system. One of 13 towns fortified by Vauban, the preserved walls and moat are built round Gravelines in the form of a star. It was a major fishing port, but over the centuries moving sands left the town 500m inland reached now by the River Aa. The communities of Grande-Fort-Philippe and Petite-Fort-Philippe have been built up on reclaimed land either side of the river.

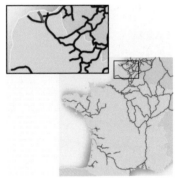

Although the town has much to offer the visitor, yachts from the UK rarely called here as there were few berths that did not dry at low water. However, a major development plan has been underway for several years, with dredging, rebuilding the Quai des Islandais, improved buoyage and generally upgrading the facilities for visitors. By 2006, Gravelines had capacity for 800 boats.

WATERWAY	PK ref	Town/*village*/≪ *lock*	Total km	
			▼	▲
RIVER AA	PK 28	**Gravelines** Vauban fortified town, with beach resorts either side of river entrance. Yacht harbour in Bassin Vauban with all facilities including cranes.	0	18
	PK 28	≪ No 63 bis		
RIGHT Canal du Mardyck (closed)	PK 24.5			
LEFT Canal de Bourbourg (9.3km 2 locks) to junction with Liaison Dunkerque-Escaut	PK 23			
RIGHT Canal de Calais (Route 20)	PK 15			
T-junction Liaison Dunkerque-Escaut	PK 11			
			▼	▲
	PK 10/120	*Watten* ⊓.	18	0

Gravelines. *Photo: Réseau Plaisance Côte d'Opale*

Route 22

Canal de Bergues: *Dunkerque ↔ Bergues*

Maximum boat dimensions: *Height above waterline* 3.24m   *Draught* 1.8m
Speed limit: 5km/h (2.7kn)
Locks: none
Distance: 8km

Much of the industrial sprawl between Dunkerque and Furnes can be avoided by taking the short (8km) stretch of canal to the Vauban fortified town of Bergues, still almost surrounded by ramparts and a moat. From Dunkerque's non-tidal yacht harbour in the Bassin de Commerce, there are several bridges to negotiate, but it is lock-free to Bergues, entering the Bergues canal just before reaching the first lock in the Canal de Furnes.

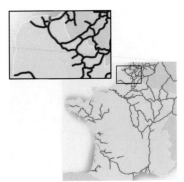

WATERWAY	PK ref	Town/*village*/≪*lock*	Total km	
			▼	▲
CANAL DE BERGUES	PK 1	**Dunkerque** (see page 175).	0	8
RIGHT Canal de la Colme (closed)	PK 7.5			
	PK 8	**Bergues** Fortified town. ♨ close to town walls.	8	0

Route 23

Canal de Furnes: *Dunkerque ↔ Furnes (Veurne, Belgium)*

Maximum boat dimensions: *Height above waterline* 3.24m   *Draught* 1.8m
Speed limit: 5km/h (2.7kn)
Lock: 1 (38.50m long x 5.05m wide) Operates April–Sept: daily 0830–1230 & 1330–1730;
Oct–Mar: Mon–Sat 0830–1230 & 1330–1730
Distance: 22km

Waterways provide a link between Nieuport, on the Belgian coastline, and Dunkerque. Nieuport has a large marina, with a holiday resort 3km north of the harbour amongst the great North Sea sand dunes. The canal between Nieuport and Furnes is in attractive rural surroundings, and the small town of Furnes has a grand market place surrounded by beautifully restored buildings. The suburbs outside Dunkerque are mainly industrial.

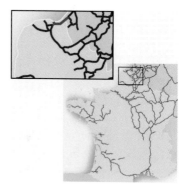

WATERWAY	PK ref	Town/*village*/≪ *lock*	Total km	
			▼	▲
CANAL DE FURNES	PK 0	**Dunkerque** (see page 175).	0	22
	PK 1	≪ *Furnes*		
Belgian border	PK 13			
Continues as **CANAL DE DUNKERQUE À NIEUPORT**			▼	▲
	(PK 22)	**Furnes** (Belgium) – 9km & 1 lock.	22	0

Route 24

River Lys (part): *Aire-sur-La Lys ↔ Deûlémont and Halluin/ Menin (Belgium)*

Maximum boat dimensions: *Height above waterline* **3.9m** *Draught* **1.8m**

Speed limit: 8km/h (4.3kn)

Locks: 7 First 5 are standard (38.50 long x 5.05m wide); Nos 6 & 7 enlarged to take longer barges. Nos 1–4 operate April–Sept: Mon–Sat 0830–1230 & 1330–1730; Sun 0930–1230 & 1330–1830. Oct–Mar: Mon–Fri by arrangement only. Nos 5–7 operate April–Sept, daily 0830–230 & 1330–1730. Oct–Mar, Mon–Sat 0830–1230 & 1330–1730

Distance: 65km

From its source near Aire-sur-la Lys and the junction with the Liaison Dunkerque-Escaut, the Lys river is navigable all the way to Ghent in the heart of Belgium. For those exploring the French waterways, the Lys offers a great opportunity of escaping the stream of heavy traffic on the 'liaison' and sampling the best of the Nord-Pas de Calais countryside along 40km of canalised river to Armentières where, for another 20km, the waterway forms the frontier between France and Belgium. Beyond Deûlémont, the river and locks have been enlarged to form an extension to the 'liaison', carrying large barges plying between France and the Schelde.

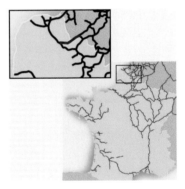

WATERWAY	PK ref	Town/*village*/≪*lock*	Total km	
			▼	▲
From Liaison Dunkerque-Escaut (Route 19)	PK 94			
LA LYS RIVER	PK 0	**Aire-sur-la Lys** ♒.	0	65
	PK 1	≪ No 1 *Fort Gassion*.		
LEFT Canal de la Nieppe (closed)	PK 4.5			
	PK 7	≪ No 2 *Cense à Witz*.		
	PK 12	*Haverskerque/St-Venant* ♒.		
	PK 12.5	≪ No 3 *St-Venant*.		
	PK 19	≪ No 4 *Merville*.		
	PK 19	**Merville** ♒.		
	PK 26	**Estaires** ♒.		
	PK 30	*Sailly-sur-la Lys* ♒.		
	PK 32.5	≪ No 5 *St-Maur*.		
	PK 38	*Erquinghem* ♒.		
	PK 40	**Armentières** ⚑ and leisure centre. Fuel. Cruiser hire	40	25
River forms frontier between France and Belgium				
	PK 41.5	≪ No 6 *Armentières*.		
RIGHT Canal de la Deûle (Route 25)				
	PK 48	*Deûlémont* ♒.		
LA LYS continues as extension to **LIAISON DUNKERQUE-ESCAUT**				
Frontier	PK 55	≪ No 7 *Comines*.	▼	▲
	PK 65	*Halluin* ♒.	65	0

Route 25

Canal de la Deûle (part): *Bauvin ⟷ Deûlémont*

Maximum boat dimensions: *Height above waterline* **5.53m** *Draught* **2.3m** (Belgian border to Lille); **3m** (Liaison Dunkerque-Escaut to Lille); **2.3m** (Lille to Deûlémont)
Speed limit: 12km/h (6.4kn)
Locks: 3 (144.60 m long X 12m wide) Operate Mon–Sat 0630–20.30; Sun 0830–1800
Distance: 35km

Canal de la Deûle is covered below from its southern end where the Deûle forms part of the Liaison Dunkerque-Escaut (Route 19) to Deûlémont where it meets La Lys river near the Belgian frontier. The Deûle waterway serves Lille, the capital of French Flanders, and the locks have been enlarged to give huge barges direct access to Lille's commercial port.

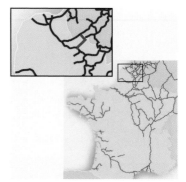

Citadelle, Lille. *Photo: Office du Tourisme de Lille*

WATERWAY	PK ref	Town/*village*/≪*lock*	Total km
			▼ ▲
T-junction: Liaison Dunkerque-Escaut (Route 19) **CANAL DE LA**	PK 0/54	*Bauvin.*	0 35
DEÛLE	PK 3.5	≪ *Don* VHF Ch22.	
	PK 4.5	*Don* ♎.	
	PK 19–17	**Lille** Sprawling industrial city – the largest in the northern region, and a major commercial port. Interesting old quarter dominated by great Vauban Citadelle. Palais des Beaux-Arts (Fine Arts museum) with important collection of Flemish and Dutch paintings with some of the Impressionists. No obvious places for visiting boats to moor up, but may be room alongside quays off through canal route by Citadelle.	
	PK 19.5	≪ *Grande Carré* VHF Ch 18.	
LEFT Canal de Roubaix navigable to lock *Marcq* (3.5km 1 lock). Restoration work underway	PK 23		
	PK 25	**Wambrechies** ♎.	
	PK 30	≪ *Quesnoy* VHF Ch 22.	
	PK 30	**Quesnoy** ♎.	▼ ▲
	PK 33.5	*Deûlémont* ♎.	35 0
Belgian border T-junction canalised River Lys (Route 24)	PK 35		

Route 26

Scarpe inférieure (lower): *Douai ↔ Mortagne du Nord*

Maximum boat dimensions: *Height above waterline* 4.7m *Draught* 3m
Speed limit: 12km/h (6.4kn)
Locks: 6 (38.80m long x 5.05m wide) Operate April–Sept: Mon–Sat 0830–1230 & 1330 –1730; Sun 0930–1230 & 1330–1830. Oct–Mar: Mon–Fri by arrangement only
Distance: 37.5km

The Scarpe inférieure or Lower Scarpe starts at Douai just off the Liaison Dunkerque-Escaut, runs roughly parallel with the canalised Escaut which it joins just below the Belgian border. It provides the opportunity of escaping the heavy 'liaison' traffic as the locks on the Scarpe can only take the smaller 38m barges. There are no major towns on the route which takes boats through a regional park, marshland drained for agriculture and forests.

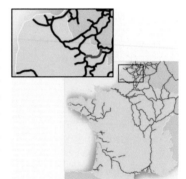

Nivelle, 4km from St-Amand-les-Eaux on the Scarpe inférieure. *Photo: Office du Tourisme de St-Amand-les-Eaux*

WATERWAY	PK ref	Town/*village*/≪*lock*	Total km	
			▼	▲
From Liaison Dunkerque-Escaut (Route 19)	PK 30		0	37.5
SCARPE INFÉRIEURE	PK 29			
RIGHT short section (1000m) of original river now closed through Douai	PK 29.5			
	PK 30	≪ No 1 *Fort-de-Scarpe.*		
	PK 37	≪ No 2 *Lallaing.*		
	PK 41.5	*Vred* ⌂.		
	PK 45.5	≪ No 3 *Marchiennes.*		
	PK 45.5	**Marchiennes** ⌂.	17	20.5
	PK 49.5	≪ No 4 *Warlaing.*		
	PK 58	**St-Amand-les-Eaux** ⌂. Casino. Abbey tower.	29.5	8
	PK 59.5	≪ No 5 *St-Amand.*		
	PK 62	*Nivelle.*		
	PK 64.5	≪ No 6 *Thun.*	▼	▲
T-junction with Escaut, border with Belgium (Route 19)	PK 66/44	*Mortagne-du-Nord* ⌂ (in Escaut).	37.5	0

Route 27

Scarpe supérieure (upper): *Corbehem ↔ Arras*

Maximum boat dimensions: *Height above waterline* **3.7m** *Draught* 1.8m
Speed limit: 8km/h (4.3kn)
Locks: **9** (38.50m long x 5.05 wide) Operate No 9: Mon–Sat 0730–1230 & 1330–1730; Sun 0830–1230 & 1330–1800. Remainder (Nos 8–1) April–Sept: Mon–Sat 0830–1730; Sun 0930–1830; Oct–Mar: Mon–Sat 0830–1730; Sun by arrangement only
Distance: 23km

The Upper Scarpe provides an interesting opportunity of escaping from the heavily-used Liaison Dunkerque-Escaut for a day-trip to Arras – a stylishly reconstructed city dating back to the Middle Ages, and heavily involved in both World Wars. A popular tourist attraction, les Souterrains is a network of tunnels beneath the city centre, some dating back to the 10th century. They have been used as wine cellars and the British housed an underground field hospital here in WWI.

If bringing the boat down the Scarpe from Arras with the idea of continuing along the Lower Scarpe, this can only be reached by entering the Liaison Dunkerque-Escaut, motoring north along the Douai bypass for 6km, through 2 locks (Courchelettes and Douai) and entering the Scarpe inférieure north of Douai. Only the first kilometre of the old route of the river through Douai (Scarpe moyenne) is navigable as far the old Courchelettes lock and *halte nautique.*

WATERWAY	**PK ref**	**Town**/*village*/≪ *lock*	**Total km**	
			▼	▲
From Liaison Dunkerque-Escaut (Route19)	PK 23.5		0	23.5
SCARPE SUPÉRIEURE	PK 22.5	≪ No 9 *Corbehem.*		
	PK 21	≪ No 8 *Brébières-Basse-Tenue.*		
	PK 20	≪ No 7 *Brébières-Haute-Tenue.*		
	PK 18	≪ No 6 *Vitry.*		
	PK 14	≪ No 5 *Biache-St Vaast.*		
	PK 14	**Biache-St Vaast** Ω.	9.5	14
	PK 11.5	*Roeux – Plouvain* Ω.		
	PK 7.5	≪ No 4 *Fampoux.*		
	PK 5	≪ No 3 *Athies.*		
	PK 2.5	≪ No 2 *St-Laurent-Blagny.*		
	PK 2	*St-Laurent-Blagny* Ω for visiting Arras.		
	PK 0.5	≪ No 1 *St-Nicholas.*	▼	▲
End of navigation	PK 0	**Arras** Capital of the Artois region. 11th century Grand Place and Place des Héros surrounded by Flemish-style houses.16th century Flemish-Gothic town hall with grand belfry. Museum in St-Vaast Benedictine Abbey houses the famous Arras tapestries. Vauban fortifications. Tours of underground passages. Presently, the town quays cannot be reached by boat, and visitors berth outside city at *St-Laurent-Blagny* (2km).	23.5	0

Route 28

Canal du Nord: *Arleux* ↔ *Pont l'Evêque*

Maximum boat dimensions: *Height above waterline* **3.7m**   *Draught* **2.4m**
Speed limit: 10km/h (5.4kn)
Locks: **19** (91m long x 5.75m wide) Operate Nos 1–7: Mon–Sat 0630–2030; Sun 0830–1800.
   Nos 8–19: Mon–Sat 0700–1900; Sun 0800–1230 & 1330–1830
Distance: 95km

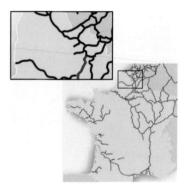

The Canal du Nord was conceived in order to carry some of the barge traffic from the congested Canal de St Quentin. Work was started in 1907 but halted during the First World War when much of what had been built was totally destroyed. Construction would only resume after WWII and this vital waterway, linking the ports and the Nord-Pas de Calais industrial region with the Oise and the Seine, was finally completed in 1965 and remains the most recently constructed of all the French waterways.

The Canal du Nord is 95km long with 19 locks and has two tunnels (Ruyaulcourt – 4354m and Panneterie – 1601m). Both tunnels are controlled with lights, and neither involve a tow as required through the longer tunnel on the more ancient Canal de St-Quentin. Traffic is kept moving through the Ruyaulcourt tunnel in both directions by using a 1000m duel waterway, allowing convoys to pass each other.

For pleasure boats making for Paris from Calais or Dunkerque, the Canal du Nord is definitely the quicker route compared with the Canal de St-Quentin. The Nord is only 10km shorter but you have to add the further distances to be covered on the Liaison Dunkerque-Escaut and the Canal Latéral à l'Oise. In total, opting for the St-Quentin, involves an extra 42km and 23 locks compared with the Nord. The other time consideration is navigating the longer tunnels. You might just miss a tow through the Canal de St-Quentin and have to wait some time for the next tug.

St-Quentin canal is still favoured by most skippers to avoid the Nord's endlessly busy traffic. There are fewer stopping places for pleasure craft on the

Canal du Nord, and the scenery is not as good with the concrete sides of the newer canal much in evidence. Provisions can be purchased from some of the Nord lock keepers.

WATERWAY	PK ref	Town/*village*/≪*lock*	Total km
			▼ ▲
Junction with the Liaison Dunkerque-Escaut (LEFT) and	PK 0	*Arleux.*	0 95
CANAL DU NORD	PK 1.5	≪ No 1 *Palluel* VHF Ch 18	
	PK 7.5	*Marquion* ♒.	
	PK 8	≪ No 2 *Marquion* VHF Ch 22.	
	PK 10.5	≪ No 3 *Sains-lès-Marquion* VHF Ch 18.	
	PK 12	≪ No 4 *Sains-lès-Marquion* VHF Ch 22.	
	PK 14	≪ No 5 *Moeuvres* VHF Ch 18.	
	PK 15.5	≪ No 6 *Graincourt-les-Havrincourt* VHF Ch 22.	
	PK 17.5	≪ No 7 *Graincourt-les-Havrincourt* VHF Ch 18.	
Tunnel (4354m)	PK 25–29.5	*Ruyaulcourt* tunnel (4354m) controlled by lights (see above) VHF 22.	
	PK 37.5	≪ No 8 *Moslains* VHF Ch 10.	
	PK 38.5	≪ No 9 *Moslains* VHF Ch 10.	
	PK 40	≪ No 10 *Allaines* VHF Ch 10.	
	PK 42	≪ No 11 *Feuillaucourt* VHF Ch 10.	
	PK 44	≪ No 12 *Cléry-sur-Somme* VHF Ch 10.	
T-junction	PK 45		
RIGHT Canal de Somme (Route 31)			
LEFT continues as **CANAL DU NORD**	PK 48	**Péronne** Town heavily fortified in 16th century. Some ramparts and the great	48 47

WATERWAY	PK ref	Town/*village*/≪*lock*	Total km
			▼ ▲
CANAL DU NORD		Porte de Bretagne survived the near total Great War destruction. Historial de la Grande Guerre, housed in the lakeside remains of the Château de Péronne, is a fascinating and moving museum devoted to the First World War. ♨ is in a quiet backwater 3km beyond junction with Canal de la Somme. Showers at adjacent camp site. 20 minutes' walk into town centre. Check depth when approaching pontoons.	
	PK 49.5	≪ No 13 *Péronne* VHF Ch 10.	
	PK 60	≪ No 14 *Epénancourt* VHF Ch 10.	
T-junction LEFT Petite Somme (Route 31)	PK 66	≪ 4, 3, 2 & 1 closed 2006	
RIGHT **CANAL DU NORD**			
Summit	PK 69.5	≪ No 15 *Languevoisin* VHF Ch 10.	
Tunnel (1040m)	PK 78.5	*Panneterie* tunnel 1058m (controlled by lights).	
	PK 82	≪ No 16 *Campagne* VHF Ch 10.	
	PK 87.5	≪ No 17 *Sermaize-Haudival* VHF Ch 10.	
	PK 92	**Noyon** Beautifully restored 12th century Gothic cathedral. Charlemagne crowned at Noyon in 768 and Hugues Capet in 987. Calvin Museum. ♨.	92 3
	PK 93.5	≪ No18 *Noyon* VHF Ch 10.	
	PK 94.5	≪ No 19 *Pont-l'Evêque* VHF Ch 10.	▼ ▲
T-junction Canal latéral à l'Oise LEFT to Chauny RIGHT to Compiègne & Paris (Route 8)	PK 95		95 0

Canal de St-Quentin: *Cambrai ↔ Chauny*

Maximum boat dimensions: *Height above waterline* 3.8m *Draught* 2.2m
Speed limit: 10km/h (5.4kn)
Locks: 40 (smallest 38.50m long x 5.05m wide) Operate Canalised Escaut 5–1: St Quentin
1–17 & 32–35 Mon–Sat 0700–1900 Sun 0830–1800; 18–31 daily 0700–1800
Distance: 105km

Canal de St-Quentin, providing a waterway link between the northern channel ports and the Oise feeding into the Seine, was built early in the 19th century. Although double locks were eventually provided, Canal de St-Quentin could not cope with the amount of traffic. Canal du Nord was commissioned in 1878 but due to a number of setbacks was not completed until 1965. Much of the traffic that had previously used the St-Quentin canal switched to the Nord. Although a greater distance compared with the Nord, more locks and the 5670m-long

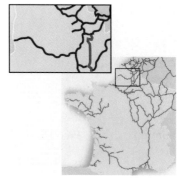

tunnel, most skippers of pleasure craft still opt for the Canal de St-Quentin in preference to the Nord unless really pushed for time. Much of the scenery is pleasantly rural woodland and great expanses of cornfields and sugar beet.

WATERWAY	PK ref	Town/*village*/≪*lock*	Total km	
			▼	▲
FROM **LIAISON DUNKERQUE-ESCAUT** bassin rond and part **CANALISED ESCAUT** to	PK 13		0	105
Cambrai	PK10	≪ No 5 *Iwuy.*		

WATERWAY	PK ref	Town/*village*/≪*lock*	Total km	
			▼	▲
CANALISED	PK10	*Bouchain* ♒.		
ESCAUT	PK 8	≪ No 4 *Thun-l'Evèque.*		
	PK 3.5	≪ No 3 *Erre.*		
	PK 1	≪ No 2 *Selles.*		
	PK 0.5	**Cambrai** Market town famous for its textiles. Ancient ramparts and boulevards. Gothic cathedral. Musée des Beaux-Arts in 18th century mansion. ⚑ just beyond Cantimpré lock.		
CANAL DE	PK 0	≪ No 1 *Cantimpré.*	13	92
ST-QUENTIN				
	PK 2 to 9.5	≪ Nos 1–6.		
	PK 11	*Masnières* ♒.		
	PK 11–17.5	≪ Nos 7–11.		
	PK 18	*Les Rues des Vignes* ♒.		
	PK 18–21.5	≪ Nos 12–14.		
	PK 23	*Honnecourt-sur-Escaut* ♒.		
	PK 23–25	≪ Nos 15–17.		
	PK 26.5	Assembly point in Macquincourt basin for tunnel traffic. Fixed departure times. Tow through first tunnel.		
Tunnel	PK 28.5–35	*Macquincourt* tunnel (5670m).		
Tunnel	PK 42–43	*Lesdins* tunnel (1098m).		
	PK 43.5	Assembly point in Riqueval basin (right bank) for N-going traffic. Fixed departure times. Tow through Macquincourt tunnel.		
	PK 45–51	≪ Nos 18–22.		
	PK 53	**St-Quentin** Industrial town (chemicals and metalworks). 12th and 15th century basilica. Musée d'Entomologie (butterflies and insects) – largest collection in Europe. ⚑ in basin on left bank just before railway bridge.	68	37
	PK 58–66.5	≪ Nos 23–25.		

WATERWAY	PK ref	Town/*village*/≪*lock*	Total km	
			▼	▲
CANAL DE ST-QUENTIN	PK 62	*Séraucourt-le-Grand* ♨.		
RIGHT Petite Somme: St-Simon to Ham. Closed 2006	PK 68			
LEFT continues **CANAL DE ST-QUENTIN**				
	PK 77–80	≪ Nos 26, 27 & 28.		
	PK 80.5	*Voyaux* ♨.		
	PK 83	**Tergnier/Fargniers** (heavy industry).	96	9
	PK 83.5–85	≪ Nos 29, 30 & 31.		
T-junction	PK 85			
LEFT 3.8km branch of Canal de St-Quentin to Canal Sambre à l'Oise (Route 30)				
RIGHT continues as **CANAL DE ST-QUENTIN** direction Compiègne & Paris				
	PK 86–92	≪ Nos 32, 33, 34 & 35.	▼	▲
	PK 92/PK 0	**Chauny** Largely industrial town with a castle and abbey. Museum displays local prehistoric archaeological discoveries and memorabilia from WWI and WWII ⚐.	105	0
Continues as Canal latéral à l'Oise direction Paris (Route 8)				
LEFT Canal de l'Oise à l'Aisne (Route 7)				

Route 30

Part canalised Sambre and Canal de la Sambre à l'Oise:
Belgian frontier/Jeumont ↔ Fargniers & Canal St-Quentin

Maximum boat dimensions: *Height above waterline* 3.5m   *Draught* 1.8m
Speed limit: 10km/h (5.4kn);
Locks: 47 (38.50m long x 5.20m wide) Operate April–Sept Mon–Sat 0830–1830; Sun 0930 –1830: Oct–Mar Mon–Sat 0830–1730; Sun by arrangement only
Distance: 123km

Towards the Belgian end of the canalised Sambre, the surroundings are mostly industrial. Before reaching these parts, the river valley is agricultural with large areas of forest. The Canal de la Sambre à l'Oise, opened in 1939, provides a commercial link between the North Sea, the Meuse basin and the Paris region.

WATERWAY	PK ref	Town/*village*/≪*lock*	Total km ▼ ▲
Frontier with Belgium	PK 54		0 123
RIVER SAMBRE	PK 53	**Jeumont** Frontier town. ⌂.	
	PK 52	≪ No 9 *Marpent*.	
	PK 48	*Boussois* ⌂.	
	PK 41.5	≪ No 8 *Maubeuge*.	
	PK 41.5	**Maubeuge** Fortified city, centre of industry ⌂.	12.5 110.5
	PK 35	≪ No 7 *Hautmont*.	

WATERWAY	PK ref	Town/village/≪lock	Total km	
			▼	▲
RIVER SAMBRE	PK 35	**Hautmont** ♨.	19	104
	PK 32	*Boussières* ♨.		
	PK 26	≪ No 6 *Quartes.*		
	PK 22	≪ No 5 *Pont sur Sambre.*		
	PK 21.5	*Pont sur Sambre* ♨.		
	PK 18	≪ No 4 *Berlaimont.*		
	PK 17.5	*Berlaimont* ♨.		
	PK 11	≪ No 3 *Sassegnies.*		
	PK 8	≪ No 2 *Hachette.*		
	PK 3	≪ No 1 *Étoquies.*		
Continues as **CANAL DE LA SAMBRE À L'OISE**	PK 0	**Landrecies** ♨.	54	69
	PK 0.5	≪ No 3 *Landrecies.*		
	PK 6	≪ No 2 *Ors.*		
	PK 8.5	*Câtillon sur Sambre* ♨.		
	PK 12	≪ No 1 *Bois l'Abbaye.*		
	PK 19	*Etreux* ⚐.		
	PK 19–27	≪ Nos 1–15.		
	PK 27	*Tupigny* ♨.		
	PK 28.5-32	≪ Nos 16–19.		
	PK 33	*Vadencourt* ♨.		
	PK 33.5–65	≪ Nos 20–35.	▼	▲
Continues as 3.8km La Fère branch of Canal de St-Quentin then RIGHT Canal de St-Quentin		**Fargniers**	123	0
		Direction north *Cambrai* and Escaut (Route 29)		
AHEAD Canal de St-Quentin		Direction Compiège & Paris (Route 29).		

Route 31

Canal de la Somme: *St-Valery-sur-Somme* ↔ *Péronne*

Maximum boat dimensions: *Height above waterline* **3.5m** *Draught* **1.8m**

Speed limit: 10km/h (5.4kn)

Locks: 21 (38.50m long x 5.10m wide) Maritime lock No 25 St-Valery operates HW -1 to HW +1. Remainder of locks operate May–Sept daily 0900–1230 & 1330–1800; Oct–April Mon–Fri by arrangement only. Weekends closed

Distance: 126km

After Gravelines, St-Valery-sur-Somme is the least used of the ports providing access to the waterways. There are two reasons for this reluctance to enter at St-Valery-sur-Somme (not to be confused with St-Valery-en-Caux, 40 miles along the coast towards Le Havre). The valleys around the Somme have been prone to flooding in the winter/spring months, and in recent years this has been so serious that several of the Somme canal locks have been out of commission for months at a time.

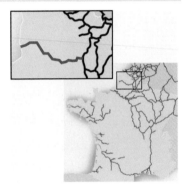

Repairs have now been completed and the lock keepers are back in business.

A glance at the coastal chart of these parts can also discourage boaters. It shows the Baie de Somme as a drying area of approximately 20 square miles, with sandbanks extending some way offshore. The *Navicarte* guide to the Somme includes a cautionary note about the bay: '*bancs de sable en déplacements constants (balisage entretenu)*' or sandbanks moving constantly (maintained buoyage).

Those boat owners familiar with the UK's east coast rivers such as the Blackwater or Orwell will be in familiar territory in the Baie de Somme and, given reasonable weather and prudent timing, the bay presents few difficulties. It is essential to locate the outer 'AT.SO' deep-water buoy. The first pair of red and green buoys (S1 and S2), marking the start of the drying channels through the sandbanks to St-Valery and Le Crotoy, are 1.7 miles to the south-east of 'AT.SO', and the distance from these outer channel buoys to the deep-water marina at St-Valery is about seven miles. The twisting channel is marked with 20 pairs of small red and green buoys.

Boats with limited power (10bhp) should aim to be at 'AT.SO' buoy 2 hours before HW to reach the marina before the ebb. Two or three days of fresh to strong onshore north-westerly to south-westerly winds build up a swell over the sandbanks, when you will have to give St-Valery a miss. Good visibility is also required.

Given reasonable conditions, St-Valery presents no great problems and the rewards are considerable for those who choose this one-time fishing harbour as their entry into the network of inland waterways. The marina is excellent with a friendly yacht club. Steeped in history, William the Conqueror departed from St-Valery for Hastings in 1066 and Joan of Arc was imprisoned here by the English en route for Rouen and her death at the stake.

These days it is a popular seaside town although apart from the marina and a dribble of water in the channel, the sea almost disappears over the horizon at low water. Med-bound yachts or those simply wanting to explore Picardy inland, have much of interest on the Grande Somme (120km with 19 locks) between St-Valery and Péronne where it becomes the Canal du Nord. To reach Péronne from Calais via the Liason Dunkerque-Escaut and then part of the Canal du Nord is a distance of 187km with 19 locks, and involves joining the endless stream of commercial traffic on these busy waterways.

On the Canal de la Somme, you can be underway for the best part of a day and not meet anyone else on the water. The first 14km pound is dead straight – a purpose-built canal to carry quite large ships up to Abbeville, passing through flat, featureless countryside. Once through Abbeville, the waterway becomes the Somme river, canalised between 1770 and 1843 to connect the industrial St-Quentin region with the sea.

The Somme countryside is predominantly flat with frequent glimpses of lakes through the trees and hedgerows as you motor by fields and woods. There are many villages with stopping places where, unlike the Liaison Dunkerque-Escaut and the Canal du Nord, you will not be troubled by the wash of passing barges. There are good quayside berths in Amiens, capital of the region. The Somme in Amiens feeds a network of miniature waterways spanned by iron bridges giving the place a Venetian feel. There are many reminders of WWI's Battle of the Somme, and farmers are still unearthing bayonets, helmets and shells. *Historial de la Grande Guerre* – a museum devoted to WW I – is located in the Château de Péronne.

At Péronne, a 20km stretch of the Canal du Nord with 2 locks, links the Grande Somme with the Petite Somme. Paris/Med-bound skippers in previous years could rejoin the Somme for the final 16km to Ham and St Simon to link up with the Canal de St-Quentin, but in 2005 the Petite Somme was closed and boats had to stay in the heavy traffic to the end of the Canal du Nord at Pont l'Evêque, which is a much more direct route to Paris.

WATERWAY	PK ref	Town/*village*/≪*lock*	Total km
			▼ ▲
BAIE DE SOMME		**St-Valery-sur-Somme**. Roman port. Guillaume de Normandie set sail from here with 400 ships transporting 30,000 soldiers to invade Britain in 1066. Fortified *Ville Haute* where the British imprisoned Joan of Arc. 16th century gateways – Porte de Nevers and Porte Guillaume give access to the old quarter. Tourist office in the old customs house overlooking Place Guillaume le Conquérant. Narrow-gauge steam railway carries tourists right round the bay from Cayeux-sur-Mer to Le Crotoy via St-Valery. 250-berth marina with 10-T crane.	
CANAL DE LA SOMME	PK 156	≪ No 25 *St-Valery* (maritime lock).	0 126
	PK 142	≪ No 24 *Abbeville*.	
	PK 141	**Abbeville** Capital of the Ponthieu region. Much of the town was destroyed in WWII. The centre has modern pedestrian ways and shopping precincts.15th century St-Vulfran Collégiale, and distinctive pink-bricked, turreted railway station survived. ⚓ 200m upriver of lock on port side. Near town centre and hypermarket.	15 111
	PK 131.5	≪ No 23 *Port Rémy*.	
	PK 130.5	*Port Rémy* 14th century château on island. ⚓.	
	PK 125	≪ No 22 *Long*.	
	PK 124.5	*Long* Sometimes dredged ⚓ through narrow cut to starboard. Showers at camp site. Pretty village with shops and restaurants.	
	PK 117.5	≪ No 21 *Labreilloire*.	
	PK 108	≪ No 20 *Piquigny*.	

St-Valery-sur-Somme. *Photo: David Jefferson*

WATERWAY	PK ref	Town/*village*/≪*lock*	Total km	
			▼	▲
CANAL DE LA SOMME	PK 108	*Piquigny* Remains of fortified castle.		
	PK 106	*'Samara'* – the old Gallic name for the Somme. Arboretum, botanical garden and village of re-constructed prehistoric dwellings occupying 30-hectare site and providing superbly presented glimpses into the origins of mankind. ♒ for those visiting Samara by boat.		
	PK 103	≪ No 19 *Ailly*.		
	PK 98	≪ No 18 *Montières*.		
	PK 95–92.5	**Amiens** Capital of Picardy. Gothic cathedral miraculously survived the heavy bombardment of the city in two world wars. Compact city centre is a pleasing mixture of modern architecture and faithful reconstruction. Network of miniature canals spanned by iron bridges. Quai Bélu in old	61	65

WATERWAY	PK ref	Town/*village*/≪*lock*	Total km	
			▼	▲
CANAL DE LA SOMME		St Leu quarter lined with restaurants. *Les Hortillonnages* are gardens among a maze of tiny waterways on land originally drained by the Romans to grow produce to feed the army. Port d'Aval, before lock No 17, is 15 minutes' walk from the city centre. The pontoon is perfectly adequate but lacks the ambience of the upstream city quay, being beside a lorry park and main road. The Port d'Amont quay, five minutes' from the cathedral, is upstream of lock 17 round the loop in the canal north of the city centre.		
	PK 94	≪ No 17 *Amiens*.		
	PK 84.5	≪ No 16 *Lamotte*.		
	PK 79.5	≪ No 15 *Daours*.		
	PK 75	**Corbie** ⚑. Cruiser hire.	81	45
	PK 74.5	≪ No 14 *Corbie*.		
	PK 65.5	≪ No 13 *Sailly*.		
	PK 58.5	≪ No 12 *Méricourt*.		
	PK 53	≪ No 11 *Froissy*.		
	PK 51	≪ No 10 *Cappy*.		
	PK 50	*Cappy* ⚑. Cruiser hire.		
	PK 45	≪ No 9 *Frise*.		
	PK 43.5	≪ No 8 *Frise*.		
	PK 39	≪ No 7 *Sormont*.		
Junction with **CANAL DU NORD**	PK 37/PK 45			
LEFT direction Douai				
AHEAD Péronne				
	PK 48	**Péronne** Town heavily fortified in 16th century. Some ramparts and the great Porte de Bretagne survived the near total	108	18

Amiens – Quai Bélu in old St-Leu quarter. *Photo: David Jefferson*

WATERWAY	PK ref	Town/*village*/≪*lock*	Total km	
			▼	▲
CANAL DU NORD		Great War destruction. Historial de la Grande Guerre, housed in the lakeside remains of the Château de Péronne, is a fascinating and moving museum devoted to the First World War. ⚲ is in a quiet backwater 3km beyond junction with Canal de la Somme. Showers at adjacent camp site. 20 minutes' walk into town centre. Check depth when approaching pontoons.		
	PK 49.5	≪ No 13 *Péronne*.		
	PK 60	≪ No 14 *Epénancourt*.	▼	▲
T-junction RIGHT Canal du Nord to Compiègne and l'Oise (Route 28)	PK 66/16		126	0
LEFT Petite Somme closed to navigation (2006)				

Bassin du Nord-Est

The canals in the Bassin du Nord-Est for the most part serve to link up the major waterways of France, Germany, Belgium and Luxembourg.

- Route 32, the Canal des Ardennes with Route 6 Canal latéral à l'Aisne & the canalised Aisne provide the east-west link between the Meuse, which serves Belgium, Holland and Germany, and the Oise which connects with the Seine and Paris.
- Routes 33 & 37, now called Canal de la Meuse and Canal des Vosges were previously known as the Northern and Southern branches of the Canal de l'Est. Combined, the two canals are 394km long and carry traffic from the Belgian border to the Saône and the Rhône.
- Route 34, the Moselle River is the north – south link between Luxembourg, Germany and the Rhine and the Saône/Rhône.
- Route 35, Canal de la Marne au Rhin, is the west – east link between Paris and Strasbourg/the Rhine.

Those boat owners who have reached Paris *en route* for the Mediterranean have the choice of several routes southwards. If the Marne route is chosen, then Route 36, Canal de la Marne à la Saône will take them to within a few kilometres of the canal junction at St-Jean-de-Losne. Those skippers, Med-bound having entered the waterways at Calais or Dunkerque, if they decide to give Paris a miss, leaving the capital well to the east, will head for Vitry-le-François and Route 36.

Canal de la Marne à la Saône. *Photo: CDT de la Marne*

Route 32

Canal des Ardennes: *Pont-à-Bar* ←→ *Vieux-lès-Asfeld*

Maximum boat dimensions: *Height above waterline* 3.5m *Draught* 1.8m

Speed limit: 8km/h (4.3kn)

Locks: 44 (38.50m long x 5.10m wide) Operate No 7 Meuse – No 1 Sauville (summit) & Nos 1–26 mid Mar–early Nov daily 0900–1900, mid June–mid Sept Mon–Sat 0700–1900, Sun 0900–1900, early Nov–mid Mar daily 0730–1730; No 27 Rilly-sur-Aisne April–Oct Mon–Fri 0700–1800, weekend 0700–1230 & 1330–1800, Nov–Mar 0730–1730; Nos 5 Attigny – 14 Vieux-lès-Asfeld April–Oct daily 0700–1800, Nov–Mar daily 0730–1730

Distance: 88km

Although the Canal des Ardennes is one of several canals providing a link between the Meuse and the Oise, it is not greatly used by commercial traffic but attracts pleasure boats in moderate numbers to the pleasant rural surroundings of forest and fields.

Entering the canal from the Meuse, the first 7 locks climbing 15m to the summit at Le Chesne are operated by hand-held electronic boxes which are handed out or handed back at lock No 1 when descending towards the Canal latéral à l'Aisne or, depending on which way you are travelling, lock No 50 Revin or No 35 Mouzon both on the Canal de la Meuse (the previously named Canal de l'Est – Branche Nord).

Beyond the summit at Le Chesne, motoring towards the Aisne canals, 37 locks achieve a drop of 100m. There are two staircases: Nos 1 – 13 and 14 – 26. These locks are automatically operated. When you leave one lock you break a light beam which sends an operating signal to the next lock. This may put you off from stopping somewhere between locks for lunch or a drink, but this is possible providing you contact the controller at lock 26 (tel 03 24 71 44 88).

WATERWAY	PK ref	Town/*village*/≪*lock*	Total km
			▼ ▲
Entry from River Meuse (Route 33) **CANAL DES ARDENNES**	PK 0	≪ No 7.	0 88
	PK 1	*Pont-à-Bar* ⚑. Fuel.	
	PK 1–17	≪ Nos 6–2.	
	PK 17	*La Cassine* ♨.	
	PK 20.5	≪ No 1 *Sauville.*	
Summit	PK 28.5	*Le Chesne* ♨.	
Receive/return at lock No 1 lock control box	PK 30–38.5	≪ Chain – nos 1–26 (26 locks in 8km).	
	PK 39	≪ No 27.	39 49
LEFT Embranchement de Vouziers (4 locks 12km)	PK 0	*Rilly* ♨.	
	PK 12	**Vouziers** ♨.	
CANAL DES ARDENNES		(Note PK and lock numbering adopted as continuation of Embranchement.)	
	PK 17	≪ No 5	
	PK 18	*Attigny* ♨ Fuel.	
	PK 20–33.5	≪ Nos 6–9.	
	PK 36.5	**Rethel** ⚑.	63.5 24.5
	PK 38.5–41	≪ Nos 10 & 11.	
	PK 46	*Château-Porcien* ♨.	
	PK 48–56	≪ Nos 12 & 13.	
	PK 58	*Asfeld* ♨.	▼ ▲
	PK 0	≪ No 14.	88 0
Continues as Canal latéral à l'Aisne (Route 6)	PK 0		

Route 33

Canal de la Meuse (previously known as Canal de l'Est Branche Nord): *Givet* ↔ *Troussey*

Maximum boat dimensions: *Height above waterline* **3.6m** *Draught* **1.8m**
Speed limits: in river **10km/h** **(5.4kn)** Canal bypasses **6km/h** **(3.2kn)**
Locks: **59** (min 38.50m long x 5.10m wide) Operate No 59 Les 4 Cheminées mid Mar–early Nov daily 0900–1900, early Nov–mid March daily 0730–1730; Nos 58–28 mid Mar–early Nov daily 0900–1900, mid June–mid Sept Mon–Sat 0700–1900, Sun 0900–1900, early Nov–mid Mar daily 0730–1730; Nos 27–1 Troussey June–Aug daily 0900–1900, Sept–May by arrangement
Distance: 272km

Over 900km long and rising in the Haute-Marne *département*, the Meuse extends in a northerly direction into Belgium and Holland where it divides – the northern arm branching off through Dordrecht and out into the North Sea.

Before reaching the Belgian border, the Ardennes mountainous countryside is spectacular with great forests dominating the views from the river. It is an area forever associated with World War I battles, and before these grim times this border territory was constantly being disputed.

WATERWAY	PK ref	Town/*village*/≪*lock*	Total km	
			▼	▲
Frontier with Belgium	PK 0		0	272
RIVER MEUSE	PK 1	≪ No 59 *Les 4 Cheminées.*		
	PK 4	**Givet** Fortified border town. ⋈.	4	268
	PK 7	≪ No 58.		
Tunnel (565m)	PK 7.5			

WATERWAY	PK ref	Town/*village*/≪*lock*	Total km
			▼ ▲
RIVER MEUSE	PK 8.5–13	≪ Nos 57 & 56.	
	PK 14	*Vieux-Wallerand* 🛏.	
	PK 17–22.5	≪ Nos 55 & 54.	
	PK 25	*Haybes* 🛏.	
	PK 25.5	≪ No 53.	
	PK 28	**Fumay** ⚑.	28 244
	PK 30.5–33	≪ Nos 52 & 51.	
	PK 39	**Revin** ⚑.	39 233
Collect/return control box for Ardennes locks	PK 39	≪ No 50 *Revin.*	
Tunnel (224m)	PK 39		
	PK 40.5–45.5	≪ Nos 49 & 48.	
	PK 48	*Les Dames de Meuse* 🛏.	
	PK 50	≪ No 47.	
	PK 49	*Laifour* 🛏.	
	PK 54	≪ Nos 46.	
	PK 63	*Bogny sur Meuse* 🛏.	
	PK 64	≪ No 45.	
	PK 70	*Joigny sur Meuse* 🛏.	
	PK 70–79	≪ Nos 44 & 43.	
Continues as **CANAL DE LA MEUSE**	PK 80	**Charleville Mézières** Fortified town ⚑. Cruiser hire.	80 192
	PK 81.5–84.5	≪ Nos 42 & 41.	
	PK 87	*Lumes* 🛏.	
	PK 95	≪ No 40.	
RIGHT Canal des Ardennes (Route 32)	PK 96.5		
	PK 100–107	≪ Nos 39, 38 & 37.	
	PK 108	**Sedan** Fortified town ⚑. Cruiser hire.	108 164

Bassin du Nord-Est: Canal de la Meuse

WATERWAY	PK ref	Town/*village*/≪*lock*	Total km	
			▼	▲
CANAL DE LA MEUSE	PK 113	≪ No 36.		
Collect/return control box for Ardennes locks	PK 122.5	≪ No 35 *Mouzon.*		
	PK 123	**Mouzon** ⌂.	123	149
	PK 131–142	≪ Nos 34, 33 & 32.		
	PK 149	**Stenay** Fortified town ⌂.	149	123
	PK 149–155.5	≪ Nos 31, 30 & 29.		
	PK 162	**Dun-sur-Meuse** ⌂. Cruiser hire.	162	110
	PK 162–173	≪ Nos 28–25.		
	PK179	*Consenvoye* ⚓.		
	PK 179–196	≪ Nos 24–20.		
	PK 202	**Belleville-sur-Meuse** ⚓.	202	70
	PK 203.5	**Verdun** Fortified town ⚓.	203.5	68.5
	PK 204–217	≪ nos 19–15.		
	PK 217	*Dieue* ⚓.		
	PK 223–226	≪ Nos 14 & 13.		
	PK 228	*Troyon* ⚓.		
	PK 231	*Lacroix sur Meuse* ⚓.		
	PK 231–234	≪ Nos 12 & 11.		
	PK 241	**St-Mihiel** ⚓. Showers at camp site.	241	31
	PK 241.5–248	≪ Nos 10, 9 & 8.		
	PK 252	*Sampigny* ⚓.		
	PK 255–266	≪ Nos 7, 6 & 5.		
	PK 266	*Euville* ⚓.		
	PK 270.5–272	≪ Nos 4–1.		
	PK 272	*Troussey.*	272	0
T-junction: Canal de Marne au Rhin (Route 35)	PK 272	LEFT direction Strasbourg. RIGHT direction Paris.		

Route 34

River Moselle: *Sierck-les-Bains* ↔ *Neuves-Maisons*

Maximum boat dimensions: *Height above waterline* 5.1m *Draught* 3m

Speed limits: Between Sierck les Bains and Metz **30km/h (16kn)** in canalised river; **12km/h (6.4kn)** in canal
Between Metz & PK 333 **15km/h (8kn)** in canalised river; **12km/h (6.4kn)** in canal
Between PK 333 & PK 349 **15km/h (8kn)** in canalised river; **6km/h (3.2kn)** in canal
Between PK349 & PK 394 (Neuves-Maisons) **12km/h (6.4kn)**

Locks: **16** (176m long x 12m wide) Operate between PK 243 & PK 283 daily 24/24; between PK 283 & PK 347 daily 0530–2330; between PK 347 & PK 394 mid April–early Nov Mon–Sat 0600–2000, Sun 0900–1900, early Nov–mid April daily 0730–1730

Distance: 151km

The Moselle river rises in the Vosges *département* flowing past Metz to the German/Luxembourg border where it forms a part of the frontier between these two countries. It meets up with the Rhine at Koblenz. Enlarged between Neuves-Maisons and its confluence with the Rhine, this busy section of the Moselle can take the largest barges.

Pleasure craft have not been overlooked as there are many stopping places where it is possible to moor up clear of the wash of passing traffic. Parts of the river are predominantly industrial, particularly around Neuves-Maisons and Metz which are centres for the steel industry. Other parts are attractively wooded but it is just over the German border that the scenery is particularly striking as the river enters this prestigious wine-producing region.

WATERWAY	PK ref	Town/*village*/≪*lock*	Total km	
			▼	▲
RIVER MOSELLE				
Luxembourg/ German frontier	PK 243	≪ *Apach.*	0	151
	PK 246	**Sierck-les-Bains** Much fought-over frontier town in beautiful surroundings. Dominated by 11th century castle from which there are fine views ⚲.	3	148
	PK 258	≪ *Koenigsmaker.*		
Canal bypass	PK 269	**Thionville** Industrial town. Once strongly fortified, town claimed by Luxembourg and Spain until finally occupied by the French in 1659 ⚑.	26	125
	PK 269.5	≪ (double) *Thionville.*		
End canal bypass	PK 273			
Canal bypass	PK 277			
	PK 277.5	≪ (double) *Richemont*		
	PK 283	≪ (double) *Talange.*		
	PK 283	**Hagondange** ⚲.	40	111
End canal bypass	PK 288			
LEFT Canal de Jouy (closed)	PK 294			
	PK 297	≪ (double) *Metz.*		
	PK 299	**Metz** Ancient Gallic town fortified by the Romans. Major administrative, commercial and cultural centre. St-Étienne Cathedral. Attractive old quarter ⚑. Cruiser hire.	56	95
	PK 302	**Scy Chazelles** 12th century church. Robert Schuman's house ⚑.	59	92
	PK 307	≪ *Ars sur Moselle.*		
LEFT Canal de Jouy (closed)	PK 308.5			
	PK 311	*Corny-sur-Moselle* ⚲. Camp site.		
Canal bypass	PK 317.5.			
	PK 318	≪ *Pagny-sur-Moselle.*		

216

WATERWAY	PK ref	Town/village/≪lock	Total km
			▼ ▲
RIVER MOSELLE	PK 318	*Pagny-sur-Moselle* ♨.	
End canal bypass	PK 326		
	PK 327& 328	**Pont-à-Mousson** Fortified town. Industrial and cultural centre. 18th century Abbey des Prémontrés ♨ (2).	85 66
Canal bypass	PK 331		
	PK 332	≪ *Blénod.*	
End canal bypass	PK 336		
Canal bypass	PK 339		
	PK 340	*Millery* ♨.	
End canal bypass	PK 341		
Canal bypass	PK 343		
	PK 344	≪ *Custines.*	
End canal bypass	PK 345		
LEFT Canal de la Marne au Rhin	PK 346.5	To Strasbourg (Route 35 – page 218).	
RIGHT **RIVER MOSELLE**	PK 347	*Pompey* ♨.	
	PK 347	≪ *Pompey.*	
	PK 354	*Liverdun* ♨.	
	PK 356	≪ *Aingeray.*	
	PK 364	≪ *Fontenoy.*	
RIGHT Canal de la Marne au Rhin (Route 35)	PK 369	**Toul** Fortified by Vauban. Tourist centre of Lorraine. Ancient ramparts and twin-towered cathedral. Wine cellar tours ⚑.	126 25
AHEAD **RIVER MOSELLE**	PK 371.5	≪ No 53 *Toul.*	
	PK 379.5	≪ *Villey-le-Sec.*	
	PK 387	*Maron* ♨.	
	PK 394	≪ *Neuves-Maisons.*	
	PK 394	**Neuves-Maison** Industrial town	151 0
Continues as Canal des Vosges		To Corre & Saône (Route 37).	

Part Canal de la Marne au Rhin: *Vitry-le-François* ←→ *Réchicourt*

Maximum boat dimensions: *Height above waterline* **3.6m** *Draught* **1.8m**
Speed limit: 6km/h (3.25kn)
Locks: 121 (38.50m long x 5.10m wide) Operate Nos 70 St-Étienne – 18 Longeaux: June–Aug daily 0900–1900, Sept–May by arrangement; Nos 17 Menaucourt – 1 Tombois (summit) & Nos 1 Mauvages – 27 Toul (summit) & Nos 26 Jarville-la-Malgrange – 2 Réchicourt: mid Mar–early Nov daily 0900–1900, mid June–mid Sept Mon–Sat 0700–1900, Sun 0900–1900, early Nov–mid Mar daily 0730–1730
Distance: 222km

This west-east waterway, over 300km long, connects the Seine basin with the Rhine. Starting at Vitry-le-François in the Champagne region, it crosses the Bassin du Nord-Est and enters the Bassin du Rhin where it terminates in the centre of Strasbourg. For the most part, the Marne au Rhin traverses the spectacular Alsace-Lorraine region, climbing to two summit levels – the first with a 4785m tunnel near Mauvages (passage through by tow in convoy) and the second with two tunnels (475m and 2307m) near the Vosges mountains.

There is another tunnel (867m) at Foug near Toul. These three tunnels are controlled by lights. The first 199km from Vitry-le-François to the summit at Réchicourt are detailed below. The continuation of Route 35 (Réchicourt to Strasbourg) is in the next section, Le Bassin du Rhin, (page 230).

WATERWAY	PK ref	Town/*village*/≪*lock*	Total km	
			▼	▲
Junction – Canal latéral à la Marne (Route 5), Canal de la Marne à la Saône (Route 36) & **CANAL DE LA MARNE AU RHIN**	PK 0	**Vitry-le-François** ⚐ (see page 105).	0	222
	PK 3–19	≪ Nos 70–64.		
	PK 19	*Pargny-sur-Saulx* ♆.		
	PK 19–41	≪ Nos 63–43.		
	PK 43	*Fains Veel* ♆.		
	PK 43–46	≪ Nos 42–39.		
	PK 47	**Bar-le-Duc** Principal town of Meuse *département*. Remains of castle in Ville Haute. ⚐.	47	175
	PK 48–62	≪ Nos 38–23.		
	PK 62	**Ligny en Barrois** ⚐.	62	160
	PK 63–84	≪ Nos 22–2		
	PK 85	*Demange aux Eaux* ♆.		
Summit	PK 85	≪ No 1 *Demange*.		
AHEAD Houdelaincourt (3km) end of spur navigation				
LEFT Mauvages tunnel (4,785m)	PK 86.5			
End of tunnel	PK 91.5			
	PK 94–102.5	≪ Nos 1–12.		
LEFT Canal de la Meuse (Route 33)	PK 111			
RIGHT **CANAL DE LA MARNE AU RHIN**				
	PK 116	*Pagny sur Meuse* ♆.		

Bassin du Nord-Est: Canal de la Marne au Rhin

WATERWAY	PK ref	Town/*village*/≪lock	Total km ▼	▲
CANAL DE LA MARNE AU RHIN	PK 120	*Lay St Rémy* ⨅.		
Foug tunnel (867m)	PK 120.5			
End of tunnel	PK 121.5			
	PK 122	≪ No 14 (double).		
	PK 122.5	*Foug* ⨅.		
	PK 123–129.5	≪ Nos 15–25.		
	PK 130	**Toul** (see page 217) ⚑.	130	92
	PK 130–131.5	≪ Nos 26, 27 & 27b.		
T-junction with Moselle				
RIGHT Épinal & alt route to Nancy				
LEFT direction Nancy	PK 369			
	PK 364–347	3 ≪ *Fontenoy, Aingeray, Pompey.*		
T-junction				
LEFT Moselle to Metz				
RIGHT **CANAL DE LA MARNE AU RHIN** direction Nancy & Strasbourg	PK 153.5	≪ *Clévant.*		
RIGHT	PK 154	≪ *de Jonction.*		
	PK 158	*Champigneulles* ⨅. Fuel.		
	PK 164	**Nancy** Principal town of Lorraine in the heart of an important industrial region. Old university town. Fine example of baroque town planning, much of which remains. Magnificent public squares, largest, Place Stanislas, surrounded by palaces. 16th century Ducal Palace. ⚑. Fuel.	164	58

WATERWAY	PK ref	Town/*village*/≪ lock	Total km
			▼ ▲
CANAL DE LA MARNE AU RHIN	PK 166	≪ Nos 26 (double).	
RIGHT Embranchement de Nancy (Canal de jonction) 10km 18 locks	PK 168	Alternative route between Toul & Nancy.	
	PK 168.5–172	≪ No 25 (double) & 24 (double).	
	PK 176	*Varangéville* ⚓.	
	PK 177	≪ No 23 (double).	
	PK 178	**Dombasle** Industrial town ⚓.	178 44
	PK 179	≪ No 22.	
	PK 181	*Sommerviller* ⚓.	
	PK 181–182.5	≪ Nos 21 & 20.	
	PK 183	*Crévic* ⚓.	
	PK 187–189.5	≪ Nos 19 & 18.	
	PK 191	*Einville-au-Jard* ⚓. Fuel.	
	PK 195–198.5	≪ Nos 17 & 16.	
	PK 200	*Parroy* ⚓.	
	PK 203	≪ No 15.	
	PK 205	*Xures* ⚓.	
	PK 206–208	≪ Nos 14 & 13.	
	PK 209	*Lagarde* ⚑ Cruiser hire.	
	PK 209.5–215	≪ Nos 12, 11 & 10.	
	PK 216	*Moussey* ⚓.	
	PK 217–219.5	≪ Nos 9, 8, & 7.	▼ ▲
Summit Route 35 to Strasbourg continues in Section 7 (page 230)	PK 222	≪ No 2 *Réchicourt*.	222 0

Route 36

Canal de la Marne à la Saône: *Vitry-le-François* ↔ *Maxilly-sur-Saône*

Maximum boat dimensions: *Height above waterline* 3.5m   *Draught* 1.8m

Speed limit: 6km/h (3.2kn)

Locks: 114 (38.50m long x 5.10m wide) Operate late Mar–early Nov Mon–Sat 0800–1200 & 1330–1800, Sun by arrangement only, early Nov–late Mar Mon–Sat by arrangement only

Distance: 224km

Those Med-bound boat owners who have opted for the Marne route down to the Saône may be wondering if they made the right choice when climbing the Marne à la Saône's 71 locks to the summit and source of the Marne and then descending 43 locks to meet up with the Saône a kilometre downstream of Maxilly. Comparison of the Bourbonnais route with the Marne route (both via Paris) will show that the overall number of locks is virtually identical, although the Bourbonnais route is 68km shorter. The alternative Bourgogne route has considerably more locks (see pages 5 and 122–3 for comparisons).

Those entering France at Dunkerque or Calais who have elected to keep well to the east of Paris and make for Reims will use the Canal de la Marne à la Saône which links the Champagne region with Burgundy (sometimes referred to as Le Canal entre Champagne et Bourgogne). The only towns near the water are St-Dizier and Chaumont, so it might be prudent to stock up and re-fuel at Vitry-le-François. Ports de Plaisance are at Orconte (PK 14), St-Dizier (PK 28), Viéville (PK 93), Chaumont (PK 110), Rolampont (PK 138) and Champigny les Langres (PK 148).

Most of the Marne à la Saône locks to the summit are worked by lock keepers, each operating a string of 4 or 5 or even more. In the drop down from the summit to the Saône, the first 22 locks are in 19km of canal, but all these locks have been mechanised, and as you leave one lock, the sequence to operate the next one is automatically tripped. There is still some commercial traffic on this waterway, but even with no delays passing through the locks and opening bridges (many automated), reckon on 50-60 hours to cover the entire canal, and bear in mind that the locks are rarely worked on Sundays.

WATERWAY	PK ref	Town/*village*/≪*lock*	Total km	
			▼	▲
T-junction Canal latéral à la Marne (Route 5) Canal de la Marne au Rhin (Route 35)				
CANAL DE LA MARNE À LA SAÔNE	PK 0	**Vitry-le-François** ♒. (see page 105).	0	224
	PK 1–9	≪ Nos 71, 70, 69 & 68.		
	PK 9	*Écriennes* ♒.		
	PK 11–13.5	≪ Nos 67 & 66.		
	PK 13.5	*Orconte* ⚑.		
	PK 15–26.5	≪ Nos 65, 64, 63, 62, 61 & 60.		
	PK 28	**St-Dizier** Once fortified town, now industrial. ⚑ just before lock.	28	196
	PK 28	≪ No 59.		
	PK 30–46	≪ Nos 58, 57, 56, 55, 54, 53,& 52.		
	PK 46	*Bayard* ♒. Shops.		
	PK 48–57	≪ Nos 51, 50, 49, 48 & 47.		
	PK 57	*Autigny le Grand* ♒.		
	PK 59–61.5	≪ Nos 46 & 45.		
	PK 63	*Joinville* ♒. Shops.		
	PK 63.5–70.5	≪ Nos 44, 43, 42 & 41.		
	PK 72	*Donjeux* ♒. Shops.		
	PK 73–84	≪ Nos 40, 39, 38, 37 & 36.		
	PK 84.5	*Froncles* ♒. Shops.		
	PK 87–91.5	≪ Nos 35, 34 & 33.		

Bassin du Nord-Est: Canal de la Marne à la Saône

WATERWAY	PK ref	Town/*village*/≪lock	Total km	
			▼	▲
CANAL DE	PK 93	*Viéville* ⚑.		
LA MARNE À	PK 94.5–109	≪ Nos 32, 31, 30, 29, 28, 27, 26 & 25.		
LA SAÔNE	PK 109.5	**Chaumont** Capital of Haute-Marne *departément*. Medieval town with castle remains and magnificent viaduct ⚑. Cruiser hire.	109.5	114.5
	PK 110.5–123	≪ Nos 24, 23, 22, 21, 20, 19, 18 & 17.		
	PK 124	*Foulain* ♨.		
	PK 126–36	≪ Nos 16, 15, 14, 13, 12, 11 & 10.		
	PK 139	*Rolampont* ⚑. Shops.		
	PK 139–148	≪ Nos 9, 8, 7, 6, 5, 4 & 3.		
	PK 149	*Champigny les Langres* ⚑.		
	PK 150	≪ No 2.		
Summit	PK 152.5	≪ No 1 *Batailles*.		
Tunnel (4820m)	PK 155			
End of tunnel	PK 160			
New numbering for Saône direction locks	PK 162–168.5	≪ Nos 1, 2, 3, 4, 5, 6, 7, 8, 9, 10 & 11.		
	PK 169.5	*Piépape* ♨.		
	PK 169.5–210.5	≪ Nos 12 to 39 inclusive.		
	PK 214.5	*Renève* ♨.		
	PK 217.5–223	≪ Nos 40, 41, 42 & 43.	▼	▲
	PK 222.5	*Maxilly-sur-Saône* ♨.	224	0

T junction:
Petite Saône
(Route 13)
LEFT direction
Corre
RIGHT direction
St-Jean-de-Losne

Route 37

Canal des Vosges (previously known as Canal de l'Est Branche Sud): *Neuves-Maisons ↔ Corre*

Maximum boat dimensions: *Height above waterline* 3.6m   *Draught* 1.8m

Speed limit: 6km/h (3.2kn)

Locks: **93** (38.50m long x 5.10m wide) Nos 47–16 (Moselle side) & Nos 3–28 (Saône side) are manual locks with mobile lock keepers; operate mid Mar–early Nov by arrangement only, June–Aug daily 0900–1900, early Nov–Feb by arrangement only. Nos 15–2 (Moselle side) & Nos 29–46 (Saône side) automatic (control box); operate mid Mar–early Nov daily 0900-1900, mid June–mid Sept Mon–Sat 0700-1900, Sun 0900–1900, early Nov–mid Mar daily 0730–1730

Distance: 122km

Linking the Moselle and the Benelux countries with the Saône, Rhône and Mediterranean, this canal is now named after the *département* through which it flows. The man-made canal runs alongside the Moselle river, climbing up to Épinal, and then passes through the dense forests of the Vosges.

Bassin du Nord-Est: Canal des Vosges

WATERWAY	PK ref	Town/*village*/≪*lock*	Total km	
			▼	▲
From canalised Moselle (Route 33)		≪ *Neuves-Maisons.*		
CANAL DES VOSGES	PK 25	**Neuves-Maisons** Industrial town.	0	122
	PK 26-28	≪ Nos 47 & 46.		
Embranchement de Nancy (Route 34) 10km 18 locks page 221	PK 28.5			
	PK 30	*Richardménil* ♒.		
	PK 31.5-60	≪ Nos 45-31.		
	PK 60	**Charmes** Many reminders of religious and military heritage ⚑.	35	87
	PK 61-71	≪ Nos 30-25.		
	PK 71	*Nomexy* ♒.		
	PK 72-77.5	≪ Nos 24-20.		
	PK 78	**Thaon les Vosges** ♒.	53	69
	PK 78.5-83	≪ Nos 19-15.		
LEFT Embranchement d'Épinal (3350m)	PK 83.5			
		Épinal Once noted for cotton weaving and lacemaking. Fine park on Castle Hill. St Maurice Basilique (13th century) ⚑.	58.5	63.5
	PK 83.5-86.5	≪ Nos 14-1.		
	PK 97	≪ No 1.		
	PK 97	*Girancourt* ♒.		
	PK 98-108.5	≪ Nos 2-18.		
	PK 109	*Forges d'Uzemain* ♒.		
	PK 109-113	≪ Nos 19-23.		
	PK 113	*Thunimont* ♒.		
	PK 114	≪ No 24.		
	PK 115	*Harsault* ♒.		
	PK 115.5-118	≪ Nos 25-28.		

WATERWAY	PK ref	Town/*village*/≪*lock*	Total km
			▼ ▲
CANAL DES	PK 119	*Hautmougey* ⚓.	
VOSGES	PK 119.5–125	≪ Nos 29–34.	
	PK 125	**Fontenoy-le-Château** Mediaeval town, once fortified ⚓. Cruiser Hire.	100 22
	PK 126–134	≪ Nos 35–39.	
	PK 134	*Pont du Bois* ⚓.	
	PK 136–136.5	≪ Nos 40 & 41.	
	PK 137	*Selles* ⚓.	
	PK 139	≪ No 42.	
	PK 141	*Passavant* ⚓.	
	PK 143–146	≪ Nos 43, 44 & 45.	
	PK 147	*Corre* ⚓.	
	PK 147	≪ No 46.	122 0

Continues as
Petite Saône
(Route 13)

Fontenoy-le-Chateâu. *Photo: Crown Blue Line*

Le Bassin du Rhin

The Rhine basin consists of that part of the Rhine forming a frontier between France and Germany (Route 40). At the southern end of this river border, the waterway becomes the Grand Canal d'Alsace as the great river sweeps off towards Basel/Bâle and Switzerland. Beyond the northern end of the frontier, the Rhine extends right into the heart of Germany. The river still carries a huge tonnage of barge traffic, and hire cruisers are not permitted on the Rhine or the Grand Canal d'Alsace.

Also within the Rhine basin is the northern branch of the Canal du Rhône au Rhin which feeds into Strasbourg (Route 39). Years ago, craft could navigate along the entire length of the Rhône au Rhin canal between Strasbourg and the Saône, avoiding the fast-flowing Rhine altogether, but the 70km section between Rhinau and Mulhouse has been closed for many years and, travelling south, the southern branch of the Rhône au Rhin canal can only be accessed from the Rhine at Niffer. (Route 14).

The basin also includes 91km of the Canal de la Marne au Rhin (part Route 35) between the second summit at Réchicourt and Strasbourg. This east-west canal system links Paris with the Rhine basin.

Canal de la Marne au Rhin near Saverne. *Photo: Crown Blue Line*

Extending northwards from this second summit of the Marne au Rhin at Réchicourt is the Canal de la Sarre (Houillères, meaning coalfields, having been dropped from the original name of the canal with the decline in the industry). This route (38) extends over the border into Germany and, bordered by lakes, is being developed for pleasure use.

Route 35 (part)

Part Canal de la Marne au Rhin: *Réchicourt ↔ Strasbourg*

Maximum boat dimensions: *Height above waterline* **3.6m** *Draught* **1.8m**
Speed limit: 8km/h (4.3kn)
Locks: 33 (38.50m long x 5.10m wide) Operate: No 2 Réchicourt mid Mar–early Nov daily 0900–1900, mid June–mid Sept Mon–Sat 0700–1900, Sun 0900–1900, early Nov–mid Mar daily 0730–1730; Nos 18 Henridorf – 51 Schiltgheim mid Mar–early Nov Mon–Sat 0700–1900, Sun 0900–1900, mid June–mid Sept daily 0700–1900, early Nov–mid Mar by arrangement only
Distance: 91km

This eastern end of the Canal de la Marne au Rhin (see page 218) between the second summit reached at lock No 2 Réchicourt and Strasbourg is more appropriately included in Section 7 Le bassin du Rhin. Although a relatively short length of canal within the administration of the bassin Rhin, they can claim to have some of the most interesting parts of the Marne au Rhin canal.

The Alsace countryside is delightful with picture-postcard villages, the elegant town of Saverne and, of course, the grand city of Strasbourg. Add to this the amazing working boat lift at St-Louis–Arzviller which raises/lowers boats 45m in 4 minutes, replacing the adjacent staircase of 17 locks which could take a whole day to negotiate, and you can understand why the main cruiser hire operators on this canal base their craft at this eastern end.

WATERWAY	PK ref	Town/*village*/≪*lock*	Total km	
			▼	▲
Continued from Section 6 page 221 **CANAL DE LA MARNE AU RHIN**				
Summit	PK 222	≪ No 2 *Réchicourt.*	0	91
LEFT Canal de la Sarre 76km 30 locks (Route 38)	PK 227.5			
	PK 236	*Xouaxange* ♒.		
	PK 240.5	*Hesse* ⌷ Fuel.		
	PK 245.5	*Niderviller* ♒.		
Niderviller tunnel (475m) traffic lights	PK 248			
End of tunnel	PK 248.5			
Arzviller tunnel (2306m) traffic lights	PK 249.5			
End of tunnel	PK 251.5			
St-Louis– Arzviller boat lift (see page 230)	PK 255			

The inclined plane, St-Louis–Arzviller.
Photo: Crown Blue Line

WATERWAY	PK ref	Town/*village*/≪*lock*	Total km	
	PK 256–258.5	≪ Nos 18, 19, 20 & 21.		
	PK 259	**Lutzelbourg** ⌷ (Port du Milieu).		
	PK 259	≪ No 22.		
	PK 259	**Lutzelbourg** ⌷ (Port du Bas).	37	54
	PK 260–268.5	≪ Nos 23, 24, 25, 26, 27, 28, 29 & 30/31.		
	PK 269	**Saverne** ⌷ opposite magnificent Château des Rohan.	47	44
	PK 270–283.5	≪ Nos 32–41.		
	PK 286	**Hochfelden** ♒.	64	27
	PK 288–289	≪ Nos 42 & 43.		
	PK 291	*Waltenheim* ♒.		

Le Bassin du Rhin: Canal de la Marne au Rhin

Picturesque Lutzelbourg on Canal de la Marne au Rhin. *Photo: Crown Blue Line*

WATERWAY	PK ref	Town/*village*/≪ lock	Total km	
			▼	▲
CANAL DE LA	PK 291–305.5	≪ Nos 44–49.		
MARNE AU	PK 307	**Souffelweyersheim** ⌂.	85	6
RHIN	PK 307–310.5	≪ Nos 50 & 51.		
RIGHT (after lock No 51) River l'Aar (no entry)				
RIGHT River L'Ill (no entry)	PK 311.5		▼	▲
AHEAD locks/ *avant port*/Rhine (no entry into lock/Rhine)	PK 313	**Strasbourg** Capital of Alsace region. Famous cathedral and university. Palais de l'Europe housing the European Council.	9	0
RIGHT		Bassin des Remparts.		
RIGHT		Bassin Dusuzeau, Bassin d'Austerlitz & Bassin de l'Hôpital (⚓).		
LEFT Canal du Rhône au Rhin – Nord branch (Route 39)				

Route 38

Canal de la Sarre: *Gondrexange ←→ Sarreguemines and Saarbrüken (Germany)*

Maximum boat dimensions: *Height above waterline* 3.7m   *Draught* 1.8m

Speed limit: 8km/h (4.3kn)

Locks: 30 (38.50m long x 5.20m wide) Operate: Nos 1–15 mid Mar–early Nov by arrangement only; Nos 16–26 & 28–30 mid Mar–early Nov daily 0900–1900; No 27 mid Mar–early Nov daily 0900–1200 & 1300–1900; early Nov–mid Mar by arrangement only

Distance: 76km to frontier

One of just three waterways crossing the French/German border (the other two being the Rhine and the Moselle), the Sarre canal was built to transport coal by water. Originally called the Canal des Houillières de la Sarre or Canal of the coalmines of the Sarre, Houillières has disappeared from the name of the waterway with the decline in the Alsace coal mining industry, leaving much of the French end of the Sarre to a moderate number of pleasure craft.

The facilities for boats along the canal are good, but you will need to give a day's notice of your cruising plans to pass through the first 15 locks, which reflects the modest use of the canal. You will be accompanied by a travelling lock keeper on this section. The next 15 locks are worked automatically with an allocated press-button control box.

Maybe the Sarre will become more popular. At the Marne au Rhin end, the canal is flanked by large lakes and then it cuts through acres of forest. The last 10km beyond Sarreguemines is canalised river which represents the French/German border. Five kilometres beyond the frontier, the old German town of Saarbrücken has an excellent Port de Plaisance where Connoisseur Holidays Afloat have set up a charter base.

The Saar (the name of the river in Germany) has been developed in recent years to take substantial barges which can now reach the Moselle from Saarbrücken.

Le Bassin du Rhin: Canal de la Sarre

WATERWAY	PK ref	Town/*village*/≪*lock*	Total km	
			▼	▲
T-junction with Canal de la Marne au Rhin	PK 0	*Gondrexange* (on the Canal de la Marne au Rhin). Nearby *Gondrexange* lake with bathing beach.	0	76
CANAL DE LA SARRE	PK 2	*Houillon* ⚓ Fuel.		
	PK 5.5–19.5	≪ Nos 1–13.		
LEFT Canal des Salines (closed)	PK 20	*Mittersheim* Another lake, used for watersports ♒.		
RIGHT **CANAL DE LA SARRE**				
	PK 20–33	≪ Nos 14–17		
	PK 33	*Harskirchen* ♒.		
	PK 33.5–45.5	≪ Nos 18–21		
	PK 51.5	*Wittring* ♒.		
	PK 51.5–63.5	≪ Nos 22–27		
	PK 64	**Sarreguemines** Border town famous for its pottery, with a museum devoted to ceramics. ⚓ Fuel.	64	12
	PK 65–72.5	≪ Nos 28, 29 & 30		
CANALISED RIVER SARRE	PK 65–76			
Frontier	PK 76			
Canalised River Saar for 5km			▼	▲
		Saarbrücken (Germany) ⚓. Cruiser hire.	76	0

Route 39

Canal du Rhône au Rhin (Branche Nord):
Strasbourg ↔ Rhinau

Maximum boat dimensions: *Height above waterline* **3.65m**   *Draught* **2.2m**
Speed limit: 8km/h (4.3kn)
Locks: **13** (min 38.50m long x 5.10m wide) Operate: Nos 86–79 mid Mar–early Nov daily
   0800–1900, early Nov–mid Mar by arrangement only; Nos 78, 77, 76 & Rhinau mid
   Mar–early Nov daily 0900-1800, early Nov–mid Mar by arrangement only
Distance: 36km

This short length of canal, running parallel with the Rhine from Strasbourg for 30km, is primarily used by charter boats. These craft are not permitted to enter the Rhine either at Strasbourg or at the southern end of the navigable section of this northern branch of the Canal du Rhône au Rhin. Privately owned craft can use this canal and enter the Rhine through the lock just below Rhinau to continue a passage south. There are plans to open up the abandoned section between the north and south branches of the canal. In the meantime, this northern section can be covered in about 6 hours.

WATERWAY	PK ref	Town/*village*/≪*lock*	Total km	
			▼	▲
	PK0	**Strasbourg** (see page 232).	0	35.5
Canal de jonction	PK 0.5	≪ No 86.		
	PK 1	**Strasbourg** Bassin de l'Hôpital ⚓ & yacht club.	1	34.5
LEFT **CANAL DU RHÔNE AU RHIN** (Branche Nord)	PK 2	≪ No 85.		
	PK 4.5	≪ No 84.		

Le Bassin du Rhin: Canal du Rhône au Rhin (Branche Nord)

WATERWAY	PK ref	Town/*village*/≪ *lock*	Total km	
			▼	▲
CANAL DU	PK 8.5	≪ No 83.		
RHÔNE AU RHIN	PK 11.5	≪ No 82.		
(Branche Nord)	PK 15	≪ No 81.		
	PK 18	*Krafft* ⌂.		
	PK 19.5	≪ No 79.		
	PK 22.5	≪ No 78.		
	PK 25	≪ No 77.		
	PK 28.5	*Boofzheim* ⚑. Cruiser hire.		
AHEAD canal				
under restoration	PK 28.5	≪ No 76.	▼	▲
LEFT Branch to	PK 31.5		31.5	0
lock *Rhin* (3.5km)		≪ *Rhin* VHF Ch 18.		
Access to Rhine				
(except for hired				
cruisers)				

Strasbourg. *Photo: Crown Blue Line*

Route 40

Rhine and Grand Canal d'Alsace: *Lauterbourg* ←→ *Basel/Bâle*

Maximum boat dimensions: *Height above waterline* **6.7m** *Draught* **2.1m**
Speed limit: **20km/h** (**10.8kn**) when river in flood, otherwise no limit
Locks: **10** (min 185m long x 12m wide) Operate all year 24/24
Distance: 184km

The Rhine is one of the great rivers of Europe, flowing through Switzerland, Germany and Holland. It connects with the Mediterranean via the Canal du Rhône au Rhin and there are waterway connections with the North Sea and the Black Sea. It forms part of the frontier between France and Germany and then, at the southern end, sweeps off to Basel/Bâle and its source in the heart of Switzerland.

This guide is only concerned with that part of the great river forming a natural border between France and Switzerland. It is primarily of interest to those boat owners passage-making from Germany to the Mediterranean – the other options being the canalised Saar River (Route 38) or the Moselle River (Route 34). Hire cruisers are not permitted on the Rhine which carries considerable commercial traffic ranging from barges to cruise ships and coasters.

Over the years, considerable work has been carried out on the Rhine either side of Strasbourg, leaving a general impression of a well-maintained motorway for waterbourne commercial traffic. The river has not been developed for pleasure boats so there are few places to stop. It will be prudent to plan the night stopover well in advance; failure to make one of the recognised *ports de plaisance* by night-fall will mean an uncomfortable berth where there will be no escaping the wash of passing traffic which continues all through the night.

Le Bassin du Rhin: Rhine and Grand Canal d'Alsace

WATERWAY	PK ref	Town/*village*/≪ *lock*	Total km	
			▼	▲
From Germany	PK 354	Customs post.	0	184
RHINE	PK 349	**Lauterbourg.**	5	179
	PK 335.5	**Beinheim** 3 ⚑.	18.5	165.5
	PK 334	≪ *Iffezheim* VHF Ch 18.		
	PK 313.5	**Offendorf** 4 ⚑.	40.5	143.5
	PK 309	≪ *Gambsheim* VHF Ch 20.		
	PK 295.5	Northern entrance to **Strasbourg** (see page 232).	58.5	125.5
	PK 291.5	Southern entrance to **Strasbourg**.	62.5	121.5
Access to Canal de la Marne au Rhin (Route 35) and Canal du Rhône au Rhin (Branche Nord) (Route 39)				
	PK 287.5	≪ *Strasbourg* VHF Ch 22.		
	PK 272	≪ *Gerstheim* VHF Ch 20.		
RIGHT Canal du Rhône au Rhin (Branche Nord) (Route 39)	PK 258			
	PK 256	≪ *Rhinau* VHF Ch 22.		
	PK 240	≪ *Marckolsheim* VHF Ch 20.		
RIGHT Canal de Colmar (23km 3 locks)	PK 226.5	**Colmar** (23km) Interesting medieval city. Capital of Alsace. ⚑.		
Continues as **GRAND CANAL D'ALSACE (RHEIN-SEITENKANAL)**	PK 226.5			
	PK 226	*Breisach* German commercial harbour.		
	PK 225.5	*Biesheim* ⚑ de Ile du Rhin near large camp site and activities centre.		

Colmar's 'little Venice'.
Photo: CRTA/Harrang

WATERWAY	PK ref	Town/*village*/≪ *lock*	Total km	
			▼	▲
GRAND CANAL D'ALSACE (RHEIN-SEITENKANAL	PK 224.5	≪ Vogelgrun VHF Ch 22.		
	PK 210.5	≪ Fessenheim VHF Ch 20.		
	PK 193.5	≪ Ottmarsheim VHF Ch 22.		
RIGHT Canal du Rhône au Rhin (Branche Sud) (Route 14)	PK 185.5			
	PK 179	≪ *Kembs* VHF Ch 20.		
Crosses Swiss frontier to			▼	▲
Basel/Bâle	PK 170		184	0

Brittany and Pays-de-la-Loire

The Canals of Brittany

Pays-de-la-Loire

The Brittany Canals

These waterways provide an interesting inland route between the English Channel and the Bay of Biscay, avoiding what, for small to medium length boats (8-10m), might be too much of a slog by sea round the outside of Finistère. Yachts and motor boats from the Channel Islands and from Normandy and the North Brittany harbours (having draughts not exceeding 1.2m and height above waterline less than 2.5m) make good use of these waterways to reach the popular cruising ground off the west coast of Brittany. Unlike many of those making for the Med via the waterways, owners of sailing craft mostly take their lowered masts with them, reckoning on fewer scrapes and hazards *en route* along the more tranquil Brittany canals with hardly any commercial traffic and no strong currents or *mistral* that may well be encountered on the more exposed and broader waters of the Rhône.

Route 41 covers this waterway link between the Manche and the Atlantique. Both ends of Route 41 (St-Malo to Dinan: 26km and the Arzal barrage to Redon: 42km) and Brest to Châteaulin: 51km (Route 43) are available to boats with masts raised and quite deep draughts, providing opportunities for interesting Brittany excursions inland for seagoing craft.

The Nantes à Brest Canal (Routes 42 & 45 north and south of Redon) is little used by pleasure craft except for chartered cruisers around Pontivy. Finally Route 44, the Brest end of the Nantes à Brest Canal was re-opened in 2005 and is now navigable by shallow-draught boats for 81km from Châteaulin to Goariva. A boat hire operator is established at Châteauneuf-du-Faou, and the re-opening of this somewhat remote waterway may tempt more visitors gaining access from the Rade de Brest.

Navigation of the total length of the Nantes à Brest canal ceased in 1920 with the building of the hydro-electric barrage at Guerlédan, resulting in the permanent closure of 50km of the canal and barred through navigation between Pontivy and Goariva.

Pays-de-la-Loire

The estuary of the Loire attracts a few sea-going craft, joining the merchant ships that still ply between St-Nazaire and Nantes. Between Nantes and the Maine river (providing access to the Mayenne and Sarthe rivers), Loire navigation is difficult with sandbanks and strong currents. Local boats and charter fleets, based on the more tranquil rivers, are the main users of the Mayenne and Sarthe.

Route 41

Liaison Manche-Océan: *St-Malo ↔ La Roche-Bernard/ Arzal barrage*

Waterway		Distance	Locks
Rance Maritime/Ille-et-Rance Canal	St-Malo ↔ Dinan*	26km	2
Ille-et-Rance canal	Dinan ↔ Rennes	79km	47
Canalised Vilaine	Rennes ↔ Redon	89km	12
Vilaine	Redon ↔ Arzal barrage*	42km	1

no air draught restrictions for pleasure craft

Rance Maritime/Ille-et-Rance Canal: *St-Malo ↔ Dinan*

Maximum boat dimensions:
Height above waterline N/A (18.9m) *Draught* 1.6m

Speed limit: 8-10 km/h (4.3-5.4kn) in canalised river above Châtelier lock

Locks: 2 Usine Maremotrice (barrage) lock operates when there is 4m of water outside (all hours except 2 hours either side of low water at springs). On the hour for incoming craft and 20 minutes before the hour for outgoing craft. Downstream traffic – boats without masts enter lock first. Upstream traffic – boats without masts enter lock last.

In 2005, because of the considerable delay to road traffic when the road bridge across the barrage lock was being operated, experimentally the authorities ceased the openings at 1200, 1400, 1700 and 1900 during July and August.

Châtelier lock is worked over the period when the water level between the lock and the barrage is being maintained at 8.5m or more above chart datum (see below).

Distance: 26km

The passage upriver from St-Malo (or the Bas-de-Sablons Marina at St-Servan) to the mediaeval town of Dinan presents no great navigational problems, but it is essential to have an indication of EDF's time-table for operating the generators in the barrage. This will determine the artificially maintained depth in the 16.5km stretch of water between the barrage lock and the Châtelier lock which is the beginning of the Ille-et-Rance canal.

At the barrage, the great tides of the Rance are harnessed to produce hydro-electric power – the first generating station of its kind in the world. Above the barrage, the rise and fall of the river is still the same range as the sea on the other side, but the changes are achieved mechanically, in accordance with a timetable published by Electricité de France (EDF).

On most days, EDF guarantee that, between 0700 and 2100, 4m above chart datum will be maintained between the barrage and Châtelier lock. For around four hours each day between 0800 and 2000, there will be a guaranteed 8.5m. This four hour period is when Châtelier lock operates. EDF timetables are available from the *Capitaineries* in St-Malo's Bassin Vauban or at Port des Sablons, St-Servan, or you can 'phone 02 99 16 37 33 for a recorded two-day timetable in English. The information is also published in *France Ouest*.

Masts can be lowered at St-Malo (Bassin Vauban) using the self-operated 1-ton crane, at the St-Servan or Dinard marinas or at Dinan where there is a smaller crane (500kg). Fuelling is available at Port des Sablons or Dinard (3 hours either side of high water). There is no alongside fuelling in St-Malo's Bassin Vauban.

Extensive prohibited areas, marked with red buoys linked with wire ropes, are either side of the barrage. Beyond the barrage, the channel is well marked with a minimum of 2m to St-Suliac, three miles upstream, where there are visitors' buoys. When the level is being maintained at 8.5m, the Rance is a vast expanse of water bordered by fields and trees, but between St-Suliac and the Châtelier lock much of the Rance drains away outside the 8.5m maintained period. There is a well defined channel between St-Suliac and the Châtelier lock.

Once through the Châtelier lock, your boat will be in the Ille-et-Rance Canal, but still with no height above waterline restrictions up to Dinan, (another 6km) and, providing the helmsman stays in the middle of the channel (between black and white starboard-hand posts and brown port-hand posts), boats drawing up to 1.6m can reach the town quay, although after long periods of no rainfall a telephone call to the harbourmaster at Dinan (tel: 02 96 39 56 44) or the Châtelier lock keeper (tel: 02 96 39 55 66) might be prudent if the boat's draught is right on the limit.

Bassin Vauban St-Malo. *Photo: David Jefferson*

WATERWAY	PK ref	Town/*village*/≪*lock*	Total km
			▼ ▲
RANCE	PK 0	**St-Malo** Old town originally built on a small island of granite rock. Ramparts encircling the island are still intact. Almost everything inside the walls was flattened in WWII, but faithfully reconstructed retaining much of its original character. ⊃ in Bassin Vauban. Nearby beach, casino and yacht club. Convenient for crew changes with Brittany Ferries operating between Portsmouth and St-Malo. *Vedettes* to Dinard and Dinan. 2-mile walk round the top of the ramparts.	0 236.5
Barrage	PK 3	≪ *Usine Maremotrice* VHF Ch 13. See above for lock operating times.	3 233.5
	PK 15	*Plouër-sur-Rance* ⊃ with all boatyard services and 10 places for visitors. Right out in the countryside. Entry over sill when 8.5m being maintained (see above). Village 3.5km. Nearby farm shop and restaurant.	15 221.5

WATERWAY	PK ref	Town/*village*/≪*lock*	Total km
			▼ ▲
RANCE	PK 20	≪ *Châtelier* VHF Ch 14 Tel: 02 96 39 55 66. See above for lock operating times.	20 216.5
	PK 20/85	*Port du Lyvet* ⊨ . Restaurant. Cruiser hire.	20 216.5
			▼ ▲
	PK 79	**Dinan** Ancient walled town always packed with tourists. Extensive pontoons alongside town quay. Shopping centre through Porte du Jeruzal and then long climb up Rue du Jeruzal lined with leaning old houses mostly occupied by galleries and craft centres. ⊨ . Showers in *Capitainerie*. Cruiser hire.	26 210.5

Dinan. *Photo: David Jefferson*

Route 41 continued

Ille-et-Rance Canal: *Dinan* ↔ *Rennes*

Maximum boat dimension: *Height above waterline* 2.5m   *Draught* 1.2m

Speed limit: 8-10km/h (4.3-5.4kn)

Locks: 47 (27.10m long x 4.70m wide) Operate April–Oct 0900–1200 & 1400–1900. Closed Nov–Mar

Distance: 79km

Between Dinan and the summit at Sègerie lock is a magnificent gorge and three small towns: Évran, St-Domineuc and Tinténiac. Beyond Tinténiac is the final climb to the summit through Les Onze Écluses, a stairway of 11 locks, 9 of which are within a stretch of 200m.

The drop down from the summit into Rennes passes more pleasant villages, through unspoilt farming country. You can motor for the whole day and not meet another soul on the waterway, apart from a few fishermen on the bank. During the holiday season, when there will be more river traffic and, if the water level is low, the lock keepers may attempt to preserve water by waiting for two or three boats to assemble outside a lock before letting them through. This can make the pace through the Brittany canals even more leisurely.

Rennes comes as a contrast to the rest of the waterways, being the capital of the region and a centre of industry. The Ille-et-Rance Canal terminates at a T-junction in the city centre. To the right is the start of the navigable Vilaine canalised river. To the left the Vilaine enters a little-used tunnel beneath a car park, and navigation ceases a little beyond the tunnel exit.

WATERWAY	PK ref	Town/*village*/≪*lock*	Total km
			▼ ▲
ILLE-ET-RANCE	PK 79	**Dinan** (see page 245).	26 210.5
CANAL	PK 77–66.5	≪ Nos 47, 46, 45, 44, 43 & 42.	
	PK 66.5	**Évran** 𝕽.	38.5 198
	PK 62.5	≪ No 41.	
	PK 61.5	*Trévérien* 𝕽.	
	PK 61–60.5	≪ Nos 40 & 39.	
	PK 57.5	**St-Domineuc** 𝕽.	47.5 189
	PK 56.5–48.5	≪ Nos 38, 37, 36, 35 & 34.	
	PK 47	**Tinténiac** 𝕽.	58 178.5
	PK 47–45.5	≪ Nos 33 & 32.	
Start of staircase	PK 43	≪ Nos 31, 30 & 29.	
lock nos 31–21			
	PK 43	**Hédé** 𝕽 in basin between lock nos 28 & 28 (town 2km).	62 174.5
	PK 42.5	≪ No 28 *La Madeleine*. In the lock keeper's house is a permanent *Canal d'Ille-et-Rance* exhibition. In July and August open daily 1030–1230 & 1330–1800.	
	PK 42.5–41.5	≪ Nos 27–21.	
End of staircase	PK 41.5	Waiting pontoon.	
Summit			
	PK 34–25	≪ Nos 20–12.	
	PK 24.5	*St-Germain-sur-Ille* 𝕽.	
	PK 24–18	≪ Nos 11, 10, 9 & 8.	
	PK 18	*Chevaigné* 𝕽.	
	PK 15.5	≪ No 7.	
	PK 13.5	**Betton** 𝕽.	91.5 145
	PK 13–7.5	≪ Nos 6, 5 & 4.	
	PK 6	*St-Grégoire* 𝕽.	
	PK 5.5–0	≪ Nos 3, 2 & 1 (*écluse le Mail*).	
	PK 0	**Rennes** One time seat of the parliament in Brittany.The 17th century building now	105 131.5

WATERWAY	PK ref	Town/*village*/≪*lock*	Total km
			▼　　▲
ILLE-ET-RANCE CANAL		houses the law courts.The Musée de Bretagne, at 20 quai Emile-Zola, covers the history and culture of the Region. Cathédrale St-Pierre, part of which dates back to 16th century. Attractive Renaissance half-timbered houses in the old quarter behind the cathedral. Moorings alongside quai Saint-Cyr in Ille-et-Rance canal just before reaching the last lock (*écluse No 1 le Mail*).This is very central, near the old quarter.	

Route 41 continued

River Vilaine: *Rennes ↔ Redon*

Maximum boat dimensions: *Height above waterline* 3.2m　*Draught* 1.2m

Speed limit: 8–10km/h (4.3–5.4kn)

Locks: 12 (27.10m long x 4.70m wide) Operate April–Oct 0900–1200 & 1400–1900. Closed Nov–Mar

Distance: 89km

The quayside stopping off place in the centre of Rennes (see above) is pleasant enough, and there is plenty to see in the capital city of Brittany, but once the boat moves on into the Vilaine the crew will usually opt for pushing on as quickly as possible through the extensive industrial suburbs of Rennes. Pont-Réan, out in the countryside, is a good night stop to aim for, with convenient shops in the nearby village.

A few kilometres beyond Pont-Réan, after Messac, the river is riddled with hard shoals, and if

the level of the river is particularly low after a dry spring and summer, this is the stretch where trouble can be expected in any craft drawing over 1m. The general rule on this canalised section of the Vilaine was to favour the tow path side of the river, even if this meant waiting for the occasional fisherman to move his line, which may be cast more than halfway across the water; unfortunately these days much of the towpath has disappeared, but as a general guide between Rennes and Pont-Réan the tow path was on the left bank, switching to the right bank below Pont-Réan.

Between Pont-Réan and Redon there are villages with pontoons and two small towns (Guipry and Messac). Some of the pontoons are located near camping sites where visiting crews can make use of the camp showers and washing machines.

Old Redon was built along the quayside where large seagoing sailing vessels once moored and where the 18th century shipowners' houses and warehouses still stand. There is a large basin for pleasure craft where yachts can raise their masts again, preparatory to making the 30-mile passage down to the Vilaine estuary and the Bay of Biscay.

Redon is a good place for crew changes, with train services to Rennes/St-Malo, Paris and the south of France.

WATERWAY	PK ref	Town/*village*/≪ *lock*	Total km
			▼ ▲
RIVER VILAINE	PK 0	**Rennes** (see page 247–8). ♒ in Ille-et-Rance canal.	105 131.5
	PK 2–18	≪ Nos 2, 3, 4, 5 & 6.	
	PK 18	*Pont-Réan* ♒.	
	PK 21	≪ No 7 *Boël* beside a beautiful water mill in lovely surroundings.	
	PK 27	≪ No 8 *Bouëxière*, with another water mill.	
	PK 30	*Bourg-des-Comptes* ♒.	
	PK 30–40.5	≪ Nos 9, 10 & 11.	
	PK 47	**Messac** ⚑. Cruiser hire.	152 84.5
	PK 47.5	≪ No 12.	
	PK 48	**Guipry** ♒.	153 83.5
	PK 52	≪ No 13.	
	PK 62	*Port de Roche* ♒. *Langon* (1.5km).	
	PK 69	*Beslé* ♒.	

Brittany and Pays-de-la-Loire: River Vilaine

WATERWAY	PK ref	Town/*village*/≪ *lock*	Total km
			▼ ▲
RIVER VILAINE			
LEFT and RIGHT Canal de Nantes à Brest	PK 89	Redon – Lorient Route 42 Redon – Nantes Route 45	
RIGHT yacht basin AHEAD **RIVER VILAINE** to Arzal barrage (see page 251)	PK 90.5	**Redon** One time flourishing commercial port. Shipowners' elegant houses line quai Duguay-Trouin. Musée de la Batellerie de l'Ouest, quai Jean-Bart, devoted to local maritime history. 11th century St-Sauveur abbey. ⌶ in town centre. Crane (self-operated). Fuel. Cruiser hire.	195.5 41

Redon. *Photo: David Jefferson*

River Vilaine: *Redon ↔ La Roche-Bernard/Arzal Barrage)*

Maximum boat dimensions: *Height above waterline* N/A *Draught* 1.2m

Speed limit: 8–10km/h (4.3–5.4kn)

Lock: 1 Arzal barrage (85m long x 13m wide) Operates 0700–2200 in high season (July and Aug) on the hour except around low water (less than 1.5m). Early and late season the last opening time is 2000

Distance: 42km

For much of the passage downriver from Redon, there is little to see from the boat with tall reeds obscuring any distant view. There is no air draught restriction with one opening bridge 10km downstream of Redon. Port de Foleux is a useful *port de plaisance*, roughly half way between Redon and La Roche-Bernard, although it is 5km to Béganne, the nearest village.

There is no mistaking the approaches to La Roche-Bernard where the Vilaine widens out and is spanned by a grand suspension bridge. The pontoons nearest the bridge belong to the Neuf Port, then there are several moorings and the arrival pontoon with more pontoons up a small creek where the Vieux Port is located. It is only another 8km to the Arzal Barrage, the end of the waterways providing this marvellous inland link between the English Channel and the Atlantic. Just before the barrage there are marinas on both sides of the river. The Port de Camoël on the south side of the river is the quieter of the two, but Port d'Arzal by the lock on the north side has all the facilities including fuel, crane, and a bar/restaurant.

Beyond the lock it can come as something of a jolt after a couple of weeks on the waterways to have to dig out charts, avoid sandbanks in the estuary, work with the tides and study weather forecasts. The reward for tackling all those locks is a superb cruising ground including the Morbihan, La Trinité and Belle Île.

Brittany and Pays-de-la-Loire: River Vilaine

WATERWAY	PK ref	Town/*village*/≪lock	Total km
			▼ ▲
RIVER VILAINE	PK 90	**Redon** ⌐ Fuel. Crane. Cruiser hire. (see page 250).	195.5 41
LEFT Bellions lock for access to Canal Nantes à Brest (Route 45)	PK 96		
	PK 115	*Port de Foleux* ⌐ .	
	PK 122.5	**la Roche-Bernard** Land at the visitors' pontoon and report to *bureau du port* to be allocated a berth in the Neuf Port or the Vieux Port, and then climb the narrow streets up from the marinas to the Place du Bouffay in the old quarter of the town. Crane. Fuel.	228 8.5
	PK 130.5	⌐ Port de Camoël on south side and ⌐ Port d'Arzal on north side, near the barrage lock. All boatyard facilities at Port d'Arzal.	▼ ▲
Tidal **RIVER VILAINE** to the sea	PK 131	≪ *Arzal*. See page 251 for lock operating times.	236.5 0

Busy end to the weekend at the lock in the barrage at Arzal. *Photo: David Jefferson*

Route 42

Nantes à Brest Canal/Canal du Blavet/River Blavet:
Redon ←→ Lorient

Maximum boat dimensions: *Height above waterline* 2.4m *Draught* 1.4m

Speed limit: 8–10km/h (4.3–5.4kn) in the canalised rivers. 6km/h (3.2kn) in canal (summit PK 191 to Pontivy)

Locks: Redon–Josselin 17; Josselin–Pontivy 72; Pontivy–Lorient 28; total: 117 (27.10m long x 4.7m wide) Operate April–Sept daily 0830–1230 & 1330–1930. Closed Oct–Mar. Maritime lock (No 28 Polvern) just upstream of Hennebont dependant on height of water downstream of lock

Distances: Redon–Josselin 62km; Josselin–Pontivy 48km; Pontivy–Lorient 72km total: 182km

The only section of the Nantes à Brest canal to be extensively used by pleasure craft is the 62km stretch between Redon and Josselin with a mere 17 locks. With cruiser hire bases at Redon and Josselin, where there is a superb waterside castle, this is one of the main centres for chartering on the Brittany waterways.

For many years, the canal between Rohan (approaching the summit, 25km beyond Josselin) and Pontivy was closed due to inadequate pumping facilities to maintain the water level. Although the route from Redon to the sea at Lorient via Pontivy and the Blavet river has been opened up, the number of locks to tackle is somewhat daunting except for the real enthusiast with plenty of time to spare. In the 48km between Josselin and Pontivy there are 72 locks including 23 over a 4.5km stretch. Avoiding any of the distractions en route, crews would normally take about 4 days to cover this 48km.

Those who have arrived at Redon who still want to sample more of the Brittany waterways before making for the sea, might consider less arduous exploration by motoring only as far as Josselin, and then coming back to the Redon crossroads.

Brittany and Pays-de-la-Loire: Nantes à Brest Canal/Blavet

Further navigation of the Nantes à Brest canal ceases at Pontivy with the blocking of the canal by the barrage at Guerlédan. Those who do reach Pontivy with plans to make for the sea can only continue along the canalised Blavet river. At the last lock (no 28), 3km above Hennebont, it is essential to check on the state of the tide with the lock keeper because at low water there may be a danger of grounding beyond the lock in the Blavet maritime, and on exceptionally high tides, the clearance of the Hennebont bridges will be reduced.

WATERWAY	PK ref	Town/*village*/≪*lock*	Total km	
			▼	▲
NANTES À BREST CANAL	PK 95	**Redon** see page 250. ⚑. Fuel. Crane. Cruiser hire.	0	182.5
	PK 104	*St-Vincent-sur-Oust* ♒.		
RIGHT	PK 105	*l'Aff* – *Glénac* ♒(1km).		
		la Gacilly ♒ (9km) Max draught 1m.		
	PK 105.5	≪ No 19.		
	PK 112	*Peillac* ♒.		
	PK 116.5–120	≪ Nos 21 & 22.		
	PK 123.5	*St-Congard* ♒. Showers at camp site.		
	PK 125.5	≪ No 23.		
	PK 126	*St-Laurent-sur-Oust* ♒.		
	PK 129.5	≪ No 24.		
	PK 132	**Malestroit** ♒.	37	145.5
	PK 133	≪ Nos 25, 26, 27 & 28.		
	PK 140.5	*le Roc Saint-André* ♒.		
	PK 143.5	≪ No 29.		
	PK 143.5	*Montertelot* ♒.		
	PK 146–157	≪ Nos 30, 31, 32, 33, 34 & 35.		
	PK 157.5	**Josselin** Magnificent waterside castle. Small town with cobbled streets and half-timbered houses. ♒ Cruiser hire.	62.5	120
	PK 158–171	≪ Nos 36, 37, 38, 39, 40, 41, 42, 43 & 44.		
RIGHT (1km)	PK 171.5	*Les Forges* ♒ at end of narrow branch off main canal.		

The castle at Josselin. *Photo: Crown Blue Line*

WATERWAY	PK ref	Town/*village*/≪*lock*	Total km	
			▼	▲
NANTES À BREST CANAL	PK 172–181.5	≪ Nos 45–52.		
	PK 182	**Rohan** ♌. Boat yard. Cruiser hire.	87	95.5
	PK 183.5–191	≪ Nos 53–78 (*Bel Air*).		
Summit and 5km pound	PK 191–196			
	PK 196–205.5	≪ Nos 79–107.		
	PK 0	≪ No 1.		
RIGHT closed section of Nantes à Brest Canal				

Brittany and Pays-de-la-Loire: Blavet Canal

WATERWAY	PK ref	Town/*village*/≪ *lock*	Total km
			▼ ▲
AHEAD continues as **CANALISED BLAVET**	PK 1	**Pontivy** Medieval town with ramparts and moat-surrounded castle. Old town later enlarged by Napoleon as a military centre. Ω Cruiser hire.	110.5 72
	PK 2–17.5	≪ Nos 2, 3, 4, 5, 6, 7, 8 & 9.	
	PK 18	*St-Nicholas-des-Eaux* Ω.	
	PK 19.5–34.5	≪ Nos 10, 11, 12, 13, 14, 15, 16 & 17.	
	PK 36.5	*Pont-Augan* Ω. Showers at camp site.	
	PK 36.5–57	≪ Nos 18, 19, 20, 21, 22, 23, 24, 25, 26, 27 & 28.	
BLAVET maritime	PK 57		
	PK 60	**Hennebont** Fortified medieval town and river port in the Middle Ages. Ω.	169.5 13
			▼ ▲
	PK 72	**Lorient** One-time naval base and dockyard, now commercial harbour, fishing port and centre of yachting with several marinas and visitors' berths in the Port de Commerce.	182.5 0

Route 43

River Aulne/canalised Aulne: *Brest ↔ Châteaulin*

Maximum boat dimensions: *Height above waterline* **N/A** *Draught* **3.2m** (between Guily-Glaz lock and Châteaulin). Tidal between lock and Brest.
Speed limit: **8–10km/h** (4.3–5.4kn) between Guily-Glaz lock and Châteaulin
Lock: **1** Guily-Glaz (40m long x 10m wide). Operates HW -2 to HW +2 (0600–2200)
Distance: 51km

The Aulne river provides deep-draught boats with the opportunity of sampling a short stretch of attractive waterway with no headroom restrictions. For those who have battled round the outside of Ushant and Finistère, bound for the Bay of Biscay or Spain, the marinas at Camaret and Morgat are popular for stopping off for a night or two to stretch the legs, dine ashore and replenish the stores. Alternatively, passage-making boats can enter the Rade de Brest, where there is a fine marina or the skipper might consider lingering for a while inland alongside the town quay at Châteaulin.

There is water at all states of the tide up to the Térénez suspension bridge (clearance 27m). It is 19km from the bridge to the lock below Port-Launay, and the passage should be planned to arrive at the lock an hour or so before high water.

The large-scale Admiralty chart of the Rade de Brest (3429) finishes at the bridge, and from then on there is little in the way of marks to guide the navigator. The general rule is to keep right on the outside of bends, but otherwise remain in the middle of the river. Port-Launay, 2km above the lock is a pleasant small town with plenty of room alongside the quay. For most boats the end of the Aulne navigation will be the market town of Châteaulin, another 2km upriver, where there are quayside berths on both sides of the river.

Brittany and Pays-de-la-Loire: River Aulne

WATERWAY	PK ref	Town/*village*/≪*lock*	Total km	
			▼	▲
RADE DE BREST	PK 51	**Brest** Naval port and Port de Commerce. Entry prohibited to pleasure craft. Nearest marina is ⚑ du Moulin Blanc, 2 miles east of Brest.	0	51
L'AULNE RIVER	PK 32.5			
	PK 29	*Landévennec/Port Maria* Deep-water moorings and slipway.		
Suspension bridge (clearance 27m)	PK 23		28	23
	PK 4	≪ *Guily-Glaz*		
	PK 2	**Port-Launay** ♒.	49	2
			▼	▲
Beyond Châteaulin height and draught restrictions (see Route 44)	PK 0	**Châteaulin** Market town. ♒. Showers at leisure centre. Large supermarket near to quayside moorings. Cruiser hire.	51	0

Port Launay. *Photo: David Jefferson*

Route 44

Nantes à Brest Canal: *Châteaulin ←→ Goariva*

Maximum boat dimensions: *Height above waterline* 2.5m *Draught* 1.2m (Châteaulin to Kergoat) 1.1m (Kergoat to Goariva)
Speed limit: 8–10km/h (4.3–5.4kn)
Locks: 45 (27.10m long x 4.7m wide) Self-operated
Distance: 81km

This Brest end of the Canal de Nantes à Brest consists of the canalised Aulne and the canalised Hyères, the latter ceasing to be navigable between the Goariva lock and Guerlédan lake with the barrage beyond. Most of the 81km of canalised river between Châteaulin and Goariva was closed as a result of flood damage in 1995, but 10 years later this waterway through a particularly lovely part of Brittany was re-opened and provides cruising in superb surroundings for those fortunate owners of craft meeting the draught restrictions above and below the waterline. There are also cruiser hire operators at Châteaulin, Pont-Coblant and Châteauneuf-du-Faou.

WATERWAY	PK ref	Town/*village*/≪*lock*	Total km	
			▼	▲
NANTES À		**Châteaulin** see page 258 ♒. Cruiser hire.	0	81
BREST CANAL	PK 0–22.5	≪ Nos 236–227.		
	PK 23.5	*Pont-Coblant* ♒. Cruiser hire.		
	PK 24–42.5	≪ Nos 226–219.		
	PK 43.5	**Châteauneuf-du-Faou** ♒. Cruiser hire.	43.5	37.5
	PK 44–61.5	≪ Nos 218–210.		

Chateaulin. *Photo: David Jefferson*

WATERWAY	PK ref	Town/*village*/≪*lock*	Total km	
			▼	▲
NANTES À BREST CANAL	PK 63	*Maison du Canal* (small museum/ information centre).		
	PK 63–73.5	≪ Nos 209–203.		
	PK 74	*Port-de-Carhaix* ♒.		
	PK 74.5–80.5	≪ Nos 202–193.	▼	▲
End of navigation	PK 81	≪ No 192 *Goariva*.	81	0

Nantes à Brest Canal/River Erdre: *Redon ↔ Nantes*

Maximum boat dimensions: *Height above waterline* **3.0m** *Draught* **1.1m** (1.4m on River Erdre)

Speed limit: 10km/h (5.4kn)

Locks: 16 (31.50m long x 5.2m wide) Operate April–Oct 0900–1200 & 1400–1900 except for lock No 1 St-Félix giving access to the Loire in the centre of Nantes. St-Félix lock operates HW -3 to HW +3 0630–1930 April–Sept. Reduced hours outside season. Some of the locks are self-operated outside high season. There are video displays at lock No 16 and No 2 showing method of operation

Distance: 95km

The section of the Nantes à Brest canal south of Redon is used by some of the charter boats from Redon, although many of these will opt to head north from Redon in the direction of Malestroit and Josselin (Route 42). From Redon to L'Erdre River there will often be less water (1.1m) compared with the Josselin route.

Most skippers using the Brittany canals to move their boats between the Channel (St-Malo) and the Bay of Biscay (Atlantic), arriving in Redon will choose to reach the sea via the Vilaine river (Route 41) which will take less than a day against 3 days to reach Nantes with the prospect of negotiating the tidal passage down the Loire river, having gained little mileage southwards.

WATERWAY	PK ref	Town/village/≪lock	Total km	
			▼	▲
RIVER VILAINE	PK 95	**Redon** see page 250. ⚓ Fuel. Crane. Cruiser hire.	0	95
NANTES À	PK 89	≪ No 17 *Bellions* ♒.		
BREST CANAL	PK 83	*Pont Miny* ♒.		
	PK 72/73	*St-Clair/Guenrouet* ♒.		
	PK 66	≪ No 16 *Melneuf* (video).		
	PK 62–59	≪ No 15 *la Touche* & ≪ No 14 *Barel*.		
	PK 56.5	≪ No 13 *Bougard*.		
	PK 51.5	≪ No 12 *la Paudais*.		
	PK 50	*Blain* ♒.		
	PK 48.5	≪ No 11 *Blain*.		
	PK 45.5	≪ No 10 *le Terrier*.		
	PK 43.5	≪ No 9 *le Gué de l'Atelier*.		
	PK 42.5	*La Chevallerais* ♒.		
	PK 40.5	≪ No 8 *la Remaudais*.		
	PK 32	≪ No 7 *le Pas d'Héric*.		
	PK 38	*Glanet* ♒.		
	PK 31	≪ No 6 *Cramezeul*.		
	PK 30	≪ No 5 *la Haie Pacoret*.		
	PK 29	≪ No 4 *la Rabinière* ♒.		
	PK 26	≪ No 3 *la Tindière*.		
	PK 21.5	≪ No 2 *Quiheix* (video).		
T-junction	PK 21			
L'ERDRE RIVER				
LEFT		Nort-sur-Erdre (5km) ♒.		
RIGHT Nantes				
	PK 15	**Sucé-sur-Erdre** ⚓. Cruiser hire.	80	15
	PK 2	**Nantes** see page 264. ♒ (Ile de Versailles).	93	2
Tunnel (900m)	PK 1			
	PK 0	♒ (*Port Malakoff*).	▼	▲
	PK 0	≪ No 1 *St-Félix*.	95	0
Loire (Route 46)				

Route 46

Loire and Maine: *St-Nazaire* ←→ *Angers*

Maximum boat dimensions: *Height above waterline* St-Nazaire – Nantes **N/A**; Nantes – Angers **4.5m** *Draught* St-Nazaire – Nantes (tidal); Nantes – Bouchemaine (tidal/**2m**) Maine **1.6m**

Speed limits: Loire **20 km/h (10.8kn)**; reduced to **10km/h** in certain narrow sections and **6km/h** through built up areas. Maine **15km/h (8.1kn)**

Lock: 1 Tidal – on Maine between Bouchemaine and Angers (38m x 5.05m) Self-operated

Distance: 150km

The Loire is the longest river in France rising in the Massif Central and reaching the Atlantic at St-Nazaire. These days, little of the 1000km length is navigable. Deep-draught vessels still ply between the sea and Nantes, a major port 55km inland. In Nantes, smaller craft have access to the Brittany canals via the River Erdre (Route 45). The navigable Loire ceases at Bouchemaine 84km above Nantes, but boats can continue along the Maine river and through the first lock to Angers where the river divides, one arm navigable to Mayenne (124km and 45 locks; Route 47) and the other to Le Mans (133km 20 locks; Route 48).

These rivers – the Sarthe and the Mayenne – do not connect with the main network of waterways and most of the craft on these rivers are either local boats or hire cruisers (understandably not permitted to leave these tranquil waters to navigate the challenging Loire). Those visiting boats that do turn into the Loire estuary from the sea and head upriver beneath the giant suspension bridge may feel they are trail-blazing along this waterway, for few pleasure craft tackle the somewhat bleak surroundings up to Nantes. Beyond, the river scenery improves, but the effects of the tide are felt right up to Ancensis (90km inland).

The depth of the Loire, between the estuary and the Maine, is maintained by training walls, but is still affected by drought or excessive rainfall when much of the surrounding countryside can be flooded. The estuary can be particularly

exposed to the elements. The channel through many sandbanks and rocky shoals
well buoyed up to Nantes, but between Nantes and the first lock in the Maine
low Angers the channel is more difficult to follow with fewer and less promi-
nt marks and at times a disturbingly strong current.

WATERWAY	PK ref	Town/*village*/≪ *lock*	Total km	
			▼	▲
LOIRE	PK 0	**St-Nazaire** Commercial and ship-building town with extensive dockyards and port. Greatly damaged in WWII, much of it by the Royal Navy attacking the German U-boat bases. Famous for the wartime Combined Operations raid to destroy the only dry dock capable of receiving the largest of Germany's battleships. Yachts berth at the S end of the Basin de Penhoët in the dock area.	0	150
Suspension bridge	PK 12	**Paimboeuf** Commercial berths.	12	138
	PK 35	*la Martinière* Possible anchorage.		
	PK 52	**Nantes** One-time capital of Brittany, now the principal city of the Loire region. Dominated by cathedral and castle built in 15th century by the Dukes of Brittany. Henri IV signed Edict of Nantes at the castle in 1598 establishing religious freedom throughout France. Prestigeous Musée des Beaux-Arts. More museums in castle. Trentemoult Marina on south bank just before reaching Ile Beaulieu in the city centre where the Loire divides. Masts can be lowered here, but berths dry at low water. If height above waterline is no more than 4.5m to pass beneath Nantes bridges at high water, a better berth is the basin the far side of St-Felix lock (operates 3 hours either side of HW). If your air draught is less than 3.8m, you can continue through the 900m tunnel to reach city's ⚑.		

WATERWAY	PK ref	Town/*village*/≪*lock*	Total km	
			▼	▲
LOIRE	PK 70.5	*La Pierre Percée* ⚑.		
	PK 80.5	*Oudon* ⚓.		
	PK 90	**Ancenis** Quays.	90	60
	PK 102	**St-Florent-le-Vieil** ⚓. Difficult section of river. Strong current where channel narrows and shallow patches.	102	48
	PK 111	**Ingrandes** ⚓.	111	39
	PK 116	**Montjean-sur-Loire** ⚓.	116	34
	PK 125	**Chalonnes-sur-Loire** ⚓.	125	25
	PK 135	*Béhuard* ⚓.		
Continues as **LA MAINE**	PK 139	*Bouchemaine* ⚓.		
RIGHT non-navigable Loire (except for shallow draught craft)				
	PK 147	≪ *Seuil en Maine.*		
	PK 149	**Angers** Capital city of the Anjou. Fine 13th century Château du Roi René with 17 granite towers, houses the famous 14th century tapestry Apocalypse and 20th century Chant du Mode. ⚑.	149	1
			▼	▲
AHEAD La Sarthe to Le Mans (Route 48)	PK 150		150	0
LEFT La Mayenne to Mayenne (Route 47)				

Route 47

River Mayenne: *Angers* ↔ *Mayenne*

Maximum boat dimensions: *Height above waterline* 4.4m to Laval (PK 36) 2.8m between Laval and Mayenne *Draught* 1.5m
Speed limit: 10km/h (5.4kn)
Locks: 45 (minimum 30m long x 5.2m wide) Operate May–mid Sept daily 0900–1230 & 1400–2000. Reduced hours and days of operation out of season, decreasing to 1400–1600 Mon, Tues, Thurs & Fri mid Nov–end Jan
Distance: 124km

With the challenging navigation of the Loire upriver of Nantes (see Route 46), it is unlikely that many seagoing boats with suitable dimensions will reach the Maine and Angers – the southerly gateway to the Mayenne river. There is a sharp contrast between the upper 'navigable' part of the Loire, with its sandbanks, rocky shoals and swirling currents and upstream of the first lock in the Maine. There is no northern entry into the river because navigation finishes at the old town of Mayenne.

The river is understandably monopolised by crews of charter boats and local boat owners, for whom pontoons are provided at almost every village between Angers and Laval. Above Laval, there are fewer stopping off places and a restriction on the height above waterline (2.8m). Those crews that do not continue along the 35km and through 20 more locks between Laval and Mayenne miss out on a beautiful stretch of river and the interesting old town at the end of the route.

A popular diversion is to leave the Mayenne and navigate the 18km and 3 locks of the Oudon river which has two waterside towns where there are good facilities for visiting boats.

WATERWAY	PK ref	Town/*village*/≪*lock*	Total km	
			▼	▲
RIVER MAINE	(PK 124)	**Angers** (see page 265).	0	124
LEFT **RIVER MAYENNE**	PK 122		2	122
AHEAD River Sarthe (Route 48)				
RIGHT La Vieille Maine to River Sarthe	PK 119			
	PK 115.5	≪ No 45.		
	PK 113	*Juigné* ♒.		
	PK 110	*Pont-Albert* ♒.		
	PK 107.5	≪ No 43.		
	PK 106	Pruillé ♒. Showers at camp site.		
	PK 103	*Grez-Neuville* ▷. Cruiser hire.		
	PK 102.5	≪ No 42.		
LEFT River Oudon (18km 3 locks)	PK 101/18			
	(PK 16)	**Le Lion-d'Angers** ♒.		
	(PK 0)	**Segré** ▷.		
	PK 99	*Chauvon* ♒.		
	PK 97	*Montreuil-sur-Maine* ♒.		
	PK 97-93.5	≪ Nos 41 & 40.		
	PK 92	*Chambellay* ♒.		
	PK 91	*Chenillé-Changé* Pretty village with château. ▷. Cruiser hire.		
	PK 90.5	≪ No 39.		
	PK 88	*La Jaille-Yvon* ♒. Showers at camp site.		
	PK 87.5	≪ No 38.		
	PK 84	*Daon* ♒. Showers at camp site.		
	PK 82.5	≪ No 37.		
	PK 78	*Ménil* ♒. Showers at camp site.		
	PK 78-75.5	≪ Nos 36 & 35.		
	PK 72.5	*Azé* ♒.		

WATERWAY	PK ref	Town/*village*/≪*lock*	Total km	
			▼	▲
RIVER	PK 71.5	≪ No 34.		
MAYENNE	PK 70	**Château-Gontier** ⚑.	54	70
	PK 69–66.5	≪ Nos 33 & 32.		
	PK 63	*Neuville* ⚓.		
	PK 63–52	≪ Nos 31, 30, 29 & 28.		
	PK 52	*La Bénâtre* ⚓.		
	PK 48.5–45	≪ Nos 27 & 26.		
	PK 44	*Port-Rhingeard* ⚑. Cruiser hire.		
	PK 44–35	≪ Nos 25, 24, 23, 22 & 21.		
	PK 35	**Laval** Several quays and ⚑.	89	35
	PK 33.5–27.5	≪ Nos 20, 19 & 18.		
	PK 27	*St-Jean-sur-Mayenne* ⚑. Showers at camp site.		
	PK 25–1	≪ Nos 17–1.	▼	▲
End of navigation	PK 0	**Mayenne** Interesting old part of town near the right bank. ⚑.	124	0

Le-Port-Joulain near Daon. *Photo: Crown Blue Line*

River Sarthe: *Angers ↔ Le Mans*

Maximum boat dimensions: *Height above waterline* **4.4m** Angers to lock No 16 Beffes (PK 81.5); **3.9m** lock No 16 Beffes to Le Mans *Draught* **1.5m**

Speed limit: 10km/h (5.4kn)

Locks: **20** (minimum 30m long x 5.2m wide) Operate May–mid Sept daily 0900–1230 & 1400–2000. Reduced hours and days of operation out of season, decreasing to 1400–1600 Mon, Tues, Thurs & Fri mid Nov–end Jan

Distance: 133km

Like the neighbouring Mayenne river (Route 47), few seagoing craft will reach the Sarthe River from the sea by way of the Loire with its navigational hazards above Nantes. The Sarthe mostly belongs to fishermen, charter boats and local boat owners who are happy to restrict their passage-making to the delightful confines of the Maine, the Mayenne and the Sarthe. Like the Mayenne, navigation of the Sarthe ceases after about 100km with no further access to the French network of waterways. The industrial town of Le Mans is the end of the Sarthe navigation.

WATERWAY	PK ref	Town/*village*/≪*lock*	Total km	
			▼	▲
RIVER MAINE	(PK 133)	**Angers** (see page 265).	0	133
AHEAD **LA SARTHE**	PK 131.5			
LEFT La Mayenne (Route 47)	PK 131.5			
LA SARTHE	PK 127	*Écouflant* ♨. Showers at camp site.		
LEFT La Vieille Maine to La Mayenne (Route 47)	PK 127			
RIGHT Le Loir river (non-navigable)	PK 122			
LA SARTHE	PK 120.5	*Briollay* ♨.		
	PK 113.5	≪ No 20.		
	PK 113	*Cheffes-sur-Sarthe* ⚑. Cruiser hire.		
	PK 105.5	*Juvardeil* ♨.		
	PK 103	*Châteauneuf-sur-Sarthe* ⚑. Cruiser hire.		
	PK 103	≪ No 19.		
	PK 97.5	*Brissarthe* ♨.		
	PK 93	≪ No 18.		
	PK 90.5	*Morannes* ♨.		
	PK 87.5–73	≪ Nos 17, 16 & 15.		
	PK 72.5	**Sablé-sur-Sarthe** ⚑. Cruiser hire.	60.5	72.5
	PK 70	≪ No 14.		
	PK 69.5	**Solesmes** Abbey of St-Pierre. Quays.	63.5	69.5
	PK 68.5	≪ No 13.		
	PK 68.5	*Juigné-sur-Sarthe* ♨.		
	PK 63	≪ No 12.		
	PK 61	*Avoise* ♨. Showers at camp site.		
	PK 58	≪ No 11.		
	PK 57.5	*Parcé-sur-Sarthe* ♨. Showers at camp site.		
	PK 55	≪ No 10.		

WATERWAY	PK ref	Town/*village*/≪*lock*	Total km ▼	▲
LA SARTHE	PK 47	**Malicorne-sur-Sarthe** ⚑. Cruiser hire.	86	47
	PK 47-41	≪ Nos 9 & 8.		
	PK 39.5	*Noyen* ⚓. Cruiser hire.		
	PK 33–27	≪ Nos 7 & 6.		
	PK26	**La Suze-sur-Sarthe** ⚓. Cruiser hire.	107	26
	PK 23	**Roëzé-sur-Sarthe** ⚓.	110	23
Canal bypass (5km)	PK 22	≪ No 5.		
End of canal bypass	PK 17	*Fillé* ⚓.		
Canal bypass (1.5km)	PK 15	≪ No 4.		
End of canal bypass	PK 13.5			
	PK 13	**Spay** ⚑.	120	13
	PK 6–2	≪ Nos 3, 2 & 1.		
	PK 1.5	**Le Mans** Industrial suburbs, but with ⚑ in the centre near more interesting old part of the town.	131.5 ▼	1.5 ▲
End of navigation	PK 0		133	0

Solesmes Abbey, River Sarthe.
Photo: Crown Blue Line

Entre Deux Mers – the Atlantic ↔ the Mediterranean and the Rivers Baïse, Lot and Charente

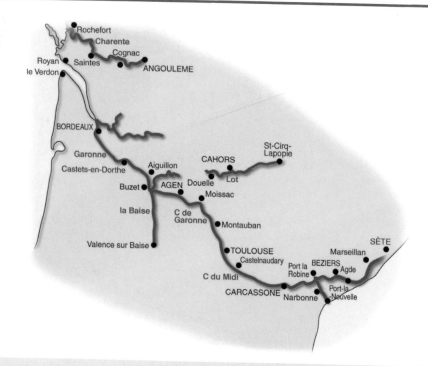

Marseillan on the Etang de Thau. *Photo: David Jefferson*

Section nine covers waterways that link the Atlantic Ocean with the Mediterranean (Route 49). A boat can start from the Atlantic port of Royan, and over 600km later motor out into the Mediterranean at Sète.

Those wanting to gain access to the Mediterranean a little earlier can leave the Canal du Midi at Le Somail and take the Embranchement to Port-la-Nouvelle (Route 50).

Also included in this Section are the Rivers Baïse and Lot (Routes 51A, B & C). The Baïse and Lower Lot can be reached from the Canal de Garonne which is part of the main network of French waterways (Route 49), but both these rivers and the Upper Lot are mostly monopolised by hired cruisers with a wealth of spectacularly beautiful stretches of river to explore.

The last route in this section (Route 52) covers the Charente River. Again, this is very beautiful and mostly used by hired boats, although the Charente can be accessed from the sea north of the Gironde estuary. The old town of Angoulême (169km inland) is the end of the river navigation, with no link up with any other waterways.

Canal des Deux Mers: *Royan* ↔ *Sète*

Maximum boat dimensions: *Height above waterline* **3.3m** at centre (reducing under some arched Canal du Midi bridges to **2.4m** at sides across **5.5m** beam); *Draught* **1.5m** (less over periods of severe drought)

Speed limit: 8km/h (4.3kn) except in harbours/mooring areas when limit reduced to 3km/h

Locks: 114 (minimum 30.00m long x 5.60m wide) Operate late Mar–early Nov daily 0900–1230 & 1330–1800; May–Sept daily 0900–1230 & 1330–1900; early Nov–Dec by arrangement only

Distance: 601km

This route from the Atlantic to the Mediterranean starts with the formidable estuary of the Gironde, then the tidal Gironde river to the confluence with the Dordogne river where the Gironde becomes the tidal Garonne until the first lock at Castets en Dorthe and the start of the Canal de Garonne which meets up with the Canal du Midi in Toulouse.

Anyone planning a dash from the Atlantic to the Mediterranean or considering bringing the boat back to the UK from the Med via these waterways should reckon on at least a couple of weeks' passage-making between Royan and Sète, and this is based on early starts to catch the first lock openings and allows little time for stopping for sightseeing. The passage will certainly take longer in the holiday season as progress through the locks on the Midi will be frustratingly slow for anyone in a hurry because of the amount of river traffic. Those who can find the time to dawdle a while on the waterways in the south of France will be amply rewarded with spectacular scenery and tempting stop-overs to sample the local cuisine and wines.

When contemplating the Canal des Deux Mers as an alternative to reaching the Mediterranean by long sea passages or transporting overland from one of the Channel ports, the first considerations must be draught and height of the vessel

Approaching the low bridge at Capestang. *Photo: Tim Hollis*

above the waterline. Any craft with a draught over 1.5m is unsuitable for this Atlantic to Mediterranean route, and 1.5m may be too much if the water levels have dropped after a long dry period. That said, the occasional grounding in these waterways will almost certainly be in soft mud. The general rule is if your boat's draught is on the limit, stick to the centre of the canal and only berth alongside recognised stopping places, exercising a cautious approach to bankside mooring and perhaps employing the dinghy to keep the boat away from the canal bank.

The height above the waterline should be no more than 3.3m at the centre and, assuming a beam of no more than 5.0m, a height of no more than 2.4m at the extremities. A boat within these dimensions will clear the bridge at Capestang (PK 189) on the Canal du Midi which has what looks like an impossibly low arch (see photo above). One British boat builder who builds boats for several of the cruiser hire operators in France uses the shape and height of Capestang to arrive at the dimensions of their canal craft in the planning stage on the basis that if their boats can clear Capestang they can pass beneath anything else on the main network.

If the height above the waterline at the sides is still right on the limit with everything dismantled or folded down, Capestang can be avoided by leaving the Midi at Le Somail and taking the 36km Embranchement de la Nouvelle to reach the Mediterranean at Port-la-Nouvelle. This allows the boat an additional 0.2m (8in) clearance at the sides.

The other consideration, which primarily applies to sailing craft is whether you have sufficient engine power to cope with the tidal Gironde and Garonne.

Approaching from the Atlantic, most yachts will initially make for Royan or the new Port-Médoc marina in the Gironde estuary and then plan the tidal passages to cover the 83km between Royan and the first lock at Castets en Dorthe. High water at Castets is four hours after HW Royan, so a yacht with modest power (say 10bhp) leaving Royan at local HW -4 or -5 will have 1–2 hours pushing a decreasing ebb and then 10 hours of flood. Anchoring in the Gironde or Garonne is not an option, but there are several stopping places en route. Those stopping points in secluded wet basins offering an escape from the fierce river currents do present a problem to some craft because leaving these basins will invariably only be possible just before high water, after which yachts may well be attempting to continue upriver against a 5 knot ebb. Port de Pauillac (28km upriver of Royan) is a popular stopping off place where a mast can be lowered if the skipper has not already opted for Royan for this operation.

The first low bridge (Pont de Pierre – clearance 3.9m) on this Atlantic to Meditarranean route is in Bordeaux, 53km inland of Royan and the sea. Bordeaux accommodates yachts, by prior arrangement with the harbourmaster, downstream of Pont de Pierre in Basin No 2 where the mast can be removed by mobile crane or there is a small crane on the Lormont Yacht Club pontoon on the east side of the river, just upstream of the giant suspension bridge Pont d'Aquitaine.

When passage-making downriver, you would leave the last lock at Castets en Dorthe around high water to tackle the shallows in the upper reaches of the tidal Garonne; a yacht making a modest 5 knots through the water will only have around 4 hours of favourable ebb and, with limited power, might succeed only in reaching the pontoon berths at Bordeaux (30km) before meeting the first of the flood. It might then take two more passages to cover the 54km between Bordeaux and Royan (again with a curtailed ebb), stopping off at Port de Pauillac which is roughly half way between the two. There are no restrictions on entry or departure times at Pauillac which is a good place to raise a mast. When you pay the modest charge at the *Capitainerie* for raising or lowering the mast, you will be presented with a bottle of wine with the complements of the harbourmaster.

Passage notes: the Atlantic to the Mediterranean

Pointe de la Négade and Pointe de la Coubre, south of La Rochelle, form the entrance to the 14-mile wide estuary of the Gironde river. These waters must be treated with considerable respect as there are numerous sandbanks and a rocky islet marked by the Cordouan lighthouse with buoyed channels either side (Passe Sud and Grande Passe de l'Ouest). There can be a 4-knot tide running in t! estuary which has to be avoided in strong wind-against-tide conditions.

The waters narrow to three miles between Royan and Point de Grave and then open up again to five miles between each bank of the Gironde river. The actual deepwater channel, narrow and well buoyed, used by deep draught merchant vessels plying between the sea and Bordeaux, is on the southerly side of the muddy waters of the Gironde with the northerly side bordered by flat, featureless barely visible countryside.

On the channel side of the river from Point de Grave in the entrance to within a few miles downstream of Bordeaux, vineyards cover the land including, 20 miles up river, vines of the Haut Médoc with waterside communal *appellations* around St-Estèphe, Pauillac, St-Julien, Margaux and Cartenac producing world-renowned red wines mostly from the Cabernet Sauvignon and Merlot grape. These vineyards of the Médoc and the Haut-Médoc, with the occasional magnificent châteaux, give the crews of yachts heading for Bordeaux a flavour of the sights to come along much of this route to the Mediterranean.

Bordeaux is a fascinating city with much of interest to tempt the crew to stay for a day or two, but it is not ideal as a stopping-off place for boats. Basin No 2 is not in the most salubrious part of the city with restricted times for entry/departure depending on the tide, and only after making arrangements in advance with the harbourmaster. Alternatively, a yacht can berth on Lormont Yacht Club's southerly pontoon if there is room, but there is no escaping the tide or wash here. Another option is to continue upstream under the Pont de Pierre for another 6km to the Port de Plaisance de Bègle which has 20 pontoon berths for visitors.

It is 58 km from the centre of Bordeaux to the first lock at Castets en Dorthe, and those boat owners who have stopped off at Bordeaux would normally make the passage on one tide, planning to arrive at the lock around high water. Apart from Bègle, the moorings between Bordeaux and Castets, listed on page 283 are isolated single pontoons in somewhat desolate surroundings where there is no escaping the current.

For those who are experiencing waterways for the first time, beyond the second chamber of the first lock is the pleasurable realisation that for the next couple of weeks or so there will be no more tidal considerations as the yacht enters the Canal de Garonne. Opened in 1856, 175 years after the Canal du Midi, this waterway would enable shipping to bypass increasingly difficult navigational hazards in the upper reaches of the tidal Garonne river between Castets en Dorthe and Toulouse.

The Canal de Garonne is 193 km long with 53 locks. Nos 52–31, 28, 27, 26, 17 and 16 are automatically operated. Once through the two basins of the first lock (écluse de Castets), crews sample the first of the many automatic locks (No 52) operated by twisting a hanging pole, entering the lock when given the green light and then pressing the illuminated green button. VNF insist that the crew member ashore operating the button should remain by the control panel throughout the operation. Immediately beyond this lock, crews can relax in still waters at the *halte nautique* de Castets en Dorthe. The essential VNF waterways licence can be obtained at the next lock (No 51).

There is a large choice of *ports de plaisance* and *haltes nautique* between the first lock at Castets and No 1 Ecluse de La Lande (193km) in the centre of Toulouse. Less crowded than the Midi, these stopping places will frequently offer, in addition to showers, water and electricity, a waterside bar or restaurant, with shops rarely more than a few minutes' away by bicycle.

There are plenty of interesting sights along the Canal de Garonne. Roughly half way along (PK 107) is Agen, administrative centre of Lot-et-Garonne Département. Approaching the town from the west, a boat negotiates a kilometre of waterway with a string of four locks and then crosses the Garonne river by one of the finest aqueducts on the French waterways. Built in 1848, the bridge is 580m long with 23 arches. The next town along the canal is Moissac (PK 64) built around the ancient superbly cloistered abbey of St-Pierre and surrounded by the gentle hills of the Tarn and Garonne covered in Chasselas vineyards and orchards.

At Montech (PK 43) there is a water slope for barges, enabling them rise or drop 14m in less than 10 minutes. They move up or down the water slope, pulled along by what looks like railway carriages with huge engines either side of the barge. Introduced in 1974, this was the first time anywhere that barges could be moved in this way. Pleasure boats still have to use Montech's five traditional locks. Those not in a hurry, might be tempted by a waterway excursion to the old fortified town of Montauban (10km – 9 locks) along a canal branch restored in 2003.

Toulouse, capital of the Midi-Pyrénées region, is considered one of the finest cities of France and an important commercial and cultural centre. At the Port de l'Embouchure in the city centre, the PK numbering comes down to 1 at the end of the Canal de Garonne, and then the waterway swings round to the left and another PK 1 marks the beginning of the 240km Canal du Midi. This waterway link to provide the inland route for shipping from the Mediterranean to the Atlantic was the brainchild of Pierre-Paul Riquet. In the 17th-century, Atlantic shipping could reach Toulouse, 300 kilometres inland, by way of the tidal Gironde and Garonne, but this was the end of the navigable waters. Riquet had the vision

Moissac. *Photo: franceafloat*

and the enterprise to create a totally man-made waterway between Toulouse and the Mediterranean. The summit would be 189m above sea level and the water in the new canal would be maintained with four reservoirs fed from streams directed from the nearby Montagne Noir (Black Mountain).

The 'Canal Royal' as it was originally called would be a vast undertaking which was started in 1667 using a workforce of 12,000 and taking 14 years to excavate what was affectionately referred to as Riquet's Ditch. He died in 1680, six months before the completion of his project with the canal within 3km of linking the Mediterranean with the Garonne. Opened in May 1681, the Canal du Midi was designated a UNESCO World Heritage Site in 1996.

Commercial traffic on the Canal du Midi virtually ceased in the 20th century, but it has been restored and maintained for recreation. It is now used by hotel barges, charter companies operating great fleets of cabin cruisers, privately owned motor boats and sailing craft dropping their masts to cut through from the Atlantic to the Mediterranean or vice versa to avoid the long slog round the bottom of Spain and Gibraltar.

The summit (Seuil de Naurouze) of the 'Canal des Deux Mers' is the pound between locks 17 and 18, which are aptly named *Océan* and *Méditerranée*. Here you can see the Obélisque de Riquet in memory of the great man. Beyond the watershed, the boat's crew adapt to the new routine in the locks, with no longer a rush of water into the lock as the sluices are opened to lower the water.

At the one-time port of Castelnaudary (PK65), you are expected to sample *cassoulet*, the local dish which is a stew made up of haricot beans, sausages and mutton. The large basin is now a base for the Crown Blue Line charter company. Carcassonne (PK 105) can claim two UNESCO World Heritage Sites if you include the Canal du Midi. It is about 30 minutes' walk from Carcassonne's excellent Port de Plaisance to the second World Heritage Site – the mediaeval fortress town called La Cité, which is ringed with 3km of ramparts and 52 towers. Inside the walls is a maze of cobbled streets with souvenir shops, cafés and restaurants catering for the daily invasion of thousands of tourists.

From the boat you can see the Pyrenees – snow-capped if you are on the waterways early or late in the season. Vineyards are still much in evidence but occasionally giving way to orchards; the landscape is dotted with Cypress trees and Mediterranean-style houses with their distinctive orchre tiles and pale blue shutters.

Much of the Canal du Midi is lined with 300-year-old plane trees, which provide much needed shade and reduce some of the evaporation of canal water. The roots prevent erosion of the canal banks and in many places are so compact that they provide a firm edge to the waterway against which boats can secure.

At Port-la-Robine (PK 168), boat owners wanting to reach the Mediterranean at the first opportunity turn right into the Canal de jonction which also avoids the low bridge at Capestang (see page 275) and gives the crew the opportunity to visit the Roman town of Narbonne. The Embranchement de la Nouvelle (Canal de jonction and Canal de la Robine between the Midi and Port-la-Nouvelle) is 36km long with 13 locks.

Beyond Capestang on the Midi is the 160m-long Malpas tunnel (PK199). No-one had ever attempted to tunnel through a mountain to take a waterway, and the rock face almost defeated Riquet. Above the tunnel is l'Oppidum d'Ensérune where archaeological discoveries from pre-Roman occupation are displayed in a small museum.

On the outskirts of Béziers (birthplace of Pierre-Paul Riquet) is the Fonserannes staircase of seven locks (PK 207) and a waterslope still occasionally used by larger craft.

At Agde (PK 232), there is a round lock with three sets of gates. Privately-owned boats can turn right and gain access to the tidal Hérault river and motor the 4km downriver to the Mediterranean port of le Grau-d'Agde. The river is prone to silting up, so it is advisable to seek advice from the Agde lock keeper.

PK 240 is the end of the Canal du Midi, marked with a light, beyond which are the open waters of the Étang de Thau. Those in sea-going craft will get a first whiff of sea air after many days spent sedately moving along the inland water-

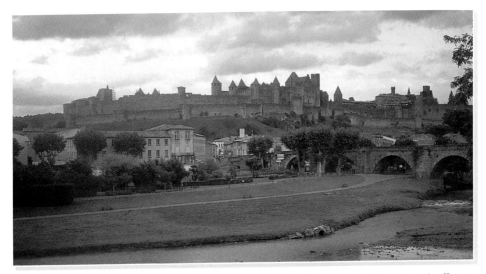

Carcassonne. Photo: David Jefferson

ways. The *étang*, classified as 'maritime waters' is a 17km-long lake and over 3km wide in some places; extensive oyster beds occupy most of the north side. Much of the *étang* or lake is shallow, particularly on the south side where there are sand-banks, and strong winds (including the local *mistral* and *sirocco*) can kick up difficult conditions for many flat-bottomed river cruisers.

Strict regulations apply to all craft crossing the Étang de Thau. Passages should not be attempted in anything over force 3, and a forecast should be obtained if in doubt (tel 08 36 68 08 34) or seek the advice of the local harbour office. The narrow channel just outside the oyster beds should be followed and there is no anchoring in the *étang*. There is a sombre warning that if the coastguards have to be employed to rescue a boat in difficulties, they will charge for their services at €150 an hour.

Having indicated these navigational warnings, it should also be mentioned that on the northerly side of the lake are two delightful fishing harbours: Marseillan and Mèze which are now mostly monopolised by pleasure boats.

Sète, at the eastern end of the Étang de Thau, is an island with the lake on one side and Mediterranean beaches on the other. Today it is the sixth largest port in France, and provides craft with an exit from the waterways to the sea. Cruise ships dock here, sharing the port with fishing boats and pleasure craft. Lifting and swing bridges operate at fixed times to allow passage through to the 300-berth yacht harbour on the Mediterranean coastline.

WATERWAY	PK ref	Town/*village*/≪*lock*	Total km
			▼ ▲
RIVER GIRONDE (tidal)	PK 95.5	**Royan** Seaside resort with several fine beaches. Modern town largely rebuilt after heavy WWII damage. Unusual 1950s cathedral. Large marina with 100 visitors' berths and all facilities.	0 601
	PK 95	*Port Bloc* on the Pointe de Grave, opposite Royan, with ferry regularly plying between the two ports. Used by local yachts but no provision for visiting craft.	
	PK 92.5	*Port du Verdon* (west bank) Restricted to commercial craft.	
	PK 92	*Port Médoc* (west bank) new (2004) 800-berth marina including 40 visitors' (tidal) berths. All facilities.	
	PK 90	*Meschers* (east bank) Wet basin (accessible HW ±2½ hrs).	
	PK 77.5	*Mortagne sur Gironde* (east bank) Wet basin (accessible HW ±2½ hrs).	
	PK 75	*Port de Goulee* (west bank) Pontoon.	
	PK 71	*Port Maubert* (east bank) Dries.	
	PK 58	*Port de Callonges* (east bank) Pontoon.	
	PK 47	**Pauillac** (west bank) Marina accessible at all states of the tide. Ideal for lowering/raising mast. Tours of local wine producers.	48.5 552.5
	PK 38	**Blaye** (east bank) Dries.	57.5 543.5
	PK 25	*Bec d'Ambès* Confluence of the River Dordogne and the Gironde.	
AHEAD **GARONNE MARITIME**			
LEFT River Dordogne and Bourg (3km)		**Bourg** Pontoon berth.	
RIVER GARONNE (tidal)	PK 0/71.5	**Bordeaux** Capital of Aquitaine region. Traces of Roman occupation. Under English rule during the Reign of Henry II.	95.5 505.5

WATERWAY	PK ref	Town/*village*/≪ lock	Total km
			▼ ▲
RIVER GARONNE		For centuries a great trading port and is still the sixth largest port in France. Industrial centre for petrochemicals, oil refineries and car plants. Remarkable Grand Théâtre. University town with many fine museums. For a short stay, possible room alongside Lormont Yacht Club pontoon on the east side of the river just upstream of the high suspension bridge (Pont d' Aquitaine). Small electric crane here for modest length light masts. Le Point du Jour marina opposite on the west side of the river discourages visiting yachts. For extended stay, lock into Basin No 1 (operates HW -1½ to HW +½) and then proceed to top end of Basin No 2. Crane for de-masting and all facilities except for alongside fuelling (none available in Bordeaux). Basin No 2 is 3km from the centre of town, and not in the most salubrious surroundings. Craft that can already clear the first of Bordeaux's low bridges Pont de Pierre (3.90m), can continue upriver to the Bègles Yacht harbour in the suburbs, 5km from the city centre.	
	PK 66	**Bègles** ⌿.	101 500
	PK 59	*Cadaujac* Port de l'Esquillot. ⚓.	
	PK 50	*Portets* ⚓.	
	PK 48.5	*Langoiran* ⚓.	
	PK 35.5	**Cadillac** ⚓.	131.5 469.5
	PK 19	*Les Arrocs* ⚓.	
LEFT Garonne	PK 193/17	*Castets en Dorthe*	150 451
AHEAD continues as **CANAL DE GARONNE**	PK 193/17	*Castets en Dorthe* ≪ No 53 (double)	150 451
	PK 192.5	≪ No 52.	
	PK 192.5	*Castets* ⌿.	

WATERWAY	PK ref	Town/*village*/≪ *lock*	Total km ▼	▲
CANAL DE GARONNE	PK 192–183.5	≪ Nos 51, 50 & 49.		
	PK 182.5	*Fontet* Matchstick museum ⚐.	160.5	440.5
	PK 181	≪ No 48.		
	PK 175.2	*Meilhan* ⚐.		
	PK 173–166	≪ Nos 47, 46 & 45.		
	PK 160.5	*Fourques* Ω.		
	PK 155.5	≪ No 44.		
	PK 155.5	*Le Mas d'Agenais* ⚐. Fuel.		
	PK 153	*Lagruère* Ω.		
	PK 150	≪ No 43.		
	PK 148	*Villeton* Ω.		
		≪ Nos 42 & 41.		
	PK 140	**Damazan** ⚐.	203	398
LEFT locks for Baïse and Garonne River for access to Lot	PK 135	(see page 293 & 294)		
	PK 135	**Buzet** ⚐. Cruiser hire.	208	393
	PK 133–125.5	≪ Nos 40, 39 & 38.		
	PK 119	*Sérignac* Ω.		
	PK 111–109	≪ Nos 37, 36, 35 & 34.		
	PK 107	**Agen** Capital of Lot-et-Garonne. Narrow streets in old quarter giving way to broad boulevards. Fashionable shops. The name of Agen is associated with prunes; try the prune preserve. 11th–16th century St-Caprais cathedral,13th century Notre Dame. Museum: ceramics, furniture, tapestries, paintings including Goya's self-portrait. ⚐. Fuel. Cruiser hire.	236	365
	PK 103	*Boé* Ω.		
	PK 97–86.5	≪ Nos 33, 32 & 31.		

WATERWAY	PK ref	Town/*village*/≪ *lock*	Total km	
			▼	▲
CANAL DE	PK 85	*Golfech* ♨.		
GARONNE	PK 81	**Valence d'Agen** ♨.	262	339
	PK 80.5–77	≪ Nos 30, 29 & 28.		
	PK 75	*Malause* ♨.		
	PK 71–67.5	≪ Nos 27 & 26.		
RIGHT lock giving access to a short section of Tarn river	PK 64			
	PK 64	**Moissac** 11th century Abbey St-Pierre, with magnificent cloisters. ⌂.	279	322
	PK 63.5–57.5	≪ Nos 25, 24, 23, 22, 21, 20 &19.		
	PK 57	**Castelsarrasin** ⌂.	286	315
	PK 55.5–47	≪ Nos 18, 17 & 16.		
LEFT water slope for commercial vessels only. Pleasure craft use adjacent staircase of locks	PK 45.5			
	PK 45–43	≪ Nos 15, 14, 13, 12 & 11.		
	PK 43	**Montech** ♨.		
LEFT Embranchement de Montauban (10 km – 9 locks) 3.4m headroom 1.6m draught	PK 43/0	Notice required. Tel. 05 63 64 73 04 or 06 62 99 44 04 previous day before 3pm to go through Tues, Wed, Thurs and before 11am previous day for Fri, Sat, Sun passage.		
	PK 4	Lock free to *Lacourt St-Pierre.* ♨.		
	PK 10	**Montauban** 12th century *bastide*. Many fine red brick buildings including the Bishop's Palace with paintings by local artist Ingres ♨.		
	PK 41	≪ No 10.		
	PK 26.5	*Grissoles* ♨.		
	PK 22.5–4	≪ Nos 9, 8, 7, 6, 5, 4, 3, 2,& 1.		

WATERWAY	PK ref	Town/*village*/≪*lock*	Total km
			▼ ▲
LEFT into **CANAL DU MIDI**	PK 0	**Toulouse** capital of Midi-Pyrénées region and fourth largest city in France. Centre of commerce and culture. Centre of Aérospatiale. Cité de l'Espace. Called *la Ville Rose,* many of its grand medieval and Renaisssance houses built with the local pink bricks. Saint-Sernin Basilica considered one of the finest Romanesque churches in the world. Port de l'Embouchure (⚓) in basin where the lateral canal meets Midi.	343 258
	PK 1–4	≪ Nos 1, 2 & 3.	
	PK 5.5	Visiting yachts are well catered for in Port St-Sauveur Port de Plaisance where fuel is available.	
	PK12	Commercial shipyard on left bank and Port-Sud at Ramonville St-Agne (⚑) on right bank.	
	PK 16–25	≪ Nos 6, 7 & 8 (no nos. 4 & 5).	
	PK 25	**Montgiscard** ⚓.	368 233
	PK 28–33	≪ Nos 9, 10 (double) & 11.	
	PK 33.5	*Négra* ⚑. Cruiser hire.	
	PK 37.5–39	≪ Nos 12 (double) & 13.	
	PK 39	*Gardouch* ⚓.	
	PK 43–47.5	≪ Nos 14, 15 (double) & 16.	
	PK 50	*Port Lauragais* Riquet Cultural and Historic Centre. Rugby museum ⚑.	
Summit marked by the Obélisque de Riquet	PK 51.5	≪ No 17 (*Océan*) and the summit .	
	PK 54	*Le Ségala* ⚑. Cruiser hire.	
	PK 56.5–61	≪ Nos 18 (*Méditerrranée*), 19 (double), 20 (triple), 21 & 22.	
	PK 65	**Castelnaudary** Famous for its cassoulet stew ⚑. Cruiser hire.	408 193

Castelnaudary. *Photo: David Jefferson*

WATERWAY	PK ref	Town/*village*/≪*lock*	Total km
			▼ ▲
CANAL DU MIDI	PK 65.5–80	≪ Nos 23 (quadruple), 24 (double), 25 (triple), 26, 27, 28, 29, 30, 31, 32, 33 & 34.	
	PK 80.5	**Bram** Gallo-Roman town built in a circular pattern around 14th century church ⌓. Cruiser hire.	423.5 177.5
	PK 86–100	≪ Nos 35, 36, 37 (double), 38 & 39.	
	PK 105	**Carcassonne** Two cities: the Bastide de St-Louis is the main commercial centre built in the reign of Louis IX with the medieval la Cité which is the largest fortress in Europe, with great outer and inner ramparts and 52 towers. In addition to the souvenir shops, cafés and restaurants, there is a château, the Basilique St-Nazaire, a theatre, Musée des Beaux-Arts and a prestigious hotel. Listed by UNESCO as a World Heritage Site in 1997 ⌓. Cruiser hire.	448 153

WATERWAY	PK ref	Town/*village*/≪*lock*	Total km	
			▼	▲
CANAL DU MIDI	PK 105-114	≪ Nos 40, 41, 42 (double), 43, 44 & 45.		
	PK 117	*Trèbes* ⚑. Cruiser hire.	460	141
	PK 118	≪ No 46 (triple).		
	PK 126.5	*Marseillette* ⚓.		
	PK 127-136	≪ Nos 47, 48 (triple), 49 (double), 50 (double) & 51 (double).		
	PK 139.5	*La Redorte* ⚓.		
	PK 142.5	≪ No 52.		
	PK 145	*Homps* ⚑. Cruiser hire.	488	113
	PK 146–149.5	≪ Nos 53, 54 (double) & 55 (double).		
	PK 151	**Argens en Minervois** ⚑. Fuel. Cruiser hire.	494	107
	PK152	≪ No 56.		
	PK 155	*Roubia* ⚓.		
	PK 157	*Paraza* ⚓.		
	PK 165	*Le Somail* In the 17th century, the inn was the resting place for passengers on the mail barge operating between Toulouse and Agde ⚑. Cruiser hire.		
	PK 168	*Port-la-Robine* ⚑. Cruiser hire.		
RIGHT 36km canal	PK 168.5	To Port-la-Nouvelle and the Mediterranean via Narbonne (Route 50).		
	PK 188	**Capestang** bridge (see page 275). Gothic Saint Etienne church. ⚓. Cruiser hire.	531	70
	PK 194	*Poilhes* ⚓.		
Tunnel (373m)	PK 199	Work on the Malpas tunnel, which was the first in the world to be dug to take a canal, almost defeated Riquet. Above the tunnel is La Maison du Malpas, a cultural centre which also has a bar to sample local wines. On top of the hill is *Ensérune oppidum* – a pre-Roman fortified village and one of the finest archaeological sites in Southern		

WATERWAY	PK ref	Town/*village*/≪lock	Total km	
			▼	▲
CANAL DU MIDI		France. Museum displays remains of Greek, Celtic and Roman occupation.		
	PK 200	*Colombiers* ⚐. Cruiser hire.	543	58
	PK 207	*Fonséranes* (≪ No 57) staircase of 6 locks (1681) with fixed times for upstream and downstream traffic. Water slope (1981) alongside restricted to occasional use by lengthier craft.		
	PK 208	≪ No 58.		
	PK 208	**Béziers** Birthplace of Pierre Paul Riquet. Magnificent cathedral St-Nazaire overlooking l'Orb river ⚓. Cruiser hire.	551	50
	PK 208.5–213	≪ Nos 59, 60 & 61.		
	PK 214	*Villeneuve les Béziers* ⚐.		
	PK 218	≪ No 62.		
	PK 222	*Port Cassafières* ⚐. Cruiser hire.		
	PK 226	**Vias** Town 1.5km to the N of canal. Mediterranean beach resort of Vias-Plage 3 km to S ⚓.	561	32
	PK 231	≪ No 63 Agde's *Bassin Rond* – an unusual lock basin with lock gates at either end with an extra pair in the south side providing access to the tidal Hérault river which has suffered from silting in recent years. Advice should be sought from Agde lock keeper to navigate the 5kms to Mediterranean port of le Grau-d'Agde.		
	PK 232	**Agde** One of the oldest towns in France, with bricks of local lava giving many buildings an almost black façade. St-Étienne cathedral (12th century). Agathois museum.	575	26
	PK 235.5	≪ No 65.		
Mediterranean end of Canal du Midi	PK 240	Base Nautique des Glenans. ⚓. Pointe des Onglous.	583	18

WATERWAY	PK ref	Town/*village*/≪*lock*	Total km
			▼ ▲
Continues as **ÉTANG DE THAU**		This 9 mile-long shallow lake or lagoon is classified as maritime waters with different rules and regulations applying to boat owners. Passages should not be attempted in any wind over force 3; craft must stick to the channel close to the oyster beds; anchoring prohibited; international rules of the road apply. A chart of the *étang* should be on board. Tel 08 36 68 08 34 for weather forecast.	
		Marseillan Yacht harbour and separate fishing harbour. Visiting yachts berth on N jetty beyond structure with starboard light in entrance. Tours and tasting at Noilly-Prat cellars and distillery.	
		Mèze Yacht harbour. Visiting yachts berth off E quay. Small beach.	
		Bouziques Yacht harbour. Surroundings mostly devoted to oyster farming industry.	▼ ▲
	(PK18)	**Sète** Large fishing port. Originally an island occupied by the Romans. Designated a port by Louis XIV. Yachts can berth in the port entrance alongside E quay. Town yacht harbour (Port St Clair) is reached through 2 lifting bridges with 2 daily openings. Access to Maritime ⚓ and the Mediterranean is through 3 more bridges via the Canal Maritime.	601 0
Canal du Rhône à Sète Beaucaire – Sète (Route 18)			

Sète. *Photo: Susan McIntyre*

Route 50

Embranchement de La Nouvelle – Canal de jonction & Canal de la Robine: *Port-la-Robine ↔ Port-la-Nouvelle*

Maximum boat dimensions: *Height above waterline* 3.3m *Draught* 1.4m

Speed limit: 8km/h (4.3kn)

Locks: 13 (40.50m long x 5.85m wide) Operate late Mar–early Nov daily 0900–1230 & 1330–1800; May–Sept daily 0900–1230 & 1330–1900; early Nov–Dec by arrangement only

Distance: 36km

For boats that entered Le Canal des Deux Mers from the Atlantic making for the Mediterranean, this is the first opportunity of leaving the Midi, and taking two short canals to reach the sea at Port-la-Nouvelle. It also avoids having to pass beneath the low arched bridge at Capestang and provides the opportunity of visiting the ancient town of Narbonne.

WATERWAY	PK ref	Town/*village*/≪lock	Total km	
			▼	▲
From **CANAL DU MIDI**	PK 168	*Port-la-Robine* ⚐.		
CANAL DE JONCTION	PK 0		0	36
	PK 0.5	≪ *Cesse.*		
	PK 1	≪ *Truilhas.*		
	PK 1.5	≪ *Empare.*		
	PK 2	≪ *Argeliers.*		
	PK 3	≪ *St-Cyr.*		
	PK 3.5	*Sallèles d'Aude* ⌂.		
	PK 3.5	≪ *Salleles.*		

ATERWAY	PK ref	Town/*village/*≼ *lock*	Total km ▼	▲
CANAL DE JONCTION	PK 5	≼ *Gailhousty.*		
Continues as **CANAL DE LA ROBINE**	PK 0		5	31
	PK 0	≼ *Moussoulens.*		
	PK 4	≼ *Raonel.*		
	PK 8.5	≼ *Gua.*		
	PK 9	**Narbonne** Interesting old town, a seaport long ago until silting up occurred. Boulevards now where ramparts used to be. 13th century former Archbishop's palace. 13th-14th century St-Just cathedral dominates restored medieval quarter. Museum with local Roman artefacts. ⚐. Cruiser hire.	14	22
	PK 9.5	≼ *Narbonne.*		
	PK 18	≼ *Mandirac.*		
	PK 29	≼ *Sainte Lucie.*	▼	▲
	PK 31	**Port-la-Nouvelle** Commercial and fishing port with resort-type development. Mast can be stepped/lowered in Port de Commerce ⚐.	31	0

The development of the Rivers Baïse and Lot

In recent years, the river Baïse and two sections of the River Lot have been developed for pleasure boats, and several cruiser hire companies have established bases along these beautiful waterways. The Baïse can be accessed from the Canal de Garonne through the double lock at Buzet-sur-Baïse, but most of the river is normally only available to boats with a draught up to 1m. Those boats with a suitable draught wishing to explore the Baïse turn right once through the Buzet double lock (Route 51A).

It is more difficult to access the Lot Aval (downstream section – Route 51B) from the Canal de Garonne. From the Buzet double lock, it is a left turn, another lock and then a 4km continuation to the Garonne end of the Baïse to the lock at St-Léger. Unless there has been a marked absence of rainfall over the preceeding months, there will usually be 1.5m of water in this short downstream section of the Baïse.

Villeneuve on the River Lot. *Photo: Crown Blue Line*

The lock at St-Léger gives access to the fast-flowing Garonne river (normal depth he 1.5m). Crews of charter boats must then report to the *Service Navigation* at the St-Léger lock and then board a small tug which will secure the charter boats alongside and then motor the 4.6km-length of the Garonne river, as far as the Nicole lock which provides access to the Lot Aval (Route 51B) which is normally navigable by boats with a 1.5m draught. A similar operation is necessary in the other direction to access the Baïse from the Lot via the Garonne. There is a modest charge for this service. There can be a 7-knot current in the Garonne. Progress is slow upriver and you should reckon on around two hours for the passage through the locks and the tow. In recent years in the late summer there has been insufficient water in the Garonne to make the transfer between the Baïse and the Lot.

Boat owners making the passage on the Garonne in their own craft between the St-Léger and Nicole locks, can proceed unaccompanied, but are strongly advised to consult with the lock keepers before locking out, and may experience a delay until other traffic has assembled. The lock keepers also operate the tug.

The Lot river is a vast reclamation project, one of the largest in France. The Lot Aval (downstream section) has been extended from Villeneuve-sur-Lot another 25km to Fumel, making 78km of navigable waterway. The Lot Amont (upstream section) is a stretch of navigable waterway extending from above the huge hydro-electric dam at Luzech for 64km to Crégols (Route 51C). With no access either end to the Lot Amont and a depth of only 1m, this section of the river is almost exclusively used by operators of hire fleets and local boat owners. There are long-term plans to restore the Lot between Fumel and Luzech, and extend the navigable waterway a further 45km beyond Crégols to Capdenac. When completed this would provide 236km of navigable river.

On the Lot river. *Photo: France Afloat*

Route 51A

River Baïse: *St-Léger* ↔ *Valence-sur-Baïse*

Maximum boat dimensions: *Height above waterline* 3.0m *Draught* 1.0m (1.5m downstream of Lavardac except in periods of drought)

Speed limit: 6km/h (3.24kn)

Locks: 21 (30m long x 5.20m wide downstream of Lavardac; 30m long x 4.20m wide upstream of Lavardac) Operate April–Oct. Apart from the double lock Graziac with a lock keeper, the remainder of the locks are self-operated by inserting a card. The self-operated locks in the Lot et Garonne *département* (Nos 1–15) can be worked April–Sept 0900–1900 & Oct 0900–1800. In the Gers *département* (Nos 16–19 & 21) April–Sept 0900–2000 & Oct 0900–1800. No 20 Graziac operates 0900–2000 except in April and early Sept–Oct 1000–1630

Distance: 65km

WATERWAY	PK ref	Town/*village*/≪*lock*	Total km	
			▼	▲
RIVER BAÏSE	PK 0	≪ No 1 *St-Léger*. Short-stay pontoon for users of lock (giving access to River Garonne – see pages 293–4).	0	65
	PK 4.5	≪ No 2 *Buzet*.		
RIGHT double lock entry/exit from Canal de Garonne (pages 293–4)	PK 5			
	PK 11	*Feugarolles* ♒.		
	PK 15	*Vianne* ♒.		
	PK 15-17.5	≪ Nos 3 *Vianne* & 4 *Lavardac*.		
	PK 18	**Lavardac** Fortified town with ancient Gallo-Roman fort. ♒.	18	47
	PK 20.5-27	≪ Nos 5 *St-Crabary*, 6 *Serbat*, 7 *Baspaume* & 8 *Nérac*.		

TERWAY	PK ref	Town/*village*/≪*lock*	Total km
			▼ ▲
RIVER BAÏSE	PK 27.5	**Nérac** ⌐. Cruiser hire.	27.5 37.5
	PK 29.5–44.5	≪ Nos 9 *Nazareth*, 10 *La Saubole*, 11 *Racaillau*, 12 *Pacheron*, 13 *Lapierre*, 14 *Vialères* & 15 *Moncrabeau*.	
	PK 44.5	*Moncrabeau* Ω.	
	PK 49.5-53	≪ Nos 16 *Autiège*, 17 *Beauregard* & 18 *Condom*.	
	PK 53.5	**Condom** Main town of the Armagnac region where barges loaded brandy for Bordeaux. 16th century Cathedral St-Pierre. Ω. Cruiser hire.	53.5 11.5
	PK 54.5-64	≪ Nos 19 *Gauge*, 20 *Graziac* (double) & 21 *Flaran*.	▼ ▲
End of navigation	PK 65	**Valence-sur-Baïse** Ω.	65 0

Nérac on the River Baïse. *Photo: Crown Blue Line*

Route 51B

River Lot (Aval): *Nicole ↔ Fumel*

Maximum boat dimensions: *Height above waterline* **3.5m**   *Draught* **1.5m**
Speed limit: **10km/h (5.4kn)** in the river; **6km/h (3.24kn)** in canal bypasses
Locks: **7** (32.50m long x 5.20m wide) Operate April–Oct 0900–1900
Distance: 78km

WATERWAY	PK ref	Town/*village*/≪*lock*	Total km	
			▼	▲
RIVER LOT (AVAL)	PK 0	≪ *Nicole* Waiting pontoons either side of lock.	0	78
	PK 3	≪ *Aiguillon.*		
	PK 10	≪ *Clairac.*	10	68
	PK 10	**Clairac** ⚓.		
	PK 18.5	*Granges-sur-Lot* ⚓.		
	PK 22.5	**Castelmoron-sur-Lot** ⚓.	22.5	55.5
	PK 23	≪ *Castelmoron.*		
	PK 23.5	*Port Lalande* ⚑. Cruiser hire.		
	PK 25	*le Temple-sur-Lot* ⚓.		
	PK 27	*Fongrave* ⚓.		
	PK 32	**Ste-Livrade-sur-Lot** ⚓.	32	46
	PK 39.5	*Casseneuil* ⚓.	39.5	38.5
	PK 50	**Villeneuve-sur-Lot** ⚓.	50	28
	PK 51.5	≪ *Villeneuve*		
	PK 59.5	*St-Sylvestre-sur-Lot* ⚓.		
	PK 68	*Lustrac* ⚓.		
	PK 68	≪ *Lustrac.*		
	PK 75.5	≪ *St-Vite.*	▼	▲
End of navigation (2006)	PK 78	**Fumel.**	78	0

Route 51C

River Lot (Amont): *Luzech ↔ Crégols*

Maximum boat dimensions: *Height above waterline* 4.4m   *Draught* 1.0m
Speed limit: 10km/h (5.4kn) in the river; 6km/h (3.24kn) in canal bypasses
Locks: 14 (30m long x 5m wide) Self-operated April–mid Sept sunrise -30 minutes to sunset +30 minutes
Distance: 64km

WATERWAY	PK ref	Town/*village*/≪*lock*	Total km	
			▼	▲
RIVER LOT	PK 0	**Luzech** ♌.	0	64
(AMONT)	PK 1	*Caïx* ♌.		
	PK 3.5	*Parnac* ♌.		
	PK 12.5	≪ *Cessac.*		
	PK 13	*Douelle* ♌.		
	PK 19.5	≪ *Quai Mercuès.*		
	PK 22	*Pradines* ♌. Shops in *Labéraudie* (1.5km).		
	PK 25-28	≪ *Labéraudie & Valentré.*		
	PK 28	**Cahors** Capital town of the Lot *département.* Several quays. Cathedral and many old buildings.	28	36
	PK 29.5-33.5	≪ *Coty & Lacombe.*		
	PK 34	*Laroque-des-Arcs* ♌.		
	PK 36.5	*Lamagdelaine* ♌.		
	PK 37.5	≪ *Arcambal.*		
	PK 39	*Arcambal* ♌.		
	PK 40.5-44.5	≪ *Galessie & Vers.*		
	PK 45	*Vers* ♌.		
	PK 46.5-49.5	≪ *Planiol & St-Géry*		

Le Pont Valentré at Cahors. *Photo: CDT Lot*

WATERWAY	PK ref	Town/*village*/≪*lock*	Total km	
			▼	▲
RIVER LOT	PK 49.5	*St-Géry* Quays either side of lock		
(AMONT)	PK 56.5	≪ *Bouziès.*		
	PK 58	*Bouziès* Quay. Hotel.		
	PK 59-61.5	≪ *Ganil & St-Cirq.*		
	PK 62	**St-Cirq-Lapopie** Quays either side of bridge.	62	2
			▼	▲
End of navigation	PK 64	*Crégols.*	64	0

St-Cirque-Lapopie on the River Lot.
Photo: Crown Blue Line

Route 52

River Charente: *Rochefort ↔ Angoulême*

Maximum boat dimensions: *Height above waterline* **3.5m**
Draught Estuary to Cognac **1.5m**   Cognac to Angoulême **1.0m**

Speed limits: Estuary to Tonnay-Charente **12kn**; Tonnay-Charente to Port-du-Lys **12km/h (6.5kn)**; Port-du-Lys to Angoulême **10km/h (5.4kn)**

Locks: **21** (34m long x 6.5m wide) Self-operated except for the first lock (St-Savinien). This lock and the next (La Baine) are open 0800–2000. Waterway closed Nov–mid Mar. Locks should not be used after sunset.

Distance: 169km

On the Biscay coast, between La Rochelle and the Gironde estuary is the entrance to the River Charente, which was claimed by Henry IV to be the most beautiful river in his kingdom. It is not connected to any other navigable waterway, but facilities for pleasure boat users have been improved over the 169km from the outer estuary buoys to the old fortified town of Angoulême.

The towns of Jarnac and Cognac have long been associated with the production of brandy, and nearly all the great names have established their distilleries here. The unmistakable perfumed air leads you to the likes of Hennessy, Remy Martin, Otard and many more, reason enough for sampling the delights of the Charente.

WATERWAY	PK ref	Town/*village*/≪ *lock*	Total km
			▼ ▲
RIVER	PK 102	Outer *Fontenelles* buoy in estuary.	0 169
CHARENTE	PK 97	*Port-des-Barques* Oyster beds.	
	PK 87	*le Port Neuf* ♒. Moorings.	
	PK 84.5	*Soubise* ♒.	
Transporter bridge	PK 80.5	After recent restoration, the *pont transbordeur* ferries foot passengers across the river in a cradle or gondola, suspended from rails on the metal structure high above.	
Downriver limit for chartered river boats	PK 77	**Rochefort** 17th century naval port and arsenal. *Corderie Royal*, nearly 400m long, where ropes were made for the French navy. Replica of 1780 frigate *Hermione* under construction. Maritime museum. No 1 and 2 basins now used as yacht harbours with all facilities except fuel. Harbours accessed through lock which operates HW –45 mins to HW +1 hr (0530–2230). Waiting pontoon outside the lock.	24 144

Rochefort. *Photo: David Jefferson*

WATERWAY	PK ref	Town/*village*/≪ *lock*	Total km ▼	Total km ▲
RIVER CHARENTE	PK 70	**Tonnay-Charente** Fishing port. Ω.	32	137
	PK 49.5	≪ *St-Savinien.*		
	PK 49	**St-Savinien** ⚐. Cruiser hire.	53	116
	PK 42	*Port d'Envaux* Ω.		
	PK 40	*Taillebourg* Ω.		
	PK 27	**Saintes** Roman occupation. Germanicus' Arch, once forming part of the bridge, is now sited alongside the river.1st century amphitheatre. 11th century Abbaye aux Dames. Archaeological museum with some fine Gallo-Roman remains Ω. (extensive quays). Cruiser hire.	75	94
	PK 16	*Chaniers* Ω. Showers at camp site.		
	PK 15.5	≪ *la Baine.*		
	PK 10	*Dompierre-sur-Charente* Ω. Showers at camp site.		
	PK 1	*Chérac* Ω.		
Boundary between *départements*	PK 0/66	*le Port du Lys* Waterski centre.	102	67
	PK 61.5	≪ *Crouin.*		
	PK 59	**Cognac** Centre of the industry with houses of Hennessy, Martell, Otard, Remy Martin all located here and offering guided tours and tastings. ⚐ rarely has any places for visitors, but the quayside either side of the entrance can be used. Public quay below Pont St Jacques on opposite bank. Cruiser hire.	109	60
	PK 58	≪ *Cognac.*		
	PK 52	*St-Brice Château* Ω.		
	PK 51.5	≪ *Garde Moulin*		
	PK 47.5	*Bourg-Charente* Restaurant gastronomique. Shop. Ω.		
	PK 47	≪ *Bourg-Charente.*		

Cognac. *Photo: David Jefferson*

WATERWAY	PK ref	Town/*village*/≪*lock*	Total km
			▼ ▲
RIVER CHARENTE	PK 44	**Jarnac** Another centre of the cognac industry. House of Courvoisier. ⚑. Extensive quays. Cruiser hire.	124 45
	PK 43	≪ *Jarnac.*	
	PK 40.5	≪ *Gondeville.*	
	PK 37	≪ *Saintonge.*	
	PK 37	*Saintonge* ♨. 11th century Bassac Abbey 1km.	
	PK 35.5	*Graves* ♨ convenient for visit to local Pineau producer (Jean-Louis Brillet).	
	PK 34	≪ *Juac.*	
	PK 33	*St-Simon* 17th century centre for barge building. La Maison des Gabarriers is a museum devoted to history of the barges and river traffic.	
	PK 31	≪ *Vibrac.*	
	PK 26.5	**Châteauneuf-sur-Charente** Old town. ♨ on Île de la Fuie just below bridge.	141.5 27.5

Index